Cooperative Learning in Social Studies

A HANDBOOK FOR TEACHERS

Robert J. Stahl, Editor

Arizona State University, Tempe

Addison-Wesley Publishing Company

Menlo Park, California • Reading, Massachusetts • New York
Don Mills, Ontario • Wokingham, England • Amsterdam • Bonn
Sydney • Singapore • Tokyo • Madrid • San Juan
Paris • Seoul • Milan • Mexico City • Taipei

Ethel K. Smith Library

Wingate University
Wingate, North Carolina 28174

DEDICATION

This book is dedicated to my mother, Mary Yirga Stahl.

ACKNOWLEDGMENTS

Managing Editor: Michael Kane
Project Editor: Priscilla Cox Samii
Production: Kane Publishing Services, Inc.

This book is published by the Innovative Division, an imprint of the
Alternative Publishing Group of Addison-Wesley.

ISBN 0-201-81786-1

2 3 4 5 6 7 8 9 10-CRS-99 98 97 96 95 94

Contents

Foreword

ROBERT J. STAHL

Cooperative learning is an often-claimed but not well-understood approach to social studies instruction. Many individuals see nothing new in cooperative learning because they "have used cooperative learning for years." For all too many educators, cooperative learning is equated with any group activity or project since all members of these groups are expected to cooperate in order to complete their assignments. However, even though cooperation among students in groups can occur and does occur quite often, having students cooperate in group settings is not the only characteristic of effective cooperative learning groups. As this book emphasizes, there is much more to cooperative learning than simply having students work and cooperate in small groups.

No book, including this one, will answer every question social studies teachers may raise concerning cooperative learning. An exhaustive book on this topic was not attempted. Instead, this volume provides a practical handbook on a selected set of highly effective and widely used cooperative learning strategies written in such a way as to make each strategy easy to use in primary- through secondary-level classrooms. Authors were challenged to produce in each chapter a highly readable, classroom-friendly, how-to-do-it discussion of a specific cooperative learning strategy. Practical, easy-to-follow guidelines are included so that teachers will be comfortable working with each strategy, one at a time. Whenever possible, classroom examples and scenarios are included to illustrate the strategy being discussed. In other instances, generic checklists, forms, and tables appropriate across all grade levels and subjects are provided for teachers to reproduce and use.

The intent is to provide teachers with a handbook to guide them toward successful completion of the cooperative learning strategies selected. Ultimately, classroom teachers like yourself will judge how well the authors and I have delivered what we set out to accomplish.

1.

Cooperative Learning: A Social Studies Context and an Overview

ROBERT J. STAHL

The notion of cooperation is an especially important one in social studies education. The historical focus of the social studies on citizenship and a more recent focus on civic competency assume that individuals function in, participate in, and contribute to their communities, societies, and nations within which survival, progress, and personal enhancement are not possible without cooperating effectively with others. Indeed, a community, society, and nation cannot exist nor long endure unless individuals are willing to cooperate with one another. Furthermore, one cannot be a good citizen or maintain one's civic competencies without having the conceptions, behaviors, and attitudes needed to cooperate with diverse individuals within a constantly changing, pluralistic world. The social studies profession has accepted the responsibility of helping students acquire what is needed to participate and cooperate effectively in social settings and in society.

Purpose of This Chapter

The purpose of this chapter is to provide a brief overview of cooperation and cooperative learning within the context of social studies education. The following section builds upon the ideas provided in the introduction to this chapter. Then, two important questions are answered.

The first concerns results that are likely to occur from using cooperative learning. These results have served as reasons to use this approach in social studies classrooms. The second question outlines the essential elements that group tasks and behaviors are to meet in order to reap the full benefits of this approach. This overview is completed with a challenge that teachers can maximize student success and growth by acting on their own to use cooperative learning rather than hoping that something "out there" will produce the results they expect.

A Context for Cooperation and Cooperative Learning in the Social Studies

Social studies educators at all levels have students study groups that depend heavily on their members cooperating with one another. Elementary students study communities, including their own towns or cities, and the various social roles individuals carry out within their respective communities. Middle-level students examine life within the Greek city-states, expeditions by explorers or conquerors to new territories, and efforts of small groups of settlers to organize to form new communities in distant lands. Meanwhile, high-school students study the cooperative efforts of the framers of the United States Constitution, the cooperation involved in trading raw materials and finished products across state and national borders, and the many ways that citizens of various nations cooperated during the world wars in support of their nations' war efforts.

Even though these are studied, all too often students do not consciously consider how cooperation played or plays important roles in the success or failure of each of these groups or activities. For example, although elementary students may study the duties of police, fire, and safety persons in their local communities, they rarely study how and why they cooperate with one another and others in their community to make it a community. Students study groups and some of their activities as though the cooperation, compromise, and mutual support among the individuals involved did not exist. To better understand the achievements of these groups, students should take time to examine systematically the cooperative behaviors and attitudes that contributed to the success and/or failure of these groups. As students comprehend the power of positive cooperation in specific situations, they are more likely to value cooperating in everyday life situations they encounter in the future. However, learning about how members of other groups have cooperated—or failed to cooperate—is not cooperative learning.

Instead of studying the cooperative activities of others, students can learn to cooperate effectively within social studies classrooms through the actual practice of cooperative behaviors, attitudes, and abilities. Teachers can structure group tasks and provide guidance so that students go beyond the study of cooperation among others. Indeed, students can actually engage in and master effective, empowering cooperative behaviors, attitudes, and abilities as they work together cooperatively to ensure that all members of their group are academically successful. Cooperative learning strategies enable students to experience firsthand many of the benefits of cooperation and of particular cooperative behaviors and abilities. This is especially so as students realize how their own academic and social growth is enhanced by working cooperatively with peers in structured academic tasks.

Social studies teachers can move beyond the study of and expected use of cooperation within their classrooms. They can take steps to arrange for students to acquire specific behaviors, attitudes, and abilities that will enable each student to cooperate effectively in many settings with diverse populations. Of equal importance, students can engage in cooperative behaviors that actually promote the academic learning and psychological enhancement of others. This cooperation and these cooperative behaviors will not occur unless students complete the necessary work together in group settings *as a group*. They must come to trust that what they give to and share with their groupmates will enable their groupmates, their group as a whole, and, eventually, their own selves to succeed well beyond what nearly all could attain on their own.

Although individuals in groups tend to cooperate with one or several others in their groups, not all groups are structured in ways that make them cooperative learning groups. The key to using cooperative learning groups effectively is to structure the groups, group tasks, and postgroup activities in ways that meet the requirements of this approach to instruction. These requirements and specific how-to-do-it strategies compatible with these requirements are described in this volume.

Cooperative Learning in Light of a Social Studies Curriculum Framework

Appropriate cooperative learning groups can enable students to learn the academic content and skills targeted within local and state social studies curriculums and many of the social behaviors, attitudes, and abilities posited as valued goals of social studies education. According to the National Council for the Social Studies (NCSS), the basic goal of social studies education is to "prepare young people to be humane, rational, participating citizens in a world that is becoming increasingly interdependent" (*Social Education*, 1979, p. 262). The social studies is the only area of the school and curriculum that focuses on the preparation of citizens. Furthermore, social studies education is committed to fostering human dignity, rational thinking, humane and civil behaviors, and active, responsible participation in the social, political, and economic life in the many communities of which one is a member. This commitment requires more than the memorization of details from the social and behavioral sciences or one's life experiences. Students must become active learners within several social communities so that understanding, perceptions, and actions concerning and impacting on others and themselves enhance human dignity and improve the human condition.

Cooperative learning, especially when heterogeneous groups are formed and then meet for prolonged periods of time, provides opportunities for students to expand their social communities and to converse with individuals of different academic skills and ethnic backgrounds from their own and who are different in gender and race. In appropriate structured cooperative learning group tasks, students learn to cooperate with one another as individuals, as groupmates, and as "academic colleagues." They come to better understand one another as unique individuals who deserve to be respected and whose dignity they need to enhance and protect. As students cooperate to learn and to help each member of their group also learn, they more fully appreciate both the uniqueness of each individual and the benefits and power of unique individuals working together in a group as a group to enhance all those involved. Through cooperative learning, the classroom becomes an environment within which students engage in direct face-to-face interactions that can enhance their own dignity and self-esteem while contributing to enhancement of these for all others in their group. In essence, cooperative learning provides opportunities for students to learn, practice, and live the attitudes and behaviors that reflect the goals of social studies education.

Knowledge[1]

To be successful both within academic areas and in life, students need appropriate knowledge. At the same time, the school as a social institution is responsible for helping young people acquire knowledge. In particular, social studies curriculums and instruction are responsible for helping students acquire knowledge from and about the social and behavioral sciences and knowledge that will enable them to be humane, rational, and participating citizens in their many communities.

Social studies teachers must do more than present information to students or place them in contact with relevant information by such means as textbooks, visual aids, videotapes, and guest speakers. Students must think about and consider this information and have feedback that their personal comprehensions and understandings are viable. They must rehearse this information so that it is retained and later retrieved for use in future situations. By considering information in appropriate ways, students construct the knowledge base needed to study academic subjects as well as a foundation for living in an ever-changing world.

One primary and highly successful role of cooperative learning is to help students learn academic content. Through cooperative learning, students acquire the knowledge they need about the social studies topics targeted. Furthermore, as they interact in their groups, they gain higher comprehension of the information, concepts, and procedures than when studying on their own. These consistent strong effects make this approach highly compatible with the academic and knowledge goals of social studies education.

Abilities

According to the NCSS, abilities provide the means of achieving knowledge and citizenship objectives as well as represent intellectual, data processing, and human relations competencies in their own right. Students need to acquire, practice, and voluntarily impose sound ways of thinking to process the information they encounter and to shape and

---

[1] This area of student learning and the three that follow in this section are emphasized as critical ones for social studies education by the National Council for the Social Studies (1979).

refine ways of thinking, perceiving, and behaving in academic and social situations. What constitutes sound thinking and what results from such thinking directly influence the knowledge one constructs, the decisions one makes, and the actions one takes. In addition, abilities associated with human relations and interactions demand involvement with others and feedback from others as to the appropriateness and adequacy of one's social attitudes, perceptions, and behaviors. Cooperative learning groups can provide the environments and structures to help students acquire, practice, and refine the many intellectual, information processing, human relations, and social interaction abilities valued by social studies educators. In the process of working together and interacting with one another and with relevant content, students engage in many thinking processes and behaviors aligned with these abilities. When group processing abilities are taught to students and used by them, students come to provide the feedback, criticisms, challenges, and support that allow many of them to make major progress toward becoming skillful users of these abilities.

Valuing

Individuals cannot live in any social group or study any topic, event, or data without engaging in valuing. As noted in the NCSS curriculum guidelines (1979), value orientations are the foundations of social institutions, and the value positions of individuals and groups have consequences for action. In other words, after infancy it is rare that one thinks, decides, or acts free of his or her values. Young people are expected to develop the values that will enable them to achieve the goals of social studies education and the academic disciplines—which themselves reflect value choices. In addition, students need to have feedback concerning their valuing processes and the applications of the results of these processes. For instance, to act in ways to enhance and protect the human dignity of others requires valuing processes and values that comprehend and cherish human dignity. Like adults, students can never be free from engaging in valuing processes. As they receive feedback about their valuing processes and the results these bring, students can refine and modify as well as preserve sound valuing processes and the values that result within the context of the social communities and world in which they live.

Cooperative learning groups enable students to engage in valuing as they consider how to act, think, and decide within their groups and with one another. Valuing processes and values are also used as students engage in academic study and consider the meaning and use of selected content, concepts, and events. Through what they say, write, and do in these groups, students give evidence of their valuing. Within these same group settings, students have an opportunity to practice and field test their valuing processes and the results. They receive feedback, encouragement, discouragement, and support, as appropriate, both from their peers and from the teacher who monitors their group work. Since the results of valuing eventually emerge in the form of decisions and actions that take place in social situations and in relation to others, cooperative learning can provide a powerful mirror for the valuing processes of each student.

Social Participation

According to the NCSS, within a democratic society, social participation requires that individual behavior be guided by the values of human dignity and rationality and be directed toward the resolution of problems confronting society for the improvement of the human condition. For this goal to be a reality, young people need ample opportunities to engage in thinking, deciding, and acting that will help them acquire, value, and use these behaviors within and outside the classroom. One cannot become skilled at participating in society unless one has had opportunities to practice participation attitudes and behaviors over extended periods of time in meaningful social situations. Students need to engage in activities in which they must act to enhance and preserve the human dignity of others. They must encounter situations during which rational thinking is needed to deal with social situations and problems. They must also have practice engaging in such behaviors as compromise, negotiation, cooperation, consensus, and majority rule, which are fundamental to functioning within a democratic community. Therefore, social participation is not something just to be studied within social studies classrooms. Rather, it is a way of acting. Furthermore, it should be a way of acting that students continually engage in within the social studies classroom.

Cooperative learning strategies provide ample opportunities for students to engage in behaviors that define, refine, and reinforce social participation attitudes, abilities, and behaviors. Students come to respect others, treat others with dignity, and encourage the use of rational thinking as they work together to complete common goals. They engage in such actions as compromise, negotiation, cooperation, consensus, and majority rule as they work to complete their assignments and to help ensure that every member of their group learns. As students deal with learning the content and abilities expected, they find themselves resolving conflicts, handling problems, and making choices that reflect personal and social situations they are likely to find in real-world situations. By using cooperative learning, students can make major progress toward developing the attitudes, values, and behaviors that will enable them to participate in their communities in ways that are consistent with the goals of social studies education.

This section describes, albeit briefly, how cooperative learning can be used to enhance social studies instruction toward the achievement of valued social studies education goals and objectives. The intent is not to provide details on how cooperative learning operates in the classroom to attain these goals and objectives. Rather, the intent is to argue that cooperative learning as an instructional alternative is highly compatible with what social studies educators desire as long-term outcomes of social studies curriculum and instruction.

The next section describes a number of results gained from appropriate cooperative learning structures and groups. The results listed reinforce the claims above that cooperative learning can contribute much to helping students attain the knowledge, abilities, valuing, and social-participation attitudes and values we desire. The section is followed by a summary of the essential elements of cooperative learning. These elements are what separate cooperative learning from other group activities and tasks.

What Do Students Gain by Working in Cooperative Learning Groups?

The proponents of cooperative learning emphasize the need for teachers to structure their student groups and group tasks, because only in this way are the many positive results of this approach likely to occur. The following list reveals the results of numerous studies done in K–12 classrooms. Although these cannot be guaranteed in every instance, they do reflect what can be attained and maintained when the requirements of cooperative learning are met. These likely results appear to be well worth the work needed to set up appropriate cooperative learning lessons and units. Compared to students engaged in noncooperative learning classrooms, cooperative learning students tend to:

- achieve higher scores on academic tests, especially those aligned with targeted outcome objectives.
- have higher proficiency in critical reasoning abilities and strategies.
- have higher levels of intrinsic motivation to learn.
- be less disruptive as individuals and as group members.
- engage in more and higher quality on-task, academic, and group interaction behaviors.
- actually work cooperatively in small-group settings toward attaining a common goal.
- possess many of the positive attitudes necessary for working effectively with others.
- have more positive attitudes toward teachers, principals, and other school personnel.
- have more positive attitudes toward learning, school, and the subject-matter content.
- be more willing to share and interact positively within group settings.
- form greater numbers of friendships based on human qualities.
- have more positive relations with individuals of different ethnic or racial groups.
- voluntarily increase their personal contact with other students in a variety of contexts.
- be more willing to state and discuss their own ideas in public.
- have more positive self-concepts and self-esteem.
- have greater feelings of psychological acceptance of themselves as persons.
- have greater interest in and willingness to engage in academic study.[2]

---

[2] The research studies and research reviews from which this list was generated include Aronson et al. (1978), Cohen (1986), Johnson and Johnson (1987, 1989, 1992), VanSickle (1992), and Slavin (1990, 1992).

Every successful cooperative learning strategy and group task, whether for one class period, one week, or one month, will not achieve all of these outcomes in every instance. The list suggests results that are likely to occur *only when cooperative learning groups operate effectively over extended periods of time.*

Another way to interpret this list is from the perspective of reasons for using cooperative learning. These outcomes reflect many of the reasons why teachers enter the profession and continue to work with students. Isn't the fact that cooperative learning, when used appropriately, is likely to achieve a number of these highly valued outcomes reason enough to try it out in your classroom? As one teacher announced after reading a list like that above, "Until I found out what cooperative learning could accomplish, I was hesitant to use it. Now, I have every reason to try to make it work and no reasons not to!" It is hoped that this list provides results that are reason enough for you, the reader, to implement cooperative learning in your classroom.

Advocating cooperative learning and carrying it out in the classroom are two separate matters. Cooperative learning groups and tasks are different from many traditional group activities. The section that follows describes the essential elements that distinguish cooperative learning from alternative uses of groups in the classroom.

What Are the Essential Elements of Cooperative Learning?

To be successful in setting up and having students complete tasks as cooperative learning groups, a number of essential requirements must be met. The exact number, name, and order of these requirements vary from author to author. However, nearly all agree that the elements listed below are essential.

A. *Clear set of specific student learning outcome objectives.* To meet this requirement, teachers must start their planning by being aware of what their students are expected to know and are able to do on their own well beyond the end of the group task and curriculum unit. Regardless of whether these outcomes emphasize academic content, cognitive processing abilities, or skills, teachers should describe in very unambiguous language the specific knowledge and abilities students are to acquire and then demonstrate on their own days and weeks after their groups have quit meeting. Cooperative learning and cooperative learning groups are means to an end rather than an end in themselves. Selecting clear, specific outcome objectives before the groups are formed and the group tasks begin keeps the focus of the groups on what is to be learned rather than on what they are to do during the group activities.

These objectives do not describe what the groups are to do or accomplish (e.g., answer questions at the end of the chapter, complete a written report on a famous person in a particular historical period, construct a model or mural depicting an event or concept related to the unit being studied). Although students may be asked to do these things, the objectives must describe the specific content and abilities students are to learn and retain as a direct result of their work in groups on assignments such as these.

B. *Common acceptance of the student outcome objectives.* It is not sufficient for the teacher to select outcome objectives; students must see these objectives as their own. To meet this requirement, students must come to know and accept the fact that everyone in a group is expected to learn a common set of information and/or skills, even though not all groups are always expected to learn the same things.[3] Each group and each student must come to accept these learning objectives as ones that all its members are to attain as the learning goals for the activity or unit in which they are involved. Cases in which individual groups select their own outcome objectives require that members of the group accept these objectives as their own.

C. *Positive interdependence.* To meet this requirement, teachers must structure learning tasks so that students come to feel that they sink or swim together (Johnson and Johnson, 1992). The social studies teacher structures the group and group tasks so that as much as possible every student learns the assigned content and abilities and makes sure that all of his or her groupmates also master the same content and abilities. Teachers can structure for positive interdependence by (a) making it

---

[3] Not all cooperative learning strategies (for instance, the Co-op Co-op and group investigation strategies described in this book) require all students in the class to master the same content and skills. However, all strategies require that all members of each particular group master the content, processes, and skills that have been targeted for that group.

clear to all students that all members of their group are to master the targeted content and abilities; (b) informing students that part of their personal effort is to help every member of their group learn the content and abilities targeted; (c) providing group rewards (e.g., if all members of a group score 85 or higher on the test, all members of the group earn 10 bonus points); (d) assigning specific complementary roles to each group member (e.g., one student is the checker, another the elaborator, and another the recorder); and (e) dividing the resources equally among all members. In addition, teachers are encouraged to find other means to ensure that students work to help every groupmate succeed.

D. *Face-to-face interaction.* Here students are to arrange themselves so that from the beginning to the end of their group work they are positioned and postured so that they face one another for direct eye-to-eye contact and face-to-face academic conversations. This positioning helps reinforce the notion of positive interdependence and makes it easier for students to promote one another's success. As they face one another, students discuss what they are studying, clarify and explain the content and procedures they are to learn, critique one another's ideas and performances, and provide appropriate feedback, support, assistance, and encouragement.

E. *Individual accountability.* Cooperative learning is intended to strengthen the academic learning of each group member. The reason why teachers put students in cooperative learning groups is so that eventually all students can be more successful as individuals than they would be studying by themselves or in noncooperative learning groups. Consequently, to ensure that each student does succeed and does take responsibility for his or her own learning, each must be held individually accountable for doing his or her own share of the work and for knowing what has been targeted to be learned.

To meet this requirement, each student is formally tested to determine the extent to which he or she has learned the targeted academic content and abilities. The teacher assesses each student's test performance and returns the results to the student as soon as possible. This element is enhanced when the teacher makes it clear in the introduction to the group study that each student is responsible for learning the targeted content and abilities as each completes the group-related tasks. If groups merely divide the work to get the assignment done, many students are not likely to learn all that is expected. The teacher must prevent such division of work and ensure that students focus on learning rather than on completing the group assignment for its own sake. Furthermore, students must know that they cannot lose themselves within the group and receive credit as a member of the group, as is often the case.

F. *Public recognition and rewards for group academic success.* To complete this element, teachers arrange for individuals and groups who meet or surpass high levels of achievement to receive ample rewards within formal public settings. Whenever possible the teacher will want to compute average scores per team and recognize teams for their collective achievement.[4] Some teachers establish an awards presentation within the class, much like presenting an Oscar for outstanding performance; others set up a permanent display on a bulletin board along with a public announcement; still others invite outside professionals such as the principal or department chair to attend an awards ceremony. The specific awards vary, with the critical criterion that the awards must be something valued by the students. As much as possible, these awards should be given on the day after the test has been given.

G. *Heterogeneous groups.* Teachers should organize the three-, four-, or five-member small groups so that as much as possible students are mixed heterogeneously according to academic abilities, ethnic backgrounds, race, socio-economic levels, and gender. When groups are heterogeneous and assigned clear academic tasks to complete, students of different academic abilities, ethnic backgrounds, race, and gender tend to interact and learn in ways that rarely are found in other instructional strategies. At the same time they tend to become tolerant of diverse viewpoints, to consider others' thoughts and feelings in depth, and to seek more support and clarification of others' positions.

In situations where heterogeneous groups cannot be formed, teachers need to structure groups using procedures that ensure as wide a range of academic abilities and backgrounds as possible. If these other procedures have to be used, students should not be allowed to form their groups based on friendships or cliques.

---

4 Excellent examples of how group grades may be analyzed and bonus points awarded based upon individual and group achievement may be found in Chapters 5, 7, and 8 on Jigsaw II, STAD, and TGT respectively.

H. *Positive social interaction behaviors and attitudes.* To complete the group tasks, students have to work together in a group as a group. However, just because students are placed in groups and expected to use appropriate social and group skills does not mean students will automatically use these skills. As students work through structured cooperative learning activities, they need to engage in such interaction abilities as leadership, compromise, negotiation, and clarifying in order to complete their tasks. To meet this requirement, the social studies teacher may need to describe the social-interaction behaviors and attitudes students are expected to use. These behaviors include leadership, trust building, communication, conflict management, constructive criticism, and encouragement. In many instances, the teacher will need to assign particular students particular group roles that match acceptable group behaviors to ensure that students consciously work on these behaviors in their groups.

I. *Postgroup reflection (debriefing) over group processes.* To meet this requirement, students spend time after group tasks have been completed to systematically reflect upon how they worked together as a team in such areas as (a) how well they achieved their group goals; (b) how they helped one another comprehend the content, resources, and task procedures; (c) how they used positive behaviors and attitudes to enable each individual and the entire group as a group to be successful; and (d) what they need to do next time to make their groups even more successful. As students debrief, they spend time discussing group maintenance, social and group processing behaviors, and particular behaviors and attitudes that promoted or prevented the group's and individual member's success.

To help students achieve this debriefing requirement, the teacher provides a structured reflection task and sufficient time after groups share their responses so that this reflection and assessment of group interaction behaviors target important group processing behaviors. This reflection is especially powerful since it provides an opportunity for each student to receive structured, focused feedback from peers on his or her social and group behaviors and attitudes. Consequently, after helping one another "get better together" in their academic learning, students have the time and the opportunity to get better together relative to their individual behaviors and attitudes in and as part of a group.

J. *Sufficient time for learning.* Each student and each group must have the time they need to spend in learning the targeted information and abilities to the extent expected. If students do not have enough time to spend learning, the academic benefits of cooperative learning will be limited (Stahl, 1992, in press).

Lists such as that above are often misinterpreted. Some teachers feel that they must use every one of these elements every time they assign students to work in groups. This is not the case. However, social studies teachers serious about implementing cooperative learning activities will need to take steps to ensure that many of these requirements are met for each cooperative learning strategy they use. More importantly, unless these elements are used frequently and correctly, teachers should not expect the many positive results that can be achieved by cooperative learning proponents.

Maximizing Student Success: It Is Within Us, "Not Out There"

One rarely enters a classroom where all students are achieving academically, affectively, and socially at the high levels they could attain. There are, thankfully, only a few educators who accept whatever their students are achieving as the very highest level they could attain. These teachers go about their jobs without modifying their own behaviors and assignments. Often these individuals hope for something "out there" to appear and suddenly change everything that happens in their classrooms. Some daydream about the good old days, days that never were, a time they perceive when nearly all their students were so much brighter, nicer, more responsible, and so on than their present-day-students—the days when teaching was so enjoyable and rewarding. One such teacher was overheard to lament, "I'd be a better teacher if I just had better students to work with." Others claimed they could be more effective if they just had more resources to use and to make available to students. Better students, more resources, more money, and better textbooks are just four things "out there" that are like the illusionary white knight who appears suddenly to save the day.

White knights exist in myths and fairy tales but rarely do they enter classrooms like yours and mine. The solution to improving student learning, self-concepts, and social abilities lies within each teacher—not "out there" beyond us. Additional resources may not come in the quality and quantity desired, and even if they did, there is certainly no reason to expect that they would be used appropriately. The failure of "teacher proof" curricular materials of the 1960s-1980s is strong evidence of that assessment. The point here is that *in the social studies classroom the teacher can make the difference that counts for students.* Indeed, with cooperative learning, we have the means to make use of a very abundant and powerful resource for teaching and for learning—our students. The issue is: will we, and how well will we, make use of our students and the instructional structures offered by cooperative learning to optimize the learning environment in our own classrooms?

Cooperative learning activities are not expected to replace all other teaching strategies in the social studies classroom. Students do need to learn how to succeed as individuals in individually important areas such as taking off in the exploration of personally interesting topics or mastering individual abilities. They also need to engage in competitive situations so that they learn to deal with the challenges and frustrations of competitive efforts as well as, in some instances, the fun of the pursuit and the challenges offered by rivalries. In cooperative learning, social studies educators have a powerful alternative to instructional approaches and strategies that focus on individuals working as individuals and within competitive-like instances most of the time. Within successful cooperative learning groups, students, indeed nearly all students, "get better together."

This chapter addresses many concerns teachers have about cooperative learning. Specific strategies and practical guidelines with classroom examples are described in the chapters that follow.

References

Aronson, E., N. Blaney, C. Stephan, J. Sikes, and M. Snapp. 1978. *The jigsaw classroom.* Beverly Hills, CA: Sage.

Cohen, E. G. 1986. *Designing groupwork: Strategies for the heterogeneous classroom.* Colchester, VT: Teachers College Press.

Johnson, D. W., and R. T. Johnson. 1987. *Learning together and alone,* 2nd ed. Englewood Cliffs, NJ: Prentice Hall.

———. 1989. *Cooperation and competition: Theory and research.* Edina, MN: Interaction Book Company.

————. 1992. Approaches to implementing cooperative learning in the social studies classroom. In R. J. Stahl and R. L. VanSickle, eds. *Cooperative learning in the social studies classroom: An invitation to social study.* Washington, DC: National Council for the Social Studies.

Johnson, D. W., R. T. Johnson, and E. J. Holubec. 1990. *Cooperation in the classroom,* rev. ed. Edina, MN: Interaction Book Company.

National Council for the Social Studies. 1979. Revision of the NCSS social studies curriculum guidelines. *Social Education,* 43 (4, April): 261-66.

Sharan, S. 1985. Cooperative learning and the multiethnic classroom. In R. E. Slavin, S. Sharan, et al., eds. *Learning to cooperate, cooperating to learn,* 255-76 New York: Plenum Press.

Slavin, R. E. 1990. *Cooperative learning: Theory, research, and practice.* Englewood Cliffs, NJ: Prentice Hall.

————. 1991. Synthesis of research on cooperative learning. *Educational Leadership,* 48 (5, February): 71-82.

————. 1992. Cooperative learning in social studies: Balancing the social and the studies. In R. J. Stahl and R. L. VanSickle, eds. *Cooperative learning in the social studies classroom: An invitation to social study.* Washington, DC: National Council for the Social Studies.

Stahl, R. J. 1992. From "academic strangers" to successful members of a cooperative learning group: An inside-the-learner perspective. In R. J. Stahl and R. L. VanSickle, eds. *Cooperative learning in the social studies classroom: An invitation to social study.* Washington, DC: National Council for the Social Studies.

————. (in press). A context for "higher order knowledge": An information-constructivist perspective with implications for curriculum and instruction. *Journal of Structural Learning and Applied Intelligence.*

VanSickle, R. L. 1992. Cooperative learning, properly implemented, works: Evidence from research in classrooms. In R. J. Stahl and R. L. VanSickle, eds. *Cooperative learning in the social studies classroom: An invitation to social study.* Washington, DC: National Council for the Social Studies.

2.

Cultivating Cooperative Group Process Skills Within the Social Studies Classroom

PATRICIA ROY

"I expected my students to get into groups enthusiastically, and then I expected to see smiling faces and better learning taking place. I was disappointed to see just the opposite!" lamented one teacher.

What went wrong? This educator later discovered that he had made an assumption that students had already mastered the skills of working together in a cooperative situation. The reality was that these students had never been taught how to work together effectively as a group.

Another high-school teacher reflected upon his first attempts at using small groups. He realized, after the first groups struggled to work as a group, that his students had the results of eleven years of independent and competitive experiences to unlearn before they could be consistently productive within a cooperative learning situation. He accepted that the norms of the traditional classroom in all academic areas have to do with preventing interaction among students, not promoting conversations between learners.

These two examples illustrate that many of the reasons why students do not immediately adopt cooperative learning strategies and use skills necessary to make these groups effective because of classroom traditions that work against their cooperation for learning. Cooperative learning classrooms are very different from classrooms in which traditional approaches to instruction and group activities are used. The chart on the next page illustrates some of these differences.

David and Roger Johnson (1989) have stated that structuring the task

Traditional Classroom	Cooperative Classroom
Do your own work	Work with others to learn
Eyes to front and be quiet	Eye to eye, knee to knee
Listen only to the teacher	Listen to group members
Learn only from teacher/materials	Learn from one's peers within a group
Work alone	Work within a small group as a group
Silence is "golden"	Productive talk is desired
Teacher only makes decisions	Students make decisions
Learners are passive	Learners are active

so that students need to work together is not enough to capitalize on the opportunity presented in a cooperative situation. The development of appropriate group and interpersonal skills is necessary so that students can work together productively without direct teacher supervision. One of the teacher's first steps when using small cooperative groups in social studies is to prepare students to work together.

One educator stated, "I can't use groups. My students don't have the skills." The reality is that students will not develop group process skills unless they are taught them directly and have an opportunity to practice those skills within a cooperative group setting. Furthermore, students must also spend time reflecting over their use of particular skills after they have completed activities during which the use of these skills was expected. Indeed, increased academic achievement and the reinforcement of interpersonal skills are two important outcomes of postgroup debriefing or processing (Yager, Johnson, and Johnson, 1986).

Rationale for the Development of Interpersonal Skills

There are numerous reasons to teach group skills that go beyond the social studies classroom. Major studies have shown that the necessary skills of a competitive work force include the ability to work with others. In the book *When Smart People Fail*, Hyatt and Gottlieb (1987) identified the nine most common reasons why people lose their jobs. The number one reason was "poor interpersonal skills." This was the major reason for a career failure and the single most important skill to acquire. Unfortunately, individuals rarely realize that their poor interpersonal skills were the real cause for their dismissal. A government study showed that 85 percent of the people who lose their jobs lose them not because of a lack of technical competence but because they could not work well with others.

Jobs are changing. Chrysler announced in a recent newspaper article that "teams" of employees now would work together to complete an automobile. New managerial skills involve knowing how to develop cooperation by working with teams, creating trust, and facilitating group decision making. In *Survival on the Fast Track*, a book that gives advice to corporate fast-trackers, the number one piece of advice to ensure that your career didn't get derailed was to "give up a competitive orientation for a cooperative one and to learn how to create a team feeling" (Kovack, 1989). The ability to work well with others is required in many industries. Studies conducted by United Airlines and the federal government revealed that 75 percent of all commercial airline accidents were due to a lack of coordination and cooperation in the cockpit.

Effective group and interpersonal skills are not necessary just so that students can interact within a cooperative learning activity; they also will benefit students when they join the work force.

Stages of Group Development

So, where does the classroom teacher start? There is no scope and sequence of group skills. Age alone does not determine the skills that should be developed. Some high-school civics teachers have discovered that they have to work on "staying with your group," just as most kindergarten teachers do. The grade level does not predict that students have had prior experience working together in groups. When it comes to working well within a group setting, a senior may need as much guidance as a first grader.

Groups have lives of their own. They progress through a variety of stages just as children move from infancy to adolescence and on to adulthood. There are at least four stages of group development: groups form, norm, storm, and then perform. Each of these stages will be described in the following section. Ideas of what the teacher can do to help students develop skills in each stage will also be discussed.

Stage One: Forming

In the forming stage, students begin learning the basics of effective cooperative group interaction. To be successful, they need to develop a clear idea of how a productive group behaves. Involving everyone, communicating and listening, giving and receiving help, getting to know others, and developing trust are important skills. Trust is accomplished when a risk-free environment is created wherein members feel free to express their thoughts and ideas without fear of ridicule. Support for and acceptance of anyone's ideas and opinions by each group member is the expected typical behavior within each group.

Teacher's Role During the Group Formation Stage

1. The teacher needs to structure group tasks very clearly and specifically. Rather than just telling groups to "work together," the specific steps and procedures that group members are to follow should be outlined. For example, the teacher may announce that "The first person to talk in your group will be the person whose first name comes first in alphabetical order. That person will explain in his or her own words how to locate a site by using longitude and latitude. All other members need to listen to make sure that they agree or disagree with the directions for locating the site. If you disagree, you are to tell the other person why you disagree. When everyone agrees on the answer, rotate to the right. That person will take the second example and so on around the group."

2. The teacher should provide experiences that help students learn about one another—especially using activities that emphasize similarities among the students. These activities are called "trust builders" or "ice breakers." These experiences can be conducted on two levels: (a) *whole class-building activities* during which students get to know all their classmates, and (b) *team-building activities* during which students learn more about only the members of their small group. For example, a people treasure-hunt activity can be used to build classroom trust and allow classmates to meet one another. For another activity, a group profile could be created for each small cooperative group.

Stage Two: Norming

Norms are rules that define how groups should interact. In other words, they describe guidelines and expectations that group members are to follow (as well as not do) all of the time. In sports, for instance, the rules are clearly defined concerning what is acceptable and unacceptable behavior. Tackling players by holding their jerseys is acceptable; but grabbing a face mask earns a penalty. Group norms might include everyone speaking for equal time periods, one person speaking at a time, each member pulling his or her own weight, and no one member dominating the group. Group members also may need to learn how to make decisions together, how to reach consensus, how to communicate and to listen, and how to help one another. Norms could also include put-downs, interruptions, and side conversations as unacceptable behavior.

Teacher's Role During the Norming Stage

1. During this stage, the teacher needs to facilitate student acquisition and refinement of the skills necessary to follow essential interpersonal and group norms. The activities included in this chapter help students understand how to work effectively with one another as a group and emphasize the importance of working together. Similar activities that focus on important group skills should be conducted during this stage of the group's development.

2. The teacher also can directly teach specific behaviors that will be required for group work. Students need to have an exact idea of what to say and what to do to put each new skill into operation. Therefore, new behavior is modeled, exact words to say are suggested and written, and attention is paid to describing appropriate nonverbal actions. One example of a direct instruction activity that helps facilitate these norms is included in this chapter.

Stage Three: Storming

Conflict among members is an inevitable stage in group development. This may seem strange, but some conflict often results as members address differences of opinion and communicate what they truly feel.

Group members can also be in conflict with the teacher. The groups might complain about the lesson structure or having to get into their groups. This stage does not mean that the groups are falling apart or that the teacher has done something wrong.

At least three areas of concern emerge during this stage.

1. *Generating new group skills.* Group members may no longer be willing to tolerate the inappropriate behaviors of others or may need to learn how to confront and cope with another member's behavior.

2. *Testing the rules and norms.* Some students will attempt to test the limits of the normative rules that have been established. Others will explore the meanings of these same rules, not always sure what behaviors are appropriate for the rules established.

3. *Reconciling one's individuality with membership in the group.* Students need to maintain their individuality and not lose their identity within the group. Students vary in their abilities to make this adjustment and successfully cope with their conceptions of themselves and their roles within the group setting.

Teacher's Role During the Storming Stage

1. The teacher needs to explain to students that conflict is a natural part of group development. It does not mean that the groups need to be dismantled, but rather that students need to learn how to work through disagreements.

2. The teacher needs to teach directly the interpersonal skills that are necessary for the management of conflict: these include describing another person's behavior without labeling or evaluating, listening actively, paraphrasing, perspective taking, describing feelings, and using "I" statements.

Stage Four: Performing

At this stage, the group can organize itself, can use all the effective group and interpersonal skills, can solve difficulties, and can work efficiently and effectively without much outside help. Placing this stage last does not mean that it takes a long period of time before cooperative groups are able to be productive. It is just that in earlier stages students need structure, guidance, and monitoring by the teacher.

Teacher's Role During the Performing Stage

1. The teacher needs to help students maintain their group skills. The balanced focus between getting the task done while preserving good working relationships needs to be maintained. The teacher makes sure groups continue to reflect upon or debrief at the end of their work sessions—although they will not need to reflect as frequently as they have done in earlier stages.

2. The teacher should act as a facilitator and consultant to groups. It is not necessary to continue to structure the group as closely as was done in earlier stages. The teacher steps back and lets the group decide how it will work together as long as the group is engaged in productive work.

It is not inevitable that all groups will progress through all these stages. Sometimes groups get stuck in one stage. All of us have probably experienced groups that became enmeshed in the conflict stage and stayed there until the group disbanded. These groups needed a facilitator to help them learn the skills necessary for working through the conflict stage and to enable them to move to the performing stage.

Time is also a factor. Groups need time to be together to develop through the stages (see Figure 2-1 below). If groups are formed and reformed every three to four lessons, groups will stay only in the forming stage.

Figure 2-1   *Stages of Group Development Over Time*

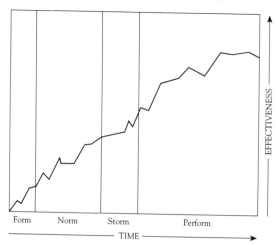

Cooperative Learning Group Skills

A list of possible group skills appears below. This listing is intended to be used as a diagnostic tool, not as a scope and sequence. It doesn't mean that kindergarten students start with "stay with your group" and high-school students focus on "disagreeing agreeably." The teacher should scan down the first column and decide which particular skills students currently use. Should students have particular skills, the teacher can move to skills listed in the next column.

Beginning	Basic	Advanced
Stays with the group	Checks	Criticizes ideas, not people
Looks at speaker	Asks questions	Describes behavior, not person
Helps complete the group's work	Acknowledges others	Perspective taking
Shares materials	Communication skills	Paraphrases
Shares ideas	• "I" statements	Problem solving
Takes turns	• Active listening	Consensus
Uses first names	• Restating	Summarizes
Talks in a soft voice	Praises	Differentiates ideas
Stays on task		Disagrees agreeably

These skills take a long time to develop. In most classrooms, students develop only about four to seven skills over an entire year. Monitoring student interactions provides the teacher with information for selecting, modifying, and assessing appropriate skills. Students can also be involved in determining the necessary skills. Another activity in this chapter will model how that discussion can be conducted.

Status Concerns Within Heterogeneous Groups

Addressing the needs of the heterogeneous classroom has been the focus of the work of Elizabeth Cohen and her colleagues (1986). Her work has demonstrated that placing students in groups does not automatically compensate for differences in academic achievement. Students bring a "status" to the group that can affect their level of participation. High-status students tend to talk more and can even dominate group interaction. Even though one of the desired outcomes of cooperative learning is increased student interaction, the opposite can result if status expectations are not addressed.

Cohen suggests training students in a number of group norms. Norms are expected working behaviors. They answer the question "How would an effective group interact?" Cohen suggests the following norms:

Everybody helps

Equal participation

Members are to explain by telling how

Members are to help their peers do things for themselves

Members are to find out what their peers think

Members are to tell why and ask why

Members are to contribute new ideas or suggestions

Members may bring other people in

Members are to ask for or give information

Members may agree when there is a good reason

Members may disagree with a good reason

Cultivating Group Interaction Skills: Practical Classroom Guidelines and Examples

The lessons and activities that follow will provide three different ways to help students learn how to work together *in and as cooperative groups* in social studies classes. The first activity is a direct approach to teaching a specific interpersonal skill. It is useful for all grade levels and is necessary to ensure that students know exactly *what to do* and *what to say* to perform a particular group skill. The second experiential learning activity, called Broken Squares, demonstrates the necessity of being aware of the needs of others during group work. The third activity is a discussion with students to facilitate their identification of interpersonal skills that need to be used when working *in and as* groups. Lastly, there is a section on conducting reflective group processing or "debriefing" tasks.

I. *Direct Instruction of Interpersonal Skills*

Some seventh-grade students were practicing how to praise their teammates. They started with saying things like "Boy, I like your hair today!" and "Great earrings!"

While any kind of praise from a seventh grader should be encouraged and treasured, this was not exactly the kind of "praise" that we wanted.

Interpersonal skills can be developed as directly as academic skills. Direct instruction of an interpersonal skill is necessary so that students have a clear idea of how to put the new skill into action. These steps for directly teaching an interpersonal skill are based on the work of Albert Bandura (1969) and have been translated by David and Roger Johnson (1987) into the following five steps.

After determining the specific, observable skill:

1. provide clear reasons why students need to learn the skill.

2. define the skill clearly.

3. provide practice for the new skill in an appropriate context.

4. provide feedback on the practice of the skill.

5. ensure review and practice of the skill over a long period of time.

What follows is an activity that teaches students how to check other members of the group. Checking, an important skill that enhances learning, ensures that every student has the opportunity to verbalize his or her understanding of the steps involved in an academic skill, and can provide a rationale for an answer or explain a concept.

This direct instructional strategy involves the following five phases:

1. a role-play situation

2. a discussion guided by the teacher

3. brainstorming by students

4. an academic activity to allow students to practice the new skill

5. processing or debriefing the activity

Materials that will be needed are:

- newsprint or large piece of butcher paper, overhead projector or chalkboard

- markers and tape
- worksheet—one copy for each group of two members
- social studies book with atlas section
- group membership roster
- list of actions for role play

Phase One: Role Play (Function: Create the need for the new skill)

The teacher begins by asking for a student volunteer to do a role play with the teacher in front of the class. (The student can be selected beforehand and given instructions on what to do or asked to participate immediately before the role play.) The student is asked to follow a set of clear directions of things to do and places to go in the classroom. For example, the teacher might ask the student to perform the following sequence of actions.

1. Go pick up a red pencil from my desk.
2. Sharpen it at the pencil sharpener.
3. Take three copies of the social studies book from the shelves and give a copy to the first person in the first three rows.
4. Pull down the map of the United States.
5. Put out two pieces of chalk.
6. Sit down at a desk, take out a piece of paper, and write your name in the upper right-hand corner.

The teacher and student complete the role-play situation twice. The first time the student cannot ask any questions or write anything down, and the teacher will not ask any questions of the student. The teacher reads the list of the six items and asks the student, "Do you understand?" As cued, the student responds "Yes" and begins to follow the directions. (The student tries to complete the activities while pretending to forget the directions.)

The second time, the teacher gives another set of directions, but this time he or she checks with the student to make sure the student does remember or knows what to do. For example, the teacher might say, "I am going to tell you to do another six things. We'll take it step by step. I will ask you questions to make sure you remember, or I will ask you how you will remember what to do next."

The student is told all of these six things to do:

1. Turn off the classroom lights.
2. Take your social studies book and put it on the top of your desk.
3. Take a dictionary from the shelf and give it to another student.
4. Write your first name on the chalkboard.
5. Take a newspaper and open it to the front page and place it on the teacher's desk.
6. Take out a piece of paper and number it from 1 to 10.

Then, the teacher asks the student questions about each action and how he or she will remember which action comes next. For example, questions like the following can be asked: "Do you remember the first step? What is it? Go practice that right now. What is the second step? How can you remember that step? In your own words, what is step three? How will you remember that this is the third step?" The teacher can give hints such as, "Remember that the second and third things you have to do have to do with books. The first is your social studies book because we are studying social studies now; the second is a dictionary." The teacher has the student practice each step one action at a time, and when the student is confident enough, he or she can perform all six steps in order.

Phase Two: Discussion Guided by the Teacher (Function: Determining the differences between the two situations)

When the second role play has been completed, the student is thanked by the teacher, who then asks that his or her classmates give a round of applause. The teacher then asks students to describe what was different between the two role plays through such questions as "What did we do in the second role play that we did not do in the first?" After sufficient wait time, students are called upon to respond. They may also be asked, "How did those things make a difference? Did they make it easier or harder to do the six steps? Why would it be easier to do the second set of steps than the first?"

Phase Three: Student Brainstorming (Function: Clearly defining the behavior)

Then say, "What I was doing in the second role play was a behavior called Checking." (Write "Checking" on a piece of newsprint or butcher paper.) "Checking is asking the other person to tell how or explain why they know something. It is getting the other person to talk. In your own words, what is the definition of checking? As we are using the term, what does checking mean?" (Students might say, "making sure someone knows how to do something, or asking another person if he or she knows how to do something.") Write a student definition under the word "Checking" on the newsprint.

This step incorporates a T-Chart. Just below the definition, draw one line horizontally across the page and another line down the center of the page so that it resembles a large letter T. This chart would take the following form.

"Checking" Sounds Like	"Checking" Looks Like

Students are asked to brainstorm words they can say to check another student's responses. They also should be asked to describe what checking looks like when students communicate nonverbally. Student responses should be recorded by the teacher on the newsprint, overhead projector, or chalkboard.

If you are the teacher, you might announce, "Checking is a skill that will be important for you to use in your cooperative groups when you work in social studies. If I were to ask you to check with members of your group, what would you say?"

Some possible checking phrases might be:

- Would you tell us why you said _____?

- Explain to me how that works.

- Please explain the answer to number _____.

- Tell us more about _____.

- What does that mean to you?

- Why is that answer correct, (student's name)?

- What is one good example of _____?

- What is the reason for that answer?

- What makes you think that way?

Next, ask students, "Is the question *Do you agree?* a good checking statement?"

Students should respond as follows: "No, because we can't tell whether someone really knows something if the person just says yes or no. The person has to explain in more detail for us to really find out if he or she knows something."

Then students are asked to think about the nonverbal ways we communicate. The teacher might say, "Our bodies sometimes tell other people how we feel even though we don't say anything." The teacher could frown or look angry and ask students what they are feeling. "We need to make sure that our bodies are showing that we care whether the other person knows the answer. If I were to videotape your group and show it to you on television but turn down the sound, what would I see that would tell me you were checking one another?"

Other student responses should be solicited and recorded on the newsprint. Some possible behaviors might include:

- direct eye contact

- leaning into the group

- sitting "eye to eye" and "knee to knee"

- one person talking at a time

- others looking at the person who is talking

Phase Four: Practicing the New Skill (Function: Initial application and rehearsal of the new skill)

The proper execution of this phase within the social studies classroom consists of two subphases described below with examples.[1]

First Subphase: Establishing a set of interpersonal skills for the learning task. As the teacher, you would inform students that they will have a chance to practice checking in their groups while they work on a review activity. For example, they may review the concepts of continent, country, and state that have been studied before. Students are arranged in

---

1 The academic lesson idea came from Cheryl Amodt.

partnerships of two. Partners can be determined by the teacher or by counting off randomly. Students should move their desks together so that they are seated side by side.

Each partnership is given one worksheet and a copy of the social studies book open to a world map. The worksheet used in this example is provided as Figure 2-2 below.

Figure 2-2 *Worksheet To Accompany the Classroom Example Relative to Continents, Countries, and States*

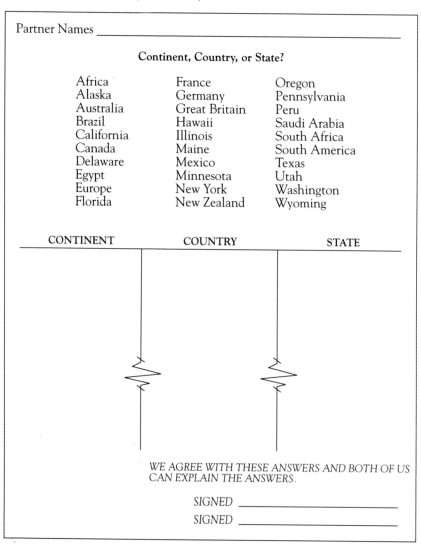

Partner Names _____

Continent, Country, or State?

Africa   France   Oregon
Alaska   Germany   Pennsylvania
Australia   Great Britain   Peru
Brazil   Hawaii   Saudi Arabia
California   Illinois   South Africa
Canada   Maine   South America
Delaware   Mexico   Texas
Egypt   Minnesota   Utah
Europe   New York   Washington
Florida   New Zealand   Wyoming

CONTINENT   COUNTRY   STATE

WE AGREE WITH THESE ANSWERS AND BOTH OF US CAN EXPLAIN THE ANSWERS.

SIGNED _____

SIGNED _____

The procedures that the partners should follow are:

1. The person with the most letters in his or her name is first. That person chooses any name from the box at the top of the worksheet page and places it in the correct column—either continent, country, or state.

2. He or she also locates the place on the map in the book.

3. The student uses one of the checking statements to ask his or her partner to explain why that specific column was chosen.

4. If both partners agree, the one who checked crosses out the name in the box at the top of the page.

5. The other partner then chooses the next place, and the same procedure is followed until all the places have been correctly categorized.

(These steps should be written on the chalkboard, overhead projector, or worksheet. Two students should be asked to demonstrate the steps for the whole class.)

Students should be informed that you, the teacher, will listen to partners work together. You will be listening especially for the ways partners check with each other. Make a tally mark for each time you hear a checking statement. When everyone has finished, let the class know how many times you heard checking statements.

Tell students that they should be able to complete this task on their own with no more than three errors. If they have four or more errors, they will need to redo the worksheet until it is 100 percent correct. Also, ask either partner to explain why each name was placed where it was. Either partner could be asked to tell why he or she chose a particular location.

Second Subphase: Facilitating the rehearsal learning task. As students work, make sure they follow the procedures, take turns, and practice using the appropriate checking behaviors. Tally the number of times you hear checking statements, and write down statements that are new. You will share these with students at the end. You might also have to intervene if a pair is not following directions. You can do that by saying, "I haven't seen you taking turns and following the steps I'd like you to practice. Whose turn is it next? It is important that you follow the procedures. I'll stand here and listen to make sure that you understand what I'd like you to do."

Phase Five: Processing (Function: Post-task conscious review of students' use of the checking behaviors)

During this phase, students discuss how well they practiced checking. Ask them to evaluate their performances by giving their partnership a grade of A, B, C, or D. "D" means very little checking was done, and an "A" indicates that students checked every time. Ask them to tell you what grade they gave and why. Randomly call on students from different pairs. Ask students to raise their hands to show how many wrote a D, how many wrote a C, and how many wrote an A or a B.

After these activities are completed, share with students the number of times you heard checking. Share other checking statements you heard as you monitored the partners. Tell the class that they will continue to work on checking until it becomes a habit.

This concludes the illustration of a direct instructional strategy for helping students to acquire a particular set of interpersonal skills appropriate for cooperative learning groups. A second strategy is described in the next section.

II. An Experiential Learning Activity

To many of our students, school is not a place where a person is concerned with how someone else is learning. In some instances, grade-conscious students don't want others to learn so that they can be at the top of the class. Sometimes students aren't concerned about or aware of what others are doing at all. The school life of many students does not involve cooperative interactions for gaining academic information and skills. As a result, many students have to learn to become sensitive to the needs of others in their group. They have to learn that in doing cooperative learning tasks, their work is not done until everyone has been successful. This can be a hard lesson to learn, especially during an academic learning task.

An Example Experiential Learning Activity: Broken Squares

The experiential cooperative activity that follows can help students become aware of the needs of other group members. This activity, entitled Broken Squares, can be used with fourth graders through adults. Broken Squares was first developed by Dr. Alex Bavelas (1973). The activity includes the following three phases.

1. Explanation of task and a set of directions

2. Activity

3. Debriefing

Materials needed are:

- one set of five squares per group of five students (such as those in Figure 2-3 on page 36)

- set of directions

- group role assignments (if teacher designates such roles)

Phase One: Explanation of Task and a Set of Directions

The teacher announces that students will be working in a group of five members. Each member will receive an envelope with a set of puzzle pieces (see Figure 2-3 on page 36). The goal is for each person to put together a complete square using the puzzle pieces available. In order to accomplish the goal, some puzzle pieces must be exchanged among group members. But there is a challenge; this exchange must be done *without any talking!* The rules for the activity are:

1. No talking—complete silence is necessary.

2. You may not point or signal to other players in any way to let them know what you need or to help them.

3. Each person must put together his or her own square. No one else may show a player how to do it or do it for him or her.

4. This is a giving game. You may not take a piece from another person, but you may give your pieces one at a time to any other member of your group. Group members can also give pieces to you or any other group member. You may not place a piece in another person's puzzle. Each person must complete it alone.

(Post these rules on the chalkboard, or overhead transparency, or make individual copies that can be given to each group.)

Phase Two: Activity

Students are informed that they can open their envelopes and take out their pieces. Announce they will have from 15 to 20 minutes to complete the activity. (Ask if anyone has done this task before. If some-

Figure 2-3 *Guidelines and Patterns for the Broken Squares Activity*

Squares are 6"x 6". One set of five squares is created for each group of five
people. All the pieces marked with the same letter should be exactly the same
size. Several combinations are possible that will form one or two squares but
only one combination will form all five squares, each 6"x 6". Letters should not
be marked on the game pieces.

Place the following puzzle pieces into envelopes:

    1. Pieces I, H, E   4. Pieces D, F
    2. Pieces A, A, A   5. Pieces G, B, F, C
    3. Pieces A, J, C

one has, ask him or her to be an observer. If you have an uneven number
of students, have the extra students act as observers. Observers can
watch to make sure that the groups follow the rules. Have these
observers say, "You need to follow the rules. You can't talk or place that
puzzle piece or . . . ." Observers can write down descriptions of how the
groups work together or what happens during the activity.)

    The teacher also needs to monitor groups to make sure that mem-
bers do not break the rules. It is possible for one member to complete
a square and block others from completing theirs. Only one combination results in everyone having a complete square. Some groups can
have difficulty with this task; others may finish right away.

Phase Three: Debriefing

When all the groups have completed their task or the time runs out, a discussion or debriefing with students should be conducted. An important component of any experiential learning activity is discussing what happened, analyzing why it happened, and generalizing applications of what the students noticed about working together to complete their squares. Of special importance is their answer to the question "What have I learned from this activity about working in any group?" Teachers cannot assume that students will learn merely from participating in the activity itself. The debriefing discussion is crucial for the long-term success of activities such as this.

Some debriefing questions you can ask students to discuss in their groups and share with the rest of the class are:

- Describe how your group worked together to complete the task. What specific problems did you have? To what extent did everything go smoothly?

- How do you feel about what happened in your group today?

- What things did you do in your group that helped you to be successful in completing the task?

- What happened during this group activity to make the work harder?

- In order to work better together, what could your group have done differently?

- In order to work better together in the future, what could your group do differently from what was done today?

- What have you learned about working in a group that could help you work with any group in the future?

Comments

One of the design features of the Broken Squares activity is the possibility that one member will complete his or her square and then sit back, unaware of others' needs. In some cases, a group member will have to break up a completed square and give pieces to others people in order to accomplish the goal of everyone having a square. These behaviors demonstrate the concepts of positive interdependence and individual accountability. *Positive interdependence* means that a group has a common goal and must help everyone accomplish the goal. *Individual accountability* means that each member is responsible for accomplishing a specific goal. These two factors are critical components of appropriate cooperative interactions. Stressing these concepts in debriefing is important, as is helping students understand the meaning and power of these concepts when translated into actual behaviors within each group.

III. *Directed Discussion*

The motivation and rationale for working in small groups come from many sources. Business leaders, industrial experts, and social psychologists all discuss the need for people to work cooperatively with others. Educational researchers have conducted hundreds of studies which reveal many cognitive and affective outcomes resulting from the use of well-structured and appropriately used cooperative learning groups. Yet, when faced with a group of third graders or skeptical seventh graders or turned-off high schoolers, do these facts make sense to the typical classroom teacher? To what extent do these results give teachers the motivation to restructure their day's activities?

Students do have experiences in groups outside of school. They team up for sports, join the Scouts or Brownies, belong to clubs or church groups, and spend time with family and peer groups. These student experiences can be used to help them realize the importance of working together in learning groups and to determine which interpersonal and groups skills should be emphasized and developed.

An Example of a Directed Discussion

This activity involves a series of questions for students to discuss with one another and then share with the rest of the class. The class is divided into groups of four students each. Each group has paper and pencils to record its ideas. The teacher should have markers and four large pieces of newsprint or butcher paper that should be posted in the room. The teacher will pose a question and give the groups from five to six minutes to brainstorm, discuss, and record their ideas. Groups will be asked to share their ideas, and the teacher will record them on the paper.

The directed discussion strategy uses examples that are typically observed in the classroom. The directions and questions provided are very close to the exact words you might use in your classroom.

Directions To Set Up the Discussion

"Your groups will be given four questions to discuss with one another about working in a group. The procedure I want you to follow is called Round Table. Each group member will be expected to give some ideas and record them on one piece of paper. I will help you determine who will go first. The first member will tell his or her ideas to the group and then record them on a piece of paper. The paper passes to the left to the second member. That person adds another idea and writes it down. The paper continues to be passed to the left until the time is up or no one has any more ideas to add. Each of you will have a turn to be a spokesperson for your group and tell the class some of the ideas your group discussed and recorded."

Discussion Questions

1. *The teacher initiates students' reflective thought about their work and experiences within the group.* The first questions would be similar to the following:

   ▪ Why is it good to work in groups?

   ▪ How do you personally benefit by working cooperatively in a group?

   ▪ What do you like about working in small groups?

   (Allow students five to six minutes to discuss and record their ideas. Monitor groups to make sure they are following directions and everyone is writing his or her ideas. Be sure they understand that they are to share their ideas aloud within the group as well as writing their ideas on paper.)

   The procedure for revealing a group's answers to the entire class is called Round Robin. Each group is given an opportunity to share their ideas with the whole classroom as the teacher asks each group to reveal one item from its list. Each group is to reveal only one idea at a time. Groups are not to repeat an idea stated by another group, they are to add only new ideas. The groups are called on in rounds and continue to share until all the ideas are announced and are written on a single sheet. The Round Robin is over when all new ideas have been revealed from all the groups.

   You can determine who the first spokesperson will be in each group—or allow students to make this decision for themselves.

2. *Students consider the advantages and disadvantages of working with close friends within their cooperative learning groups.* Students usually like to work with their friends and can sometimes challenge their teacher concerning group membership. Students need to consider and discuss situations in which they have asked to work with friends or complained when they were not with friends. State that a lot of experience has shown that working with friends isn't always the best choice. Then ask students to answer these questions among themselves in their groups:

   ▪ Why doesn't it work to be in groups with just your friends?

   ▪ Why might working in a group with your friends prevent you from doing your best?

   (Allow students to discuss and record ideas for five to six minutes using the Round Table procedure. Call time, and again record their ideas on the larger paper using the Round Robin technique. Make sure there is a new spokesperson for this round.)

3. *The teacher creates a mental picture of a meeting of an efficient, well-functioning group.* This real or hypothetical meeting could be an international group of leaders or an intergalactic meeting of cosmic leaders. Urge students to imagine that this is a very effective group. The members work well together and are immensely productive. Ask students to image themselves with this group as it works together. Then ask students to answer the question:

   ▪ While this group works, what behaviors should you see and hear?

   (Allow students to discuss and record ideas for five to six minutes using the Round Table procedure. Call time and record their ideas on newsprint using the Round Robin technique. Make sure there is a new spokesperson for this round.)

4. *Each group selects the four class-listed behaviors they feel are most important to use as they work together.* Announce that the top four to six behaviors to be identified by the class will become the expected group behaviors, or norms, for future group interaction. Each group needs to seek a consensus about the four most important group behaviors. Then the entire class will be asked to vote for four behaviors. (Allow seven to eight minutes for this consensus-seeking discussion.)

Once the group discussions are completed, ask for the decisions of each group and tally the vote on the large paper. The top four to six behaviors identified by the class should become the expected group behaviors for group interaction. These four to six behaviors, now recorded on large paper, should be posted. They are a visual reminder of the expected and effective group behaviors students should practice as they work together.

5. *Students are asked to determine dysfunctional behaviors to be avoided within their groups.* Two last questions for the class to answer cooperatively are:

   ▪ What two behaviors would you outlaw in the group?

   ▪ Sometimes it is difficult to work with other people. Situations arise in the group that are uncomfortable or that get in the way of completing the work. What two behaviors would you like to make sure never happen in your group?

   (Ask students to spend five to six minutes to discuss and then record on the large paper their possible answers. Ask each group to read its two ideas. Tell them it is acceptable to repeat another group's ideas. If two groups select the same behavior, put a tally mark next to the behavior.)

   These behaviors also can be posted with an international NO sign: a circle with a line drawn diagonally across it. These become the inappropriate behaviors that students must avoid while working together.

6. *The directed discussion strategy ends with the teacher pointing out that future group membership will be determined by ensuring that a variety of skills and talents is represented in each group.* Reemphasize that the behaviors the class has identified as important are those each student is to use and are those that the class will continue to discuss in order to make sure their groups are effective.

   This strategy can be quite effective in helping students to generate lists of acceptable and unacceptable behaviors in cooperative learning groups. One key to its success is precisely worded questions to cue students as to what specific behaviors they are to describe. The other key is sufficient uninterrupted time for student groups to generate their collective answers. The fourth strategy that follows involves students in a different set of processing tasks related to productive interaction behaviors.

IV. Systematic Debriefing

In experiential learning, a necessary component is systematic debriefing or processing the activity after its completion. This debriefing task is a time to look back on what happened during the activity, create meanings about the interactions, and examine how those meanings could apply to other situations. In other words, we do not learn just by having experiences per se but rather from reflecting upon our experiences. Debriefing is also an important component in developing and refining group skills. During this time, group members are given the opportunity to reflect back upon their experiences of working together.

Systematic debriefing has three intended outcomes:

1. description of effective behaviors that helped the group to be successful and thus should be repeated

2. description of areas for improvement

3. generalization of this learning situation to other group situations one may encounter in the future

Systematic debriefing can be accomplished in a number of ways, such as having students complete a processing form or cooperatively answering a set of open-ended questions. The most important points to remember are that debriefing tasks should focus on the positive and that students should become actively involved in the discussion.

Debriefing questions are open-ended rather than close-ended. The nature of these questions is illustrated by the following examples:

Open-ended "What are some things a group member did that helped your group to be successful today?"

Close-ended "Were you successful today?"

Questions that elicit only "Yes" or "No" answers do not facilitate students' understanding of how groups work, what makes a good group, or how their behaviors can make a difference in a group's success or failure.

One of the goals of cooperative learning groups is to help students become consciously aware of their behaviors while working in a small group. Many times, students perform group skills unconsciously and haphazardly. Appropriate debriefing heightens the awareness of effective behaviors and is designed to increase the number of times students perform these behaviors. This debriefing also increases the likelihood that the targeted interpersonal behaviors will be done consciously and deliberately.

There are two standards of a productive group: a balance between task behaviors, and maintenance behaviors. *Task behaviors* are those actions that help the group complete its work. Task behaviors include making sure everyone helps, giving ideas, asking questions, sharing materials, and so forth. Task behaviors also include any action that helps the group to be productive and accomplish their goals. *Maintenance behaviors* are those actions that help maintain good working relationships among group members. Maintenance behaviors include praising, acknowledging others' contributions, encouraging participation, and trusting. When groups first learn to work together, most of their energy is focused on completing the task. Systematic debriefing provides additional time for the group to work on its maintenance skills. Group members can identify how or why they appreciate each member's actions. This kind of positive feedback acknowledges members' contributions and maintains a balance between task and maintenance functions.

Some recent studies of cooperative learning (e.g., Yager, Johnson, Johnson, and Snider, 1986) reveal that debriefing processing has another important function: it seems to have a positive effect on achievement outcomes. In a study comparing three conditions—individualistic; cooperation without processing; and cooperation with processing—students who systematically debriefed after the cooperative group lesson learned more and retained achievement levels better than students in the other two conditions (see Figure 2-4 on page 44). So, this postgroup processing not only helps students integrate new group-skill behaviors but also helps them increase achievement levels and retain their learning.

At the beginning of the year, systematic debriefing should be conducted after every group activity. From five to ten minutes at the end of the work session is usually sufficient time for this debriefing task. As working in groups becomes more of a classroom routine, processing can be conducted less frequently—possibly once or twice a week. This debriefing can be conducted in at least three ways:

1. whole-class debriefing

2. combination whole class and small group

3. independent small group

1. Whole-Class Debriefing

At first, the teacher would model selected debriefing behaviors and strategies for the whole class. The teacher can identify effective behav-

Figure 2-4 *Illustration of the Effectiveness of Group Processing and Individualistic Learning on Student Achievement*

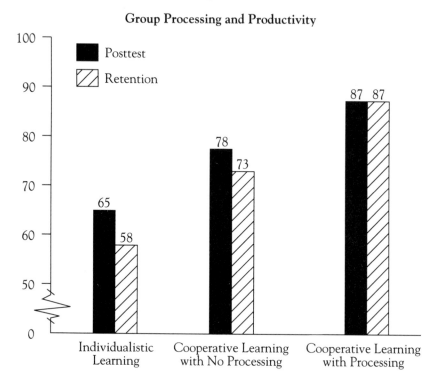

Group Processing and Productivity

iors that the entire class exhibits and create a chart recording the number of times those behaviors are performed by students. Figure 2-5 illustrates such a chart. These positive interaction behaviors are charted over a long period of time so that students can see their personal progress for each behavior. The teacher also models how to give positive feedback on

Figure 2-5 *A Table of Selected Positive Group Processing Behaviors with Frequencies Per Day for All Students in One Class*

Date	9/11	9/12	9/15	9/20	10/1	10/2	10/3			
Checking	4	5	7	10	11	10	15			
Sharing	20	25	25	27	30	30	32			
Praising	4	8	9	6	10	12	10			
Helping	7	7	12	12	15	8	10			

group behaviors and helps the class determine behaviors that could be improved upon the next time students work in groups.

Students are then asked questions about behaviors performed by anyone in their group that helped the group work well together. The teacher may repeat phrases and statements he or she heard and ask students to indicate whether these are examples of appropriate cooperative skills. For example, the teacher might repeat a student's remarks such as "Great idea, that really helped me learn today!" Students are then directed to indicate by thumbs up or thumbs down whether this is an example of a praise statement. This activity can provide new ways for students to be cooperative. A whole-class processing allows the teacher to give feedback, provide new models of behavior, and reinforce appropriate behaviors.

A special note about whole class debriefing needs to be made. It is important that in the beginning the data be reported back to the class as a whole rather than giving data back group by group. If the data are reported so that the class knows that one group shared ideas twelve times while a second group shared twenty times, and a third group shared thirty times, this can create a sense of competition among groups that can lead to some inappropriate behaviors. Such competition does not foster helping behaviors among competitors. In the beginning, it is best to create a classroom spirit of cooperation, not competition, among small groups.

2. Combination Whole-Class and Small-Group Debriefing

The teacher may bring the entire class together, with each cooperative group sitting together. In this situation, the teacher would conduct a "buzz session" with the class. In this buzz session the teacher asks a question and gives each small group a short period of time to discuss its answer together. Then, the small group shares what it discussed and another question is asked.

For example, the buzz session might involve the following tasks:

a. A group process question is asked, e.g.: "What are the ways your group checked to make sure everyone understood the material you studied today?"

b. Each group is given two minutes to answer that question and get ready to share its answer with the rest of the class.

c. Each group reports.

d. After each group has shared its answers, which may be recorded, another question is asked. Two or three questions may be asked and answered, one at a time.

The advantage of this debriefing strategy is that the teacher maintains some control over the debriefing yet still allows students to discuss their interactions with other group members. It also is a good way to monitor the discussions that students have about working in groups.

3. Independent-Group Debriefing

When students seem to understand the purpose of appropriate debriefing and have shown appropriate skills, each small group might debrief independently. There are a variety of ways to conduct independent group processing.

One method is called the "whip." In a whip, each group member, in turn, is given time to make a statement with no comments from other members. This technique allows the group to hear from every member quickly and lets everyone participate. The teacher supplies the sentence stems to which the group reacts. For example, some sentence stems could be:

- Our group works best when . . .

- The most helpful thing that happened today in our group was . . .

- Our group is great at . . .

- One thing we could do to make us an even better group is . . .

Independent debriefing can also be conducted by having students complete a written processing form. This task allows each student time to make a personal assessment of how the group worked together, to share, and then to compare this assessment with other members to find out their perceptions. Written forms can be collected and used to decide on citizenship grades or can be included in student portfolios. Some sample written processing forms are illustrated in Figures 2-6 and 2-7 on pages 48 and 49.

Debriefing processing can and should be done in a variety of ways. Varying processing procedures keeps the activity vital and interesting to the students and to the teacher. Processing helps develops interpersonal skills and affects how well group members work with one another. Taking a few minutes at the end of the groups' time to debrief systematically can increase group productivity and improve the ways in which students work together in their cooperative groups.

Epilogue

When social studies students are asked to work in small groups, they are often expected to work effectively within and as a group even though many have never had sufficient guidance on how to behave in group situations. This chapter provides a number of specific ideas and behaviors students should use within group settings. It also includes guidelines for helping students acquire, refine, and master group-interaction skills. The four strategies offer a range of instructional modes that may be used in kindergarten through grade 12 social studies to enable students to acquire group skills applicable within and beyond the classroom.

Figure 2-6   *One Sample Form for Students To Record Self-Assessment of Their Behaviors in and Contributions to a Group*

CONTINUUM STATEMENTS

1. I shared my ideas.

Never	Sometimes	Always

2. My ideas were responded to even if they were not agreed with or used.

Never	Sometimes	Always

3. I shared my opinions to reach consensus.

Never	Sometimes	Always

4. I watched the clock to complete our task within the given time.

Never	Sometimes	Always

What Happened Today?

The most helpful things that anyone did today were:

_____

_____

As a group, we are outstanding at:

_____

_____

We could do the following interpersonal skills differently to be an even better group:

_____

_____

Figure 2-7   *A Second Sample Form for Students To Record Self-Assessment of Their Behaviors in and Contributions to a Group*

REFLECTIONS

Circle one response for each sentence.
Be ready to explain why.

I contributed ideas in my group today.

a lot   some   none

I accepted others' ideas.

a lot   some   none

My ideas were accepted by others.

a lot   some   none

I disagreed with a reason.

a lot   some   none

One thing that I did differently today to help my group work better was:

_____

_____

_____

_____
Signature

References

Bandura, A. 1969. *Principles of behavior modification.* New York: Holt, Rinehart and Winston.

Bavelas, A. 1973. The five squares problem: An instructional aid in group cooperation. *Studies in Personal Psychology* (5): 29-38.

Cohen, E. 1986. *Designing groupwork: Strategies for the heterogeneous classroom.* New York: Teachers College Press.

Hyatt, C., and L. Gottlieb. 1987. *When smart people fail.* New York: Penguin Books.

Johnson, D. W., and R. T. Johnson. 1987. *Learning together and alone.* Englewood Cliffs, NJ: Prentice Hall.

————. 1989. *Cooperation and competition: Theory and research.* Edina, MN: Interaction Book Company.

Kovack, B. 1989. *Survival on the fast track.* New York: Dodd, Mead, & Company.

Yager, S., R. T. Johnson, et al. 1986. The impact of group processing on achievement in cooperative learning groups. *Journal of Social Psychology* 126 (30): 389-97.

3.

Learning Together in the Social Studies Classroom

DAVID W. JOHNSON AND ROGER T. JOHNSON

Using Cooperative Learning in the Classroom

Cooperative learning is uniquely suited for social studies courses because of its powerful impact on learning social studies content, social studies skills, democratic attitudes and beliefs, and their application to the real world. One method of cooperative learning within the social studies classroom consists of (a) the integrated use of three types of cooperative learning procedures (formal cooperative learning, informal cooperative learning, and cooperative base groups); (b) the essential components that make cooperation work (positive interdependence, face-to-face promotive interaction, individual accountability, social skills, and group processing); and (c) making classroom routines cooperative (i.e., using cooperative learning structures). This integration is depicted in visual form in Figure 3-1 on page 52.

There are three ways a teacher may use cooperative learning in the classroom. A classroom example that illustrates the above integration and these three ways is a sixth-grade classroom where students arrive in the morning and meet in their cooperative base (or home) group. Within the base groups, students welcome one another, complete a self-disclosure task (such as answering the question "What is my favorite television show?"), check one another's homework to make sure all members are prepared for the day, and tell one another to have a good day.

Figure 3-1 *Cooperative Learning*

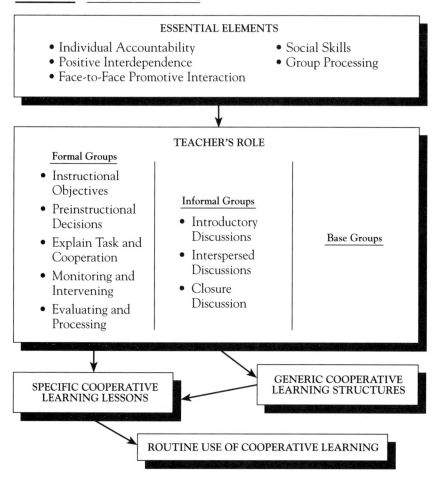

Cooperative base (or home) groups are long-term, heterogeneous cooperative learning groups with stable membership (Johnson, Johnson, and Holubec, 1992). The purposes of the base group are to give the support, help, encouragement, and assistance each member needs to make academic progress (attend class, complete all assignments, learn) and to develop cognitively and socially in healthy ways. Base groups meet daily in elementary school and twice a week in secondary school (or whenever the class meets). They are permanent (lasting from one to several years) and provide the long-term, caring peer relationships necessary to influence members to work hard consistently in school. They formally meet to discuss the academic progress of each member, provide help and assistance to one another, and verify that each member is completing assignments and progressing satisfactorily through the academic program. Base groups may also be responsible for letting absent group members know what went on in class when they miss a session. Informally, members interact every day within and between classes, discussing assignments and helping one another with homework. The use of base groups tends to improve attendance, personalizes the work required and the school experience, and improves the quality and quantity of learning. The larger the class or school and the more complex and difficult the subject matter, the more important it is to have base groups. Base groups are also helpful in structuring homerooms and on occasions when a teacher meets with a number of advisers.

Suppose our sixth-grade teacher begins a social studies lesson on world interdependence. The teacher presents a series of objects and wants students to name all the countries involved in creating the objects. To help students cognitively organize in advance what they know about the world economy, she forms informal cooperative learning dyads by having students turn to the person seated next to them and ask him or her to name the seven continents and one product produced in each continent. They are given four minutes to do so.

Informal cooperative learning groups are temporary, ad hoc groups that last from a few minutes to one class period (Johnson, Johnson, and Holubec, 1992). During a lecture, demonstration, or film they can be used to focus student attention on the material to be learned, set a mood conducive to learning, help set expectations as to what will be covered in a class session, ensure that students cognitively process the material being taught, and provide closure to an instructional session. During direct teaching the instructional challenge for the teacher is to ensure that students do the intellectual work of organizing material, explaining it, summarizing it, and integrating it into existing conceptual frameworks. Informal cooperative learning groups are often organized so that students engage in a three- to five-minute focused discussion before and after a lecture and two- to three-minute turn-to-your-partner discussion interspersed throughout a lecture.

Formal cooperative learning groups are now used in the lesson. Suppose the teacher has only two objectives for the lesson: students are to learn about global economic interdependence and improve their skill in encouraging one another's participation. Every formal cooperative lesson always has two types of objectives — academic and social skills.

In planning this particular lesson the teacher has made a number of preinstructional decisions. She has decided that (a) the group size will be three; (b) group membership will be heterogeneous; (c) each group will need a set of objects, their geography books, and a report form; (d) the room will be arranged in a certain way; and (e) certain roles will be assigned to students in their group. To implement these decisions, her thirty students count off from 1 to 10 to form triads randomly. Students then sit so they can either face one another or the teacher. The teacher then hands out the objects that include a silk shirt with plastic buttons, a cup of tea (a saucer and cup with a tea bag and a lump of sugar in it), and a Walkman® and earphones (with a cassette tape of a Nashville star) made by Phillips (a European company). She assigns members of each triad the roles of hypothesizer (who hypothesizes about the number of products in each item and their origins), a reference guide (who looks up each hypothesized country in the book to see what products it exports), and a recorder. After each item has been considered, the roles are rotated so that each student fulfills each role once.

The teacher follows with a ten-minute lecture on world economic interdependence in which she notes the following:

1. A hand-held calculator most often consists of electronic chips from the United States. It is assembled in Singapore or Indonesia, placed in a steel housing from India, and stamped with the label "Made in Japan" on arrival in Yokohama. (The trees and chemicals making up the paper and ink in the label are all made and processed elsewhere, and the plastic in the keys and body is made elsewhere.)

2. Modern hotels in Saudi Arabia are built with room modules made in Brazil, constructed by laborers from South Korea, and managed by personnel from the United States.

3. The extent of global economic interdependence is almost beyond imagining.

The teacher then *assigns the academic task* of having students name the many countries that contributed to the production of each object handed out earlier. She establishes *positive goal interdependence* by stating that it is a cooperative assignment and, therefore, all members of the group must agree on an answer before it is recorded, and all members must be able to explain each of the group's answers. *The criteria for success* are to hand in a correctly completed report form and for each member to score 90 percent or better on the test to be given the next day on world economic interdependence. The teacher establishes *positive reward interdependence* by stating that if the record sheet is accurate, each member will receive 15 points, and if all members of the group achieve 90 percent or better on the test, each member will receive 5 bonus points. *Individual accountability* is established by the roles assigned and the individual test. In addition, the teacher will observe each group to make sure all students are participating and learning. The teacher informs students that the expected social skill to be used by all students is encouraging one another's participation. She defines the skill and has each student practice it twice before the lesson begins.

While students work in their groups, the teacher monitors by systematically observing each group and intervening to provide academic assistance and help in using the interpersonal and small-group skills required to work together effectively. At the end of the lesson the groups hand in their report forms to be evaluated. Students then engage in a *debriefing process* wherein they consider how well they worked together. This debriefing includes describing three things members did to help the group achieve and one thing that could be added to improve their group next time.

Formal cooperative learning groups may last for one class period or for several weeks in order to complete specific tasks and assignments (such as decision making or problem solving, completing a curriculum unit, writing a report, conducting a survey or experiment, reading a chapter or reference book, learning vocabulary, or answering questions at the end of the chapter) (Johnson, Johnson, and Holubec, 1990).

In formal cooperative learning groups the social studies teacher completes at least these five tasks.

1. *Specifies the objectives for the lesson.* In every social studies lesson there should be at least one academic objective specifying the social studies concepts and strategies to be learned and at least one social skills objective specifying the interpersonal or small-group skill to be used and mastered during the lesson.

2. *Makes a number of preinstructional decisions.* A teacher has to decide on the size of groups, the method of assigning students to groups, the roles students will be assigned, the materials needed to conduct the lesson, and the way the room will be arranged.

3. *Explains the task and the positive interdependence.* A teacher clearly defines the assignment, teaches the required concepts and strategies, specifies the positive interdependence and individual accountability, gives the criteria for success, and explains the expected social skills to be used and mastered.

4. *Monitors students' learning and intervenes within the groups to provide task assistance or to increase students' interpersonal and group skills.* The social studies teacher systematically observes and collects data on each group as it works. When necessary, the teacher intervenes to assist students in completing the task accurately and in working together effectively.

5. *Evaluates students' learning and helps students process how well their groups functioned as a group.* Students' learning is carefully assessed and their social studies performances are evaluated. Members of the learning groups take time to consciously process how effectively they worked together as a group.

The teacher uses an *informal cooperative* learning group to close the lesson. She asks students to return to their seats, turn to the person next to them, write four conclusions they derived from the lesson, and circle the one they believed was the most important.

At the end of the class period, the *cooperative base groups* meet to review what students believe is the most important thing they were to have learned during the day, what homework has been assigned, and what help each member needs to complete the homework.

Why Use Cooperative Learning in the Social Studies Classroom?

The use of cooperative learning results in students learning the content of social studies more effectively, mastering the skills taught, adopting desirable attitudes and beliefs, increasing commitment to social participation, and applying social studies knowledge and skills in and outside the classroom.

Social Studies Content

Generally, when they learn in cooperative groups rather than competitively or individualistically, students in social studies courses attain higher achievement, retain more in long-term memory, use higher-level reasoning strategies more frequently, and are better able to apply what they learn to real-world situations. More than 375 experimental studies on achievement have been conducted over the past 90 years (Johnson and Johnson, 1989, *Cooperation and Competition*). A meta-analysis of all studies and the methodologically high-quality studies reveal that cooperative learning results in significantly higher achievement and retention than do competitive and individualistic learning (see Figure 3-2 below). The more pure the operationalization of cooperation, the higher the achievement tends to be. Cooperative, compared with competitive or

Figure 3-2   *Mean Effect Sizes for Impact of Social Interdependence on Dependent Variables*

Total Studies	Achieve	InterA	Support	S-Esteem
Coop vs. Comp	0.67	0.67	0.62	0.58
Coop vs. Ind	0.64	0.60	0.70	0.44
Comp vs. Ind	0.30	0.08	−0.13	−0.23
High-Quality Studies				
Coop vs. Comp	0.88	0.82	0.83	0.67
Coop vs. Ind	0.61	0.62	0.72	0.45
Comp vs. Ind	0.07	0.27	−0.13	−0.25
Mixed Operationalizations				
Coop vs. Comp	0.40	0.46	0.45	0.33
Coop vs. Ind	0.42	0.36	0.02	0.22
Pure Operationalizations				
Coop vs. Comp	0.71	0.79	0.73	0.74
Coop vs. Ind	0.65	0.66	0.77	0.51

Note: Coop = Cooperation; Comp = Competition; Ind = Individualistic; Achieve = Achievement; InterA = Interpersonal Attraction; Support = Social Support; S-Esteem = Self-Esteem

For a complete description of effect sizes and the data, see Johnson and Johnson (1989 *Cooperation and Competition*).

individualistic, learning tends to result in increased higher-level reasoning, more frequent generation of new ideas and solutions, and greater transfer of what is learned within one situation to another (i.e., group-to-individual transfer). When only the nearly 50 studies on social studies classes are examined, cooperation promoted higher achievement and greater retention than either competitive (effect size = .51) or individualistic (effect size = .58) learning. The results were basically the same for studies in elementary (effect size = .54), junior high (effect size = .49), and high school (effect size = .74) social studies classrooms.

In addition to actual achievement, there are a number of other issues about the way cooperative learning affects the effectiveness with which social studies content is taught. Social studies, for example, may be taught by giving answers or by asking questions. Within social studies classes students should consider the great questions that have dominated our past and determine our present and future. Leaving out analytical questions reinforces the impression that social studies is simply a series of facts, events, and people. If students are to consider the great questions, the questions must be presented in a way to encourage investigation of alternative answers and opposing points of view.

A second issue is whether students should be passive or active when they learn social studies. *Social studies learning is an active, not a passive, process or a spectator sport.* Traditional competitive/individualistically structured social studies instruction is based on the assumption that students are passive absorbers of information who store what they know in easily retrievable fragments as a result of repeated practice and reinforcement. The results have been that many students tended to learn dates, events, and people by rote and have difficulty making the necessary connections between social studies knowledge and their understandings of the world in which they live. Reading textbooks, listening to lectures, filling out worksheets, and taking tests, in themselves, do not teach social studies.

Students can increase their active construction of personal knowledge encountered during their experiences in social studies classes. Cognitive activeness is best aroused in vigorous discussions and arguments with others within structured cooperative learning groups. The active intellectual exchange inherent in cooperative learning enables students to (a) cognitively process and critically evaluate the information they encounter in social studies classes; (b) use rational reasoning processes based on inquiry, the scientific method, and inductive and deductive logic; (c) communicate their reasoning to others; and (d) apply social studies knowledge and reasoning processes to solve problems.

Social Studies Academic Skills

Learning to reason using social studies knowledge and processes in order to solve problems is a primary reason for studying social studies. Social studies academic goals also include geography skills, historiography skills, inquiry skills, the use of the scientific method, and related skills required to make sound judgments about social issues and major problems facing the person, his or her society, and the world. These skills are used by students to make sound, reasoned decisions in and outside of class.

Cooperative learning groups create environments wherein interpersonal exchanges require the use of higher-level thinking strategies, higher-level reasoning, and metacognitive strategies. Students working together cooperatively expect to teach what they learn to groupmates and engage in discussions that include explaining and elaborating what is being learned. While they work together they monitor one another's participation and contributions and give one another feedback about their ideas and reasoning. When groups are heterogeneous, students both encounter and seriously consider diverse perspectives and ideas.

Walter Savage Landor once said, "There is no more certain sign of a narrow mind, of stupidity, and of arrogance, than to stand aloof from those who think differently from us." When teachers lecture about events and people and structure competition among students, they create the conditions under which students will avoid listening to different points of view and defensively reject ideas and people that might expand their personal perspectives or prove them wrong. In order to avoid close-minded attempts to "win" in answering the great questions and to hold both their own and other people's perspectives in mind at the same time, social studies teachers must structure the learning situation in ways that promote interest, curiosity, inquiry, and open-minded problem solving. Cooperative experiences have been found to promote greater perspective-taking ability than did competitive or individualistic experiences (effect size =.57 and .44 respectively). Perspective taking resulted in better understanding and retention of others' information, reasoning, and perspectives (Johnson, 1971; Johnson and Johnson, 1989, *Cooperation and Competition*).

Attitudes and Beliefs

Social studies courses should promote such attitudes and beliefs as valuing democracy, individual liberty, social responsibility, good citizenship, civic competence, human dignity, cooperation, and diversity. Discussions within a competitive context often result in defensiveness against attitude development and change. Meanwhile, positive student attitudes can be developed, clarified, reinforced, and changed through structured discussions within a cooperative context (Johnson, 1979; Johnson and F. Johnson, 1991). Such discussions (a) demonstrate that students' reference groups value democracy; (b) lead to public commitment to the attitudes; (c) create active cognitive processing of the attitudes and the development of enduring conceptual framework; (d) result in students advocating the attitudes and beliefs to others; (e) lead to being confronted with vivid and personalized appeals to adopt democratic attitudes; and (f) provide visible and credible social models who value democracy.

Being an American is creedal rather than racial or ancestral. Within our schools we can lay the groundwork for creating a *unum* from our *pluribus*. This is done in basically four steps: by encouraging students to develop (a) an appreciation of their religious, ethnic, or cultural background; (b) an appreciation of the religious, ethnic, and cultural backgrounds of other students; (c) a strong superordinate identity of "American"; and (d) a pluralistic set of values concerning democracy, freedom, liberty, equality, justice, the rights of individuals, and the responsibilities of citizenship (Johnson and Johnson, 1992). To accomplish these four steps, diverse students must be brought together for repeated face-to-face interactions, and teachers must use cooperative learning procedures the majority of the time. The more students work in cooperative groups, the more they like one another, even when they differ in intellectual ability, handicapping conditions, race, ethnic membership, social class, and gender (Johnson and Johnson, 1987, 1992, *Cooperative Learning and Cross-Ethnic Relationships*). Not only are relationships more positive, they are also more supportive. Since the 1940s more than 106 studies have found that cooperative learning promoted greater social support than competitive (effect size = .62) or individualistic (effect size = .70) learning.

The research results reported in this section reveal that appropriate cooperative learning generates results that are consistent with the many academic, process, and social skills valued by social studies educators.

Essential Elements That Make Cooperation Work

Mastering the use of formal and informal cooperative learning procedures and cooperative base groups requires an understanding of and the abilities to implement the components essential for cooperative effort. Social studies teachers need to master the essential elements of cooperation for at least two reasons. First, they need to tailor cooperative learning to their unique instructional needs, circumstances, curriculums, subject areas, and students. Second, teachers need to diagnose the problems some students have in working with others and to intervene to increase the effectiveness of student learning groups.

Simply placing students in groups and telling them to work together does not in and of itself result in cooperative efforts. There are many ways in which group efforts may go wrong. Seating students together can result in competition at close quarters or individualistic efforts through talking. If social studies teachers are to implement cooperative learning successfully, the essential elements of cooperation need to be understood and followed.

When social studies teachers have real expertise in using cooperative learning, they will structure five essential components into instructional activities (Johnson and Johnson, 1989, *Cooperation and Competition*; Johnson, Johnson, and Holubec, 1990). Well-structured cooperative learning lessons are differentiated from poorly structured ones on the basis of these elements. These essential elements, furthermore, should be carefully structured within all levels of cooperative efforts. Each learning group is a cooperative effort, as can be the class as a whole, the teaching team, the school, and the school district. The five essential elements are as follows:

1. *Positive interdependence.* Positive interdependence is the perception that one is linked with others in such a way that one cannot succeed unless all do (and vice versa); that is, others' work benefits you and your work benefits them. It promotes a situation in which students work together in small groups to maximize the learning of all members, sharing their resources, providing mutual support,

and celebrating their joint success. Positive interdependence is the heart of cooperative learning. For a learning situation to be cooperative, students must perceive that they are positively interdependent with other members of their learning group: that is, they must believe that they sink or swim together.

Within every cooperative lesson, positive goal interdependence must be established through *mutual learning goals* (learn the assigned material and make sure that all members of your group learn the assigned material). In order to strengthen positive interdependence, *joint rewards* (if all members of your group score 90 percent correct or better on the test, each will receive 5 bonus points), *divided resources* (each group member gets a part of the total information required to complete an assignment), and *complementary roles* (reader, checker, encourager, elaborator) may also be used.

2. *Face-to-face promotive interaction.* Once teachers establish positive interdependence, they need to maximize the opportunity for students to promote one another's success by helping, assisting, supporting, encouraging, and praising one another's efforts to learn. There are cognitive activities and interpersonal dynamics that only occur when students get actively involved in promoting one another's success. This includes orally explaining how to solve problems, discussing the nature of the concepts being learned, teaching one's knowledge to classmates, and connecting present with past learning. Accountability to peers, ability to influence one another's reasoning and conclusions, social modeling, social support, and interpersonal rewards all increase as the face-to-face interaction among group members increases. In addition, the verbal and nonverbal responses of other group members provide important information concerning a student's performance. Silent students are uninvolved students who are not contributing to the learning of others as well as their own. Promoting one another's success results in both higher achievement and in getting to know others on a personal as well as an academic level. To obtain meaningful face-to-face interaction, the size of groups needs to be small (typically, two to four members).

3. *Individual accountability.* Individual accountability exists when the performance of each student is assessed as an individual and the

results are given back to the group and the individual. It is important that the group knows who needs more assistance, support, and encouragement in learning the targeted material. It is also important that group members know that they cannot "hitch-hike" on the work of others. The purpose of cooperative learning groups is to make each member a stronger individual in his or her right. Students learn together so that they can subsequently perform at a higher level as individuals separate from the group. To ensure that each member is strengthened, students are held individually accountable to do their share of the work. Common ways to structure individual accountability include (a) giving an individual test to each student; (b) randomly selecting one student's product to represent the entire group; and (c) having each student explain what he or she has learned to a classmate.

4. *Social skills.* Contributing to the success of a cooperative effort requires interpersonal and small-group skills. Placing socially unskilled individuals in a group and telling them to cooperate does not guarantee that they will be able to do so effectively. Individuals must be taught the social skills for high-quality cooperation and be motivated to use them. Leadership, decision making, trust building, communication, and conflict-management skills, for example, have to be taught and practiced just as purposefully and precisely as academic content and skills. Procedures and strategies for teaching students a number of specific social skills may be found in Johnson (1990) and Johnson and F. Johnson (1991).

5. *Group processing or debriefing.* Group processing exists when group members discuss how well they are achieving their goals and maintaining effective working relationships. Groups need to describe which member actions are helpful and unhelpful and make decisions about which behaviors to continue or change. Students must also be given the time and procedures for analyzing how well their learning groups are functioning and the extent to which students are employing their social skills to help all group members to achieve and to maintain effective working relationships within the group. Such processing (a) enables learning groups to focus on group maintenance; (b) facilitates the learning of social skills; (c) ensures that members receive feedback on their participation; and (d) reminds students to practice collaborative

skills consistently. Some of the keys to successful processing are allowing sufficient time for it to take place, making it specific rather than vague, maintaining student involvement in processing, reminding students to use their social skills while they process, and ensuring that expectations as to the purpose of processing are communicated.

These five elements are illustrated in the following classroom example.

In a primary classroom in Vancouver, British Columbia, Jean Crockett explains to her class that they are moving to a different planet in a faraway galaxy to form a new community. To survive, students must determine the survival skills, cooperative efforts, and materials needed to build a community on a different planet. She then randomly assigns students to groups of three, with the stipulation that at least one male and one female be in each group.

Students are asked to assign the roles of father, mother, or child within the new space family (*role interdependence*). They then pick a name for their family (*identity interdependence*). Their task is to make a list of fifteen items they need to build a new community on a faraway planet (they are reminded that space suits are an essential first item). *Positive goal interdependence* is established by asking students to come to consensus and make one list for the group. Group members are to sign the list, indicating that they agree with the list and can explain their choices to the rest of the class (using their own first names and the surname of their space family). *The criteria for success* are for the group to assign roles, pick a name, make a list, and behave in a way that would make their "space family" an important part of the new community. Ms. Crockett's students then move their chairs to engage in direct *face-to-face interaction* and use the *social skills* of decision making, leadership, and communication. While students work, the teacher moves from group to group observing for (a) staying with the group; (b) using twelve-inch voices; (c) using one another's names; (d) looking at the speaker; and (e) helping the group work. At the end of the lesson, students *process* (*debrief*) how well they worked together as a group and make one suggestion as to how they could work together even more effectively tomorrow.

The lesson ends with Jean Crockett randomly choosing one member from each group to contribute one item from his or her family's list (*indi-*

vidual accountability). The student is to read the selected item, explain to the class why it is important, and then write it on the chalkboard as part of a superlist. When this reporting ends, the chairs are arranged in a lift-off position. Using space music and with the teacher guiding their imagery, the rocket blasts off, leaves Earth, and flies past clouds, moon, planets, stars, and galaxies before landing on the new planet. The students don their space suits and step into their new community.

Conceptual understanding and skillful use of cooperative learning are two sides of the coin of expertise. The elements described above are critical components for constructing a sound foundation in the theory and conception of cooperative learning as an approach to classroom instruction. Developing conceptual understanding of how to teach effectively ultimately enables the social studies teacher's true teaching genius to be expressed. Once the essential elements are clearly understood and mastered, each social studies teacher can fine-tune and adapt cooperative learning to his or her specific circumstances, needs, and students.

Cooperative Structures for Classroom Routines: Practical Guidelines and an Example

In order for social studies teachers to use cooperative learning the majority of the time, they must select course routines and generic lessons that repeat over and over again and structure them cooperatively (Johnson and Johnson, 1991). These repetitive cooperative tasks provide a base upon which the cooperative classroom may be built. Examples include checking homework, preparing for and reviewing a test, drill review of facts and events, reading of textbooks and reference materials, writing reports and essays, giving presentations, learning concepts, doing projects such as surveys, and problem solving. Each of these instructional activities may be done cooperatively and, once planned and repeated several times, will become automatic in the classroom. They may also be used in combination to form an overall lesson.

To illustrate the guidelines social studies teachers might follow to enable students to master particular routines, an example relative to checking homework will be used.

Task: Bring completed homework to class and understand how to do it correctly.

Cooperation required: Students enter the classroom and meet in their cooperative learning groups. The groups should be heterogeneous in terms of social studies and reading abilities. One member (the runner) goes to the teacher's desk, picks up the group's folder, and hands out any materials in the folder to the appropriate members. The runner records how much of the assignment each member completed. The group goes through as much of the homework as time permits, comparing answers and, when necessary, dialoguing through different answers to find the most appropriate one(s). At the end of the assigned review time, the members' homework is placed in the group's folder and the runner returns it to the teacher's desk.

The *cooperative goal* is to ensure that all group members bring their completed homework to class and understand how to do it correctly. Two roles are assigned: explainer (explains step by step how the homework is correctly completed) and accuracy checker (verifies that the explanation is accurate, encourages members, and provides coaching when needed). The explainer reads the first part of the assignment and explains step by step how to complete it correctly. His or her groupmates check for accuracy. Roles are rotated clockwise so that each member does an equal amount of explaining. The group should concentrate on the parts of the assignment that members did not learn.

Expected criteria for success: All group members must complete the homework correctly and understand how to do it.

Individual accountability: Regular examinations and random selection of group members daily to explain how to solve randomly selected problems from the homework.

Expected in-group behaviors: Active participation, checking, encouraging, and elaborating by all members.

Intergroup cooperation: Whenever it is helpful, procedures, answers, and strategies are checked with another group. For instance, when one group is finished, its answers are compared with those of another group and then discussed.

Alternative to directed homework review: As an alternative, students are assigned to pairs. The teacher randomly picks questions from the homework assignment. One student in each pair explains step by step the correct procedures and answer(s). The other student listens, checks for accuracy, and prompts the explainer when he or she does not know the answer. Roles are switched for each question.

This section illustrated one of the many cooperative learning strategies that may be used to enable social studies students to complete classroom routines in more productive fashion. The guidelines provided above can be used as early as tomorrow to facilitate student learning through cooperative effort.

The Learning Together Approach

Our *learning together* approach to cooperative learning is based on the interaction among theory, research, and practice. Our conceptual framework has derived from a five-step process. First, we have reviewed and synthesized the results of nearly every study that has been conducted on cooperative learning to determine the current state of knowledge in the area (Johnson, 1970; Johnson and Johnson, 1974, 1989, *Cooperation and Competition*). Second, we formulated a series of theoretical models based on the results of the previous research and the theorizing of Morton Deutsch (1949, 1962). Third, we conducted a systematic program of research to validate our theorizing. Over the past twenty years we have conducted over eighty-five research studies on cooperative learning. Fourth, based on the theory validated by the research, we have devised a series of practical procedures for teachers. Fifth, we have developed a network of school districts throughout North America, Europe, Asia, the Middle East, and Africa within which we have trained teachers. Based on our experience in helping teachers implement cooperative learning in their classrooms, we have revised our theoretical models, conducted research studies to validate the new theory, incorporated the new findings into our recommended procedures, and helped teachers implement the modified procedures in their classrooms, which in turn has influenced us to revise our theoretical models.

Our conceptual approach requires the social studies teacher to acquire both a conceptual understanding of cooperative learning (its nature and essential components) and the skills to use that understanding to plan and teach cooperative learning lessons, strategies, and curriculum units uniquely tailored for their specific students and circumstances. We assume that each teacher faces a complex and unique combination of circumstances, students, and needs and, therefore, cooperative learning needs to be adapted and refined to uniquely fit each teacher's situation. Understanding the essential elements allows teachers to think metacognitively about cooperative learning and create any number of strategies and lessons.

Our belief is that teachers should be educated and trained to be engineers with cooperative learning, not technicians. Technicians are trained in how to teach packaged lessons, curriculums, and strategies in a lockstep (step 1, step 2, step 3), prescribed manner, without really understanding what cooperation is and what makes it work. This leaves teachers unable to adapt cooperative learning procedures and strategies to a variety of curriculums, students, and circumstances. An engineer conceptually understands cooperative learning and, therefore, can adapt it to his or her specific teaching circumstances, students, and curriculums. The goal of the conceptual approach is to develop teacher expertise in cooperative learning so that teachers can:

1. take any lesson or objective in any subject area and structure it cooperatively.

2. practice repeatedly the use of cooperative learning until they are at a routine/integrated level of use and can implement cooperative learning at least 60 percent of the time in their classrooms.

3. describe precisely what they are doing and why they are doing it in order to communicate to others the nature of cooperative learning and teach others how to implement cooperative learning in their classrooms and settings.

4. apply the principles of cooperation to other settings, such as collegial relationships and faculty meetings.

The conceptual approach is used in all technological arts and crafts. An engineer designing a bridge, for example, applies validated theory to the unique problems imposed by the need for a bridge to span a certain length from a river bank of one unique geological character to a bank of another unique geological character, in an area with specific winds, temperatures, and susceptibility to earthquakes. Teachers can engage in the same process after (a) learning a conceptualization of essential components of cooperative learning and (b) applying that conceptual model to their unique teaching situation, circumstances, students, and instructional needs. The example below illustrates how one teacher "engineered" a cooperative learning lesson around Greek philosophers and philosophy.

Ed Harris, a high-school social studies teacher, explains to his students that they are to learn the philosophies of Plato, Socrates, and Aristotle and then decide the most likely attitudes these philosophers would have toward current controversial issues such as capital punishment or voluntary abortion. He announces that while students are working together they are to demonstrate mastery of three social skills: encouraging others' participation, giving sound explanations, and summarizing. The procedure for this example cooperative learning lesson (which takes two or three class periods) follows.

1. *Philosopher groups.* Students are randomly assigned to groups of three. Each group is randomly assigned a philosopher (Plato, Socrates, Aristotle). The groups are to (a) research the attitude of the assigned philosopher and make a list of his ideas; (b) plan how each member can best teach classmates about the philosopher; and (c) ensure that all group members know and can apply the philosophy and are ready to teach. A visual aid to help teach is required. Each member needs a copy of the list and the teaching plan.

2. *Practice pairs.* Each student meets with a member of another group that researched the same philosopher and (a) presents his or her list; (b) listens carefully to the information presented by the other person; and (c) takes the best ideas and information from the other person and adds them to his or her list.

3. *Philosopher groups.* Students share what they have learned from members of the other groups. A final list of the philosopher's ideas is generated along with a plan for teaching others about the philosopher. Each member needs his or her own copy of the plan. One copy is handed to the teacher, who evaluates it.

4. *Application groups.* Students are assigned to new triads, stratified so that one member represents each philosopher in the group. First,

each member is to teach the information about his or her philosopher to the other two members and learn about the other two philosophers and philosophies. Second, the triad picks a controversial issue (such as the death penalty or voluntary abortion), decides how each philosopher would likely stand on the issue (for or against), and writes at least five reasons why its members think the philosopher would take that stand.

The groups choose the three best reasons and write a paragraph explaining why each philosopher would be for or against the issue. The paragraph has to have a topic sentence, the reasons why the philosopher would take this stand, an example clarifying each reason, and a conclusion. Each group ends up with three paragraphs, one for each philosopher.

5. *Whole-class summary.* Each group hands in one copy of each paragraph to the teacher, who grades it. One student from each group is randomly selected to present a philosopher's perspective on the controversial issue.

6. *Test.* Students individually take a test on the ideas of each philosopher. A student's base grade is determined by his or her score on the test taken individually (students can receive from 0 to 100 points). In addition, students can earn between 0 and 10 points for their philosopher group's list of ideas embraced by their philosopher; 0 to 60 points for their application group's members; 20 bonus points when all members of their application group score 90 or above on the individual test; and 10 bonus points when they were observed using targeted social skills (encouraging one another's participation, giving good explanations, and summarizing). Each student's grade is the sum of his or her test performance, the points earned by his or her philosopher and application groups, and bonus points.

7. *Group processing (debriefing).* Application groups meet and discuss how well they worked together and decide on one way to improve their efforts next time.

While the groups work, Mr. Harris systematically observes each group, intervening only when groups need help in understanding the tasks or in working together effectively.

Within this example lesson, *positive interdependence* was structured by the (a) group goal of ensuring that all members knew the assigned material and were prepared to teach or present the group's position; (b) division of resources within the application group; (c) shared rewards based upon the groups' grades for the list of ideas, written paragraphs, presentation, and the bonus points; and (d) shared identity of group membership. Students promoted one another's learning *face-to-face* in the various groups. *Individual accountability* was structured by having each student participate in the group, teach about a philosopher, take the test, and risk being selected to present to the class. The targeted *social skills* were encouraging one another's participation, giving good explanations, and summarizing. Finally, at the end of the lesson, the groups *processed* (debriefed) how well they functioned.

Gaining Expertise in Using Cooperative Learning

Gaining expertise in using cooperative learning is in itself a cooperative process that requires a team effort. It is also a complete process that places extensive cognitive and emotional demands on teachers. In order for the social studies teacher to implement cooperative learning at a *routine-use level* (where he or she can automatically structure a lesson cooperatively without extensive preplanning or conscious thought), he or she needs experience in an incremental step-by-step manner. The teacher then needs to progressively refine his or her competencies by (1) teaching a cooperative lesson; (2) assessing how well it went; (3) reflecting on how it could have been taught better; and then by (4) teaching an improved cooperative lesson; (5) assessing how well it went; and so on, repeating this cycle until the behaviors are automatized.

A support system is needed to encourage and assist teachers in a long-term, multiyear effort to improve continually their competence in using cooperative learning. With only a moderately difficult noncooperative learning teaching strategy, for example, teachers may require from 20 to 30 hours of instruction in its theory, 15 to 20 demonstrations using it with different students and subjects, and an additional 10 to 15 coaching sessions to become highly skilled. For a more difficult teaching strategy like cooperative learning, several years of training and support may be needed to ensure that teachers master it. In short, teachers may need three or more years to become effective "routine engineers" of cooperative learning in their classrooms.

To gain expertise in using cooperative learning, teachers have to help their colleagues gain expertise. The key to successful implementation of cooperative learning is the use of collegial support groups (Johnson and Johnson, 1989, *Leading the Cooperative School*). During the training sessions teachers learn about cooperative learning and the essential elements that make it work. Teachers then have to transfer this knowledge to their own classrooms and maintain their use of cooperative learning for years to come. The success of the training depends on *transfer* (teachers trying out cooperative learning in their classrooms) and *maintenance* (long-term effective use of cooperative learning). Transfer and maintenance depend on teachers themselves being organized into cooperative collegial support groups that focus on helping each member progressively improve his or her competence in using cooperative learning.

The Cooperative School— or Social Studies Department

Willi Unsoeld, a renowned mountain climber and philosopher, once stated, "Take care of each other, share your energies with the group; no one must feel alone, cut off, for that is when you do not make it." The same may be said for everyone in schools. The issue of cooperation in social studies is part of a larger issue of the organizational structure of schools. For decades, business and industrial organizations have functioned as mass manufacturing organizations that divided work into small component parts performed by individuals who worked separately from and, in many cases, in competition with peers. Personnel were considered to be interchangeable parts in the organizational machine.

Most schools today are structured as mass manufacturing organizations. Teachers work alone, in their own rooms, with their own sets of students and curriculum materials. Students may be assigned to any teacher because teachers are typically viewed as interchangeable parts in the education machine and, conversely, teachers may be given any student to teach. Schools need to change from a mass manufacturing, competitive/individualistic organizational structure to a high-performance, cooperative, and team-based organizational structure (Johnson and Johnson, 1989, *Leading the Cooperative School*). The new organizational structure is generally known as the cooperative school.

In a cooperative school, students work primarily in cooperative learning groups, teachers and building staff work in cooperative teams, and district administrators work in cooperative teams. The organizational structure of the classroom, school, and district are then congruent. Each level of cooperative teams supports and enhances the other levels.

A cooperative school and department structure begins in the classroom with the use of cooperative learning the majority of the time. Cooperative learning is used to increase student achievement, create more positive relationships among students, and generally improve students' physiological well-being (Johnson and Johnson, 1989, *Cooperation and Competition*). A secondary effect is that using cooperative learning in the classroom affects teachers' attitudes and competencies concerning collaborating with colleagues. Teachers typically cannot promote isolation and competition among students all day and be collaborative with colleagues. What is promoted in instructional situations tends to dominate relationships among staff members.

The second level in creating a cooperative school or department is to form collegial support groups, task forces, and ad hoc decision-making groups within the school (Johnson and Johnson, 1989, *Cooperation and Competition*). Just as the heart of the classroom is cooperative learning, the heart of the school and department is the collegial support group.

Collegial support groups are small cooperative groups whose purpose is to increase teachers' instructional expertise and success. The focus is on improving instruction in general and increasing members' expertise in using cooperative learning in specific.

Task force groups plan and implement solutions to schoolwide issues and problems such as curriculum adoptions and lunchroom behavior. Task forces diagnose a problem, gather data about the causes and extent of the problem, consider a variety of alternative solutions, make conclusions, and present recommendations to the entire faculty.

Ad hoc decision-making groups are used during faculty meetings to involve all staff members in important decisions. Ad hoc decision-making groups are part of a small-group/large-group procedure in which staff members listen to a recommendation, are assigned to small groups, meet to consider the recommendation, report their decisions to the entire faculty, and then participate in a whole-faculty decision as to what the course of action should be. The use of these three types of faculty cooperative teams tends to increase teacher productivity, morale, and professional self-esteem.

The third level in creating a cooperative school and its departments is to implement administrative cooperative teams within the district (Johnson and Johnson, 1989, *Leading the Cooperative School*). Administrators are organized into colleagial support groups to increase their administrative expertise and success. Administrative task forces and ad hoc decision-making groups are also used. When administrators compete to see who is the best administrator in the district, they are unlikely to be able to promote cooperation among staff members of the school. The more the district and school personnel work in cooperative teams, the easier it will be for teachers to use cooperative learning and vice versa.

Cooperative learning is more than an instructional procedure. It is a basic shift in organizational thinking and structure that extends from the classroom through the superintendent's office.

Epilogue

Cooperative learning can be used with some confidence at every grade level, in every subject area, and with any task. In addition, any social studies course objective, assignment, or lesson may be reformulated to be consistent with cooperative learning requirements. Cooperative structures can contribute to attaining many different social studies instructional outcomes simultaneously. Students will achieve higher and learn more complex cognitive skills and academic knowledge. Working cooperatively will also increase their ability to work effectively with diverse and heterogeneous peers, encourage their self-esteem and psychological health, and heighten their ability to act independently and exert their autonomy. Their interpersonal and small-group skills and their understanding of interdependence and cooperative efforts will be enhanced immeasurably.

As we have emphasized, cooperative learning is far more than a seating arrangement. To be effective, teachers have to structure cooperative learning situations so that students perceive that they sink or swim together, interact face to face to provide each other help and support, are accountable for doing their fair share of the work, utilize interpersonal and small-group skills, and process ways to improve the effectiveness of the group. It is these essential components that differentiate cooperative learning from traditional classroom groupings. Social studies teachers need to learn an *expert system* of how to implement cooperative learning to create unique adaptations to their specific circumstances, students, and needs. With the essential elements they can generate new cooperative lessons and strategies as the need arises. They can also transfer their use of cooperative learning to create more cooperative collegial relationships, staff meetings, relationships with parents, and committees.

Finally, social studies teachers using cooperative learning are on very safe ground empirically, conceptually, and theoretically. Both the quantity and quality of the research evidence are so strong and so consistent that any social studies teacher who is not using cooperative learning the majority of the school day should feel some dissonance and unease. Indeed, it is time for social studies educators to take Heywood's statement, "Two heads are better than one," seriously.

References

Deutsch, M. 1949. A theory of cooperation and competition. *Human Relations* 2: 129-52.

———. 1962. Cooperation and trust: Some theoretical notes. In M. R. Jones, ed. *Nebraska symposium on motivation*, 275-319. Lincoln, NE: University of Nebraska Press.

Johnson, D. W. 1970. *Social psychology of education.* New York: Holt, Rinehart and Winston.

———. 1979. *Educational psychology.* Englewood Cliffs, NJ: Prentice Hall.

———. 1990. *Reaching out: Interpersonal effectiveness and self-actualization.* Englewood Cliffs, NJ: Prentice Hall.

Johnson, D. W., and F. Johnson. 1991. *Joining together: Group theory and group skills.* Englewood Cliffs, NJ: Prentice Hall.

Johnson, D. W., and R. T. Johnson. 1974. Instructional goal structure: Cooperative, competitive, or individualistic. *Review of Educational Research* 44: 213-40.

———. 1985. Impact of classroom organization and instructional methods on the effectiveness of mainstreaming. In C. Meisel, ed. *Mainstreamed handicapped children: Outcomes, controversies, and new directions*, 215-50. New York: Lawrence Erlbaum.

———. 1989. *Cooperation and competition: Theory and research.* Edina, MN: Interaction Book Company.

———. 1989. *Leading the cooperative school.* Edina, MN: Interaction Book Company.

———. 1991. *Cooperative learning lesson structures.* Edina, MN: Interaction Book Company.

———. 1992. Cooperative learning in the culturally diverse classroom. In R. DeVillar, C. Faltis, and J. Cummins, eds. *Successful cultural diversity: Classroom practices for the 21st century.* Albany: State University of New York Press.

Johnson, D. W., and R. T. Johnson. 1992. Cooperative learning and cross-ethnic relationships. In J. Lynch, C. Modgil, and S. Modgil, eds. *Prejudice, polemic or progress?* London: Falmer Press.

Johnson, D. W., R. T. Johnson, and E. Holubec. 1990. *Circles of learning: Cooperation in the classroom*, 3rd ed. Edina, MN: Interaction Book Company.

———. 1992. *Advanced cooperative learning*, 2nd ed. Edina, MN: Interaction Book Company.

4.

Social Studies and the Structural Approach to Cooperative Learning

JEANNE M. STONE AND SPENCER KAGAN

As educators, our job is to prepare students to function effectively in today's world. Our goal is to give them both the skills they need to function effectively within society and the knowledge they need to understand our ever-changing society, focusing on the people, events, and ideas that form who we are today. Teaching social studies through cooperative learning provides the means to accomplish both goals simultaneously. Cooperative learning provides a framework to teach students the socialization skills needed to succeed in today's world and the thinking skills to continually use the information they are gathering. The social studies content provides the knowledge base necessary for students to create their own integrated world view, relating events of the past to those of the present and future.

The Structural Approach[1]

The structural approach to cooperative learning is based on the definition and use of a number of distinct methods of organizing the interaction of students in a classroom. These methods are called *structures*. Structures are content free and involve a series of steps with a specific behavior expected at each step. Structures are the building blocks of a

---

[1] "The Structural Approach" is adapted from Spencer Kagan, *Cooperative Learning*.

lesson and are combined to form multistructural lessons with predictable results. Each structure provides a learning experience that when linked with other structures and experiences leads to predictable outcomes in the academic, linguistic, cognitive, and social domains.

There are numerous distinct structures, such as Round Table, Team Interview, and Numbered Heads Together. Each structure defines the social interaction patterns of the individuals in the classroom. For example, a structure may have the students think (individuals think), pair (pairs discuss), and share (individuals share with whole class). Think-Pair-Share can be used to have students respond to any question asked by the teacher or to share thoughts about a topic.

Traditional Versus Structural Approach

Looking at the traditional classroom, one of the most commonly used structures is a competitive structure called Whole-Class Question-Answer. In Whole-Class Question-Answer, students compete for the teacher's attention and praise—creating negative interdependence among students. As one student is called on, the others lose their turn. As one student errs, all others are delighted as they have a second chance to get the teacher's attention and praise. Students know that another student's failure increases their own chance for recognition. In contrast, Numbered Heads Together is a simple four-step cooperative structure.

Figure 4-1   *Structure of the Numbered Heads Together Activity*

Structure of the Numbered Heads Together Activity

1. The teacher has students number off within groups so that each student is a 1, 2, 3, or 4. (Colors or letters also can be used.)
2. The teacher gives a directive to the group, such as "Make sure everyone on the team can name the capital of California" or "Be sure each person on the team knows how to build $\frac{1}{2} + \frac{1}{16}$ using fraction bars."
3. The teacher tells the students to put their heads together to make sure everyone on the team knows.
4. The teacher calls a number (1, 2, 3, or 4), and only the students with that number can respond.

Numbered Heads Together can be used with almost any subject matter, at all grade levels, and at various places in a lesson. This structure includes all the essential elements of cooperative learning: teams, a management system, motivation and ability for students to cooperate, positive interdependence, individual accountability, and simultaneous interaction. Positive interdependence is built in; if any student on the team knows the answer, the ability of each student is increased. Individual accountability is also built into the structure because all the helping is confined to the heads-together step; there is no more helping in the responding step, when each student is on his or her own.

The simultaneous interaction during Numbered Heads Together is in contrast to the sequential interaction in Whole-Class Question-Answer; rather than one student responding when a question is posed, all students interact. When Numbered Heads Together is used, all students cooperate. The high achievers share answers because they know their number might not be called and they want their team to do well. The lower achievers listen carefully because they know their number might be called. Numbered Heads Together is a contrast to Whole-Class Question-Answer in which only the high achievers need participate; the low achievers can (and often do) tune out, leaving the student participation time more like a private conversation between the teacher and the highest achieving students.

Definition of a Structure

An important concept of the structural approach is the distinction between structures, content, and activities. A structure is the content-free *how* of instruction. It is the social organization of the classroom, involving a series of steps or elements that define interaction patterns. A structure can be used to deliver a wide range of academic content. Content is the *what* of instruction, ranging from learning about your neighborhood to world politics. When you add content to a structure, you have an activity. At any moment in a classroom, the activity occurring is defined by a combination of a structure and the content; i.e., structure + content = activity.

When Numbered Heads Together (structure) is used to practice map reading (content), an activity is formed. There are many excellent cooperative learning activities that teachers can design. Activities almost always have a specific objective, such as creating a topographical state map as a conclusion to a unit on state geography, or creating a class banner to build a positive class identity. Activities are specific and content bound, and cannot be meaningfully repeated more than a few times. Structures, however, are content-free ways of organizing group interaction and may be used repeatedly with a variety of curriculum materials and at various times in the lesson plan, across a range of grade levels.

Domains of Usefulness

There are dozens of cooperative learning structures, and each structure has a different impact on students. A structure's domain of usefulness is determined by the different roles it can have in a lesson plan. Understanding the domains of usefulness of the structures provides the teacher with the freedom to choose the best structure for a given outcome. The definition of structures allows teachers to effectively design cooperative lessons because each structure has predictable outcomes in the academic, linguistic, cognitive, and social domains. Because the structures have different domains of usefulness, a wide variety of structures have been developed. New structures are continually being designed and old structures are evolving.

The domain of usefulness of a structure is best illustrated by contrasting two similar structures, Team Discussion and Three-Step Interview (see Figure 4-2 on page 82). In Team Discussion, individual accountability is lost—some individuals may participate very little or even not at all. There is also no assurance that team members will listen to one another. In one group, for example, each individual may be talking while no one is listening. At any one moment, if one person is speaking, one fourth of the class is involved in language and idea production.

In contrast, in Three-Step Interview each person must produce and receive language. There is equal participation; there is individual accountability for listening because each student has a time to share what he or she has heard; and, since for the first two steps, students interact in pairs, one half, rather than one fourth, of the class is involved in language production at any one time.

Analysis of structures can reveal profound differences between apparently similar cooperative structures. Three-Step Interview leads to almost twice as much language production, as well as more listening,

Figure 4-2 *Team Discussion vs. Three-Step Interview Table*

Team Discussion	Three-Step Interview
STEPS	
1. Teacher asks a question.	1. In pairs, one student interviews another.
2. Teacher tells the groups to talk it over.	2. Reverse roles: interviewer becomes interviewee.
	3. Round-robin: Each student shares with the group what he or she learned in the interview.
BASIC PRINCIPLES	
Individual Accountability	
None	High (for listening)
Simultaneous Interaction	
Medium: $1/4$ participate at a time	High: $1/2$ participate at a time
Equality of Participation	
Unequal	Equal
DOMAIN OF USEFULNESS	
Reaching Consensus	
High	Low
Brainstorming	
High	Low
Sharing Personal Information	
Medium	High
Increasing Listening Skills	
Low	High

when compared to typical team discussion. Three-Step Interview is better for developing language and for sharing personal reactions. Team Discussion is the structure of choice for brainstorming and for reaching group consensus because of its open nature. When teachers are aware of the effects of different structures, they can effectively design lessons to achieve the desired results.

Different structures are useful for different objectives. Most structures are categorized by their primary functions: *class building, team building, communication, information sharing, mastery,* and *thinking skills.* Each structure has a different domain of usefulness, good for some, but not all, steps in a lesson plan, and for some, but not all, kinds of cognitive and social development. The art of structuring successful cooperative learning lessons includes analyzing the objective of a lesson and knowing which structures to use, the cooperative skills of the students, and the cognitive and social objectives of the lesson.

Using the framework for cooperative learning provided by the structural approach, social studies content can be presented to guide students in becoming effective citizens in our ever-changing world. Using cooperative learning to teach social studies provides the knowledge of events in the past and their effect on life today and the social skills students need to function in today's world. Learning in their heterogeneous teams, students begin to understand and accept the varied culture and traditions of society.

Structures for Social Studies[2]

In this section, we overview a few of the many structures that are useful for delivering social studies content (see Figure 4-3 on page 84).

Class Building

Corners, a class building structure, can be used to develop a community feeling within the classroom, to introduce a topic, or to help students appreciate the differences that are inherent in their classroom and in society as a whole. As an example, beginning a primary unit on "The

---

2 "Structures for Social Studies" is adapted from Jeanne M. Stone, *Cooperative Learning and Social Studies: A Multi-structural Approach.*

Figure 4-3 *Overview of Selected Structures**

Structure	Brief Description	Social Studies Content
Corners	**Class Building** Each student moves to a corner of the room representing a teacher-determined alternative. Students discuss within corners, then listen to and paraphrase ideas from other corners.	Students choose a historical figure they would like to meet: George Washington, Benjamin Franklin, Sacajawea, Rosa Parks.
Round Table	**Team Building** Each student in turn writes one answer as a paper and pencil are passed around the team.	Students round table the reasons the settlers began to move west.
Value Lineups	**Communication Skills** Teacher makes a statement. Students line up based on the degree to which they agree or disagree with the statement.	"All states should have equal representation in both the Senate and the House of Representatives."
Numbered Heads Together	**Mastery: Practice and Review** The teacher asks a question, students consult to make sure everyone knows the answer, then one student is called upon to answer.	Review the states and their capitals.
Team Interview	**Information Sharing** Students interview one another in turn. This is sometimes done in role.	Students each portray a different occupation and are interviewed on the pros and cons of the job.
Think Pair Share	**Thinking Skills** Students think to themselves on a topic provided by the teacher; they pair up with another student to discuss it. They then share their thoughts with the class.	After reading about a particular historical event, students think-pair-share about what change occurred because of that event.
Partners	**Division of Labor Lesson Design** Students work in pairs to create or master content. They consult with partners from other teams. Then they share their products or understanding with the other partner pair in their team.	One set of partners reads a historical account of an event, and the other set of partners reads about the same event in a historical novel.

* Adapted from S. Kagan, "The structural approach to cooperative learning." *Education Leadership*, December–January, 1989–90.

Neighborhood," a teacher may post signs in the four corners of the class-room. Each sign has a name of an occupation (with pictures of a hat or tools) that is common in the surrounding neighborhood; maybe a bus driver, a mechanic, a store clerk, and a police officer.

Students are asked to select an occupation that they feel is important to the neighborhood and write the name of the occupation on a small slip of paper. (For students who are nonwriters, the teacher may number each of the signs and have students write a number on the slip of paper or draw a matching picture.) Students group themselves under the occupation they choose. Students then pair up to discuss the reasons for selecting the occupation and talk about what the neighborhood would be like without that occupation. Students can share with the class some of the reasons for selecting their particular corner, thus helping students accept differences of opinion.

In an upper-grade classroom, historical figures pertinent to an event in history can be used instead of occupations. Having studied the Civil War, students may select from Abraham Lincoln, a slave, a slave owner, or a Confederate general. Having made their selection, students meet in corners with others who have made the same choice. Pairs discuss the feelings each person has toward the war, his or her role in it, and what effect the war had on his or her livelihood. New groups can be formed combining students from each corner, with their task to plot a strategy for uniting the country after the war.

Working with existing information, students meet to create new outcomes, a skill they will need in the real world.

Team Building

Round Table and Round-Robin are team-building structures that also work well to share or collect information among team members or for mastery. In Round Table, the teacher announces a topic and the students pass one paper and one pencil around the team, with each team member recording a response as the paper is passed to him or her. The paper continues around the table until time is called. There can be help among the teammates if one doesn't have an answer, but each member must record the answer for his or her turn. Round-Robin is used in the same way, except that instead of writing the responses, the team members share them orally. In turn, each member gives a response to the topic or question provided by the teacher. In a social studies program these structures can be used to prepare to study a new topic (round table everything you know about the American Revolution), review a topic that has just been studied (round-robin the needs that people have), or share ideas on a topic to be discussed (round table possible solutions to the problem of a town that has lost its wheat crop for the year and needs to find a way to get money to buy foodstuffs).

As students in the primary grades look at the past and the changes that have occurred, have them round-robin the things they did when they were babies. Use a class round-robin (each team reporting in turn) to record the information on a class chart. Students can round-robin again, this time round tabling the things that they can do now. After another class round-robin, have students use team discussion to make conclusions about the differences in the two lists and what these differences show.

In an upper-grade classroom, after studying the westward expansion, students can round-table the issues and events that caused the settlers problems as they moved across the continent. Selecting from these events can be the basis for a journal or log chronicling one family's move across the continent. (Providing examples such as excerpts from *Little House on the Prairie* by Laura Ingalls Wilder and *My Prairie Year: Based on the Diary of Elenore Plaisted* by Brett Harvey may help students capture the true feelings of the pioneers.)

Communication Skills

A communication skills structure that lends itself to the social studies classroom is Value Lineups. After the teacher provides a controversial statement, students must decide if they agree or disagree with the statement and to what degree. Having recorded their position (either numerically on a scale of 1-Strongly Agree to 5-Strongly Disagree or verbally "I strongly agree that . . .") on a small slip of paper, students line up, in order, with those strongly agreeing on one end and those strongly disagreeing on the other end. Topics for Value Lineups can range from the consequences of breaking classroom rules to the death penalty to whether or not students agree with a decision made by a historical figure (for example, President George Bush should not have sent American troops to the Persian Gulf).

Mastery

Numbered Heads Together (described earlier in the chapter) is a mastery structure that the students enjoy because of its game format. The teacher asks a question and the students in each team put their heads together to make sure that all the students know the answer. The teacher calls a number and one person on each team stands up to respond. In social studies, the teacher may use this structure to review the facts just covered in a textbook. If a large map is placed in the front of the room, students can be asked to identify a particular state, country, river, and so forth, and when a number is called, come to the front of the room to label the map.

Information Sharing

Team Interview, an information-sharing structure, allows students to interact with the content in a variety of different ways. Following a prompt topic or question from the teacher, one student sits on the "hot seat" as the interviewee. The other team members function as the interviewers. The interview continues until the teacher calls time, and the roles switch so that another student has a chance on the hot seat. Team Interview continues until all students have been interviewed. The flexibility of this structure is an asset to the social studies curriculum. Students can respond with their opinions on issues or current events being studied, or students can select a historical figure and be interviewed "in role." Team Interview can be especially effective if students have read a biography of the person they are portraying.

In a primary classroom, students frequently study the types of transportation. A student can become an "expert" on a particular type of transportation, pretend to be a travel agent who is selling that type of transportation, and during the team interview try to convince people to travel that particular way. Students can also pretend to be one who operates a type of transportation and can tell people what to expect on the ride they are about to take. This structure can be a great practice activity before students interview adults who work in the real world.

In an upper-grade classroom example, students have studied ancient Egyptian civilization. Having identified the occupations or roles that were important to the economic makeup of those times, each student selects one of these roles and a comparable role in today's world. During Team Interview, students share their insights as to the similarities and differences their particular role has in the two societies.

Thinking Skills

Think-Pair-Share is one of the easiest structures to implement, yet it can have a powerful impact on students. It is basically three steps. After the teacher states the topic (a question, an issue, a problem), students have independent think time. Students pair up to discuss the topic. Then some type of whole-class sharing is used. At any time during the lesson, the teacher can ask students to "think," "pair," and "share." While watching a news show, the teacher can use the commercial breaks to have students Think-Pair-Share what impact the news will have on them. While reading a social studies text, the teacher may ask students to Think-Pair-Share what event today they are reminded of, by the past event they just read about. As a teacher is getting ready to start a lesson on needs and wants, he or she may have students Think-Pair-Share what they would buy if they had one hundred dollars.

Division of Labor Lesson Design

Most social studies content is such that there is a great deal of material that must be learned. Cooperative learning structures can be used to divide the labor involved in learning the material. *Partners* allows students to learn new material with the help of a teammate.

In order to make history real to students, it helps to read a biographical sketch or volume that relates how a person has dealt with the events of a given time period. Having been introduced to the historical time period being studied, students form partners within their teams. Each set of partners on a team will learn half of the information and then meet back with their team to share what they have learned. For example, half of the class can read from the history text about life in medieval times and the other half can read selections from novels such as *Adam of the Road* by Elizabeth Gray, *The Door in the Wall* by Marguerite de Angeli, and *Harald and the Giant Knight* by Donald Carrick. After reading the material with a partner, students meet with partners from another team who have the same material. Students compare notes and ideas and then meet with their partner to prepare to tutor their other teammates. After students have tutored their teammates on the information they learned, there is time for reflection. The final step is some type of individual assessment to make sure all students have mastered all the materials. For this activity, the individual assessment may be a writing assignment to compare and contrast the historical facts and the facts presented in the novels.

In a primary classroom where the students are unable to read the information themselves, there are a variety of ways to use Partners. In looking at the past compared to the present and the differences in life-styles, the information can be presented to the students using different media. (Dividing the information by topic rather than past vs. present allows students to work from the same material, gathering information pertinent to their topic.) Again forming the teams into partners, have the same topic partners meet on the same side of the classroom—one set will be looking at transportation and occupations and the other set will look at clothing, shelter, and food. Ways to present information to students can include some of the following: watch a film or video, listen to a picture book read aloud or on audio tape, study prints or photos of life at the given time, interview adults with knowledge of the time period being studied. After students have tutored their teammates and processed the team's interaction, students are ready for an individual assessment.

Being fluent in a variety of structures, a teacher can begin to design lessons that link structure to structure—multistructural lessons—to teach toward academic (and sometimes social) objectives. The teacher selects the objective of the lesson and uses different structures to guide the students' interaction and learning toward this objective. Since no one structure is the most efficient for all objectives, the most efficient way of reaching all objectives is a multistructural lesson.

Social Studies Multistructural Lessons[3]

Understanding how structures work and what their domains of usefulness are paves the way for designing multistructural lessons. To design a

---

3   These lessons are from J. M. Stone, *Cooperative Learning and Social Studies: A Multistructural Approach.*

lesson, first the objectives are decided upon (knowledge, social, cognitive, and linguistic), and the structures are selected to best meet the objectives. The lessons beginning on the following page show how the structures can be linked to create a complete lesson.

Lesson 1: *Getting To Know Ben Franklin*
  Grades: 2–6
  Focus: History

Lesson 2 *"60 Minutes"*
  Grades: 5–8
  Focus: History, Economics, Political Science, Geography

Lesson*
Getting To Know Ben Franklin

Lesson-at-a-Glance

Grades: 2–6
Focus: History
Academic Skills:
- Understand past, present, and future
- Identify contributions Franklin made
- Make a timeline of Franklin's life

Time: One to two social studies periods

Materials:
Biography of Benjamin Franklin —handout
Small pads of paper
Long piece of yarn divided into thirds (about 15 feet)
Clip-type clothespins
Chart paper

Cooperative Learning Structures:
- Round Table
- Partners
- Brainstorming
- Lineup
- Class Round-Robin
- Think-Pair-Share

Resource List:
The Many Lives of Benjamin Franklin by Aliki
Ben and Me, Benjamin Franklin as Written by His Good Mouse Amos by Robert Lawson
Ben Franklin of Old Philadelphia by Margaret Cousins

Lesson Overview

This lesson introduces students to a historical figure of the past, Benjamin Franklin. It helps them understand more of what life was like in the past and the contributions that Franklin made. The timeline is a tool for organizing facts learned about Benjamin Franklin, as well as a way to see the relationship between the past and the present.

This lesson can easily be used as a frame to study other historical figures from the past or present. In altering the lesson, substitute references to Franklin with references to the historical figure being studied. For example, if you wanted to study George Washington Carver, you might have the students round table as many uses for peanuts as they can.

Lesson Sequence

Teacher's Note
Collect a variety of reference books for the students to use.

* This lesson is reprinted by permission of J. M. Stone from *Cooperative Learning and Social Studies: A Multi-structural Approach.* San Juan Capistrano, CA: Resources for Teachers. (In preparation)

Round Table

Listing Items with Electricity

Have the students round table as many items as they can that use electricity. As they finish, a member from each team records two or three ideas on a class chart. As students are waiting for others to finish, have them discuss historical figures that come to mind when they think about electricity.

Partners

Learning About Benjamin Franklin

Tell students that Benjamin Franklin was the person who learned that lightning was electricity. Many of them may have heard about his kite experiment. Explain that he was a famous inventor and made many contributions that are still in use today more than 250 years later (e.g., bifocal glasses, the Franklin stove).

Within the teams, have students form partners A and partners B (two students will work on the same material together). Have the partners meet on opposite sides of the room with like partners (all A's and all B's). Partners A will read about Franklin's early life and Partners B will read about his later life. Pass out a Benjamin Franklin note-taking handout to each pair.

Working in pairs, the students read the material and take notes. Students then meet with like partners, forming a group of four, and compare notes. Students separate and again work in pairs, as they prepare to tutor their teammates. Students return to their teams and share with their teammates what they learned about Benjamin Franklin.

Brainstorming

Dates in Franklin's Life

Using individual sheets for each event, have the students brainstorm as many dates and events as they can about Franklin's life. When they are done, the team arranges its events in chronological order.

Class Round-Robin

Franklin's Life

Have each team number off 1, 2, 3, and 4. Starting with one team and team member number 1, have him or her bring an event card forward to begin a class event list. Continue around the teams with each number 1 adding a new event. Start around the teams again with 2's, then 3's, then 4's. If there are events remaining, continue the round-robin, beginning again with 1's.

Lineup

Franklin's Timeline

On a long piece of yarn, label the centuries (1700, 1800, 1900, 2000). Shuffle and mix up the events from the class round-robin. If there are not enough events, prepare a few extra cards that fit into the time period (1776–Declaration of Independence) and into current times (1983–our birth year). Pass out the cards to the students and have them line up in front of the piece of yarn. Before sitting down, students clip their event card to the piece of yarn with a clothespin.

Think-Pair-Share

Important Event

Have students think about what impressed them most about Benjamin Franklin. Have them share their impressions with a partner. Create a "Benjamin Franklin was . . ." and have students record their impressions on the chart.

Extensions

■ **Team Interview** Have each student pretend he or she is Franklin during a particular event in his life. Other team members pretend they are newspaper reporters and interview him or her.

■ **Team Project** Prepare a "This Is Your Life, Benjamin Franklin" show. Each team can select an event to act out for the class. Record the events as the teams decide what they will be doing so that there will not be duplicate events.

■ Have students create a modern-day version of *Poor Richard's Almanac*. Ask each team to decide what it will include and how it will format the almanac. *Co-op Co-op* can be used to structure the activity.

■ Have students pretend they met Ben Franklin on the street today. He had invented a time machine and had traveled forward in time. Use *Three-Step Interview* to share what students feel Franklin was most surprised to see and why.

Lesson*

"60 Minutes"

Lesson-at-a-Glance

Grades: 5–8
Focus: History, Economics,
   Political Science, Geography
Academic Skills:
- Identify current events
- Analyze the social studies elements in a selected current event
- Orally report on a selected current event

Time: Two to three social studies periods
Materials:
   Copy of current news article, 1 per team
   Chart paper
   Current newspapers and news magazines
   Tape recorder (optional)
Cooperative Learning Structures:
- Think-Pair-Share
- Partner-Expert Group Jigsaw
- Team Discussion
- Numbered Heads Together
- Co-op Co-op

Resource List:
   Local daily newpapers
   U. S. News and World Report
   Time
   USA Today
   Wall Street Journal
   Television and radio news broadcasts
   Television news magazines

Lesson Overview

To reinforce the interwoven elements in social studies instruction, students will select a current event and analyze its impact on history, economics, political science, and geography. Using this information, the students will prepare an "expose" or news commentary (like "60 Minutes") on the current event they have selected.

Lesson Sequence

Teacher's Note

Prior to the lesson, students should be watching/listening to the news and/or reading the newspaper to become familiar with some of the issues in the news.

Think-Pair-Share

Naming Current Events

Have students think of one or two of the most frequently men-

---

* This lesson is reprinted by permission of J. M. Stone from *Cooperative Learning and Social Studies: A Multi-structural Approach.* San Juan Capistrano, CA: Resources for Teachers. (In preparation)

tioned current events. Have them pair up and discuss the importance of these events and why they are "hot" news items. Use *stand up and share** for the whole-class share and record the current events mentioned during the share on a chart posted in the front of the room.

Stand Up and Share All students have an idea in mind and all stand up. Starting on one side of the room, the students share their idea and then sit down. If they have an idea that is similar to one that someone else shares, they sit down as that person sits down. This simultaneous share is to be done quickly and depends on individual accountability so that each idea is shared only once. In essence, everyone's ideas are represented, but each is only mentioned one time.

Partner-Expert Group Jigsaw

Define Social Studies Disciplines

Have the students number off from 1 to 4. Have students with like numbers meet together. In each group, students will pair up (form partners) to discuss and define a different social studies discipline. Their discussion should focus on how to identify the discipline and its impact on people.

1–History

2–Geography

3–Economics

4–Sociopolitics

Partners pair in an expert group to compare information. After partners prepare to present the information to teammates, teams reunite to share information.

Team Discussion

Identify Social Studies Disciplines

Pass out the sample current news article to the students. Have the teams discuss how each discipline is involved in the article.

Numbered Heads Together

Review News Article

Use numbered heads together to review the disciplines in the news article. Use questions such as:

- How is geography a factor in the event?

- What impact can this event have on history?

- Did the influence of government ease or worsen the situation?

- Had money not been a factor, would this event still have occurred?

Co-op Co-op

Prepare a News Commentary

Each team meets to select a news topic that it would like to explore in depth. Keep a running class list, as teams select a topic, so that no topic is repeated. Once the topic is selected, students decide who will approach the article from each of the disciplines. After each student has prepared and presented his or her information to the team, the team begins preparing a news commentary that summarizes the news event and shows the effect the various disciplines have on the event. The teams make presentations to the class. Each presentation must include information from all four student reports, and all four students must present.

Teacher's Note: A variety of processing (reflection time) can be used with this lesson. One of the simplest ways is to have the students rate themselves and their team on how well they used the necessary social skills.

Teacher's Note: In evaluating an activity that is intensely involved in group work, grade students only for the report they prepared to present to their teammates and/or on an individual follow-up assignment given at the completion of this assignment. In essence, students receive grades for work that they do independently, not as a team.

Extensions

- Repeat the lesson with a historical event.

- Change the social studies disciplines the students are using to evaluate the news event. The use of culture and ethics with history and geography can change the way the students look at a particular event.

- As a *team project*, have students create a "60 Minutes" show about events occurring at school.

References

Kagan, S. 1992. *Cooperative learning.* San Juan Capistrano, CA: Resources for Teachers.

Stone, J. M. (in preparation). *Cooperative learning and social studies: A multi-structural approach.* San Juan Capistrano, CA: Resources for Teachers. (In preparation)

5.

Jigsaw II: Cooperative Learning with "Expert Group" Specialization

RONALD L. VANSICKLE

The Jigsaw II Strategy: Introduction

Social studies teachers find Jigsaw II a valuable way to teach historical and social scientific knowledge and to develop citizenship skills. Jigsaw II tends to motivate students to work more persistently than usual. Student interdependence, created by task specialization, and team members' ability to hold one another individually accountable for their contributions to achieving the group goal motivate them. Research on the academic achievement effects of Jigsaw II (e. g., Mattingly and VanSickle, 1991) shows that students generally achieve at higher levels *under the conditions of individual accountability and appropriate group reward* Jigsaw II provides (Slavin, 1986, 1990). The attitudes and social abilities involved in cooperative efforts to learn and to demonstrate academic achievement are consistent with valued citizenship abilities and attitudes, including political participation, problem solving, communication, and commitment to promoting the general welfare.

When Jigsaw II is used effectively and when it is given sufficient time to succeed, students are more competent in their knowledge and abilities during in-class and out-of-class situations where these are applicable. Many also find the home-team and expert-group work desirable because these make learning a more cooperative and a greater social experience contrasted to a competitive or an individualistic experience. The public recognition students and teams receive for good work is perceived by students as worthwhile, regardless of the students' ages, thus increasing the level of satisfaction students experience in school.

Overview of the Jigsaw II Strategy

Students who study social studies by means of Jigsaw II work together in cooperative teams to attain knowledge and abilities aligned with the student outcomes of a unit of study. Students are grouped initially into heterogeneous *home or base-group* teams of mixed academic and social characteristics such as gender, race, and ethnic diversity.

Students also work together in *expert groups*. To form expert groups, each team sends representatives to join with representatives from all the other teams so that all teams are represented in all expert groups. The teacher assigns a different part of the unit's work to each expert group. Members of an expert group study their part of the unit intensively and become "experts" in the assigned information, concepts, and abilities. This typically involves carefully studying the textbook or outside references, such as library books or periodicals. They also communicate what they have learned to their fellow experts. In addition, members of each expert group prepare a plan to teach their peers in their respective home teams. Development of teaching aids, such as charts or outlines, might also be necessary.

After the expert groups complete their study and planning, the initial teams reform, and each team member teaches his or her expertise. The responsibility of each home group is to ensure that every member masters the information and abilities for all sections of the unit encompassed by the Jigsaw II tasks. These heterogeneous groups are provided ample time to ensure that the expertise is shared and that the required learning occurs and is verified within the group by group members.[1]

Students must accept from the outset that the purpose of Jigsaw II

---

[1] Students need to be provided guidance as to how they can check to verify that each member of their home group has mastered the information and is very likely to retain the important information and abilities beyond the end of the class period. In addition, teachers need to allow students enough time for each home-group student to do an adequate job of teaching and verifying learning and to learn the new information shared by other experts in the group.

group tasks is not just to complete a series of individual and group activities in order to cover the material or complete specially constructed worksheets called "expert sheets." Students are expected to master and retain the knowledge and abilities targeted via the worksheets so that they can use this knowledge and these abilities equally well after the groups have stopped meeting. In other words, while correctly completing the expert sheets is required, merely completing these sheets is insufficient to fulfill the major purpose of Jigsaw II.

After the teams complete the assigned learning tasks over one or more class periods, all students take an individual test.[2] Since each student is personally accountable for his or her achievement, the chapter/unit test score is recorded for each individual. Students are assigned improvement points relative to the extent of their improvement above their individual base scores. Individual improvement points for each student are also combined to produce team total and average improvement points that represent each team's scores for that test and unit.[3] Depending on the team scores, the teacher provides public recognition appropriate to the quality of learning demonstrated.

Group rewards in the form of highly relevant recognition are based on a sum of the individual team members' academic performances as determined by their improvement over their base scores. The group cannot be successful in demonstrating strong performance unless all team members do their jobs of teaching their expertise and working to achieve the unit objectives. In this way, students hold one another individually accountable for their performances. Individual accountability for contributions to a group academic goal promotes positive classroom norms and encourages academic achievement and cooperation.

---

[2] A limited version of Jigsaw II that many teachers use is to divide students into home and expert teams in order to help students learn targeted content and skills. These students are then given individual tests. However, these teachers do not check each student's quiz or unit test scores against his or her prior (or base) score and do not compute scores for each team. While a jigsaw activity can occur with home base and expert teams meeting, a complete Jigsaw II strategy cannot occur unless students take individual tests, the scores are considered in light of base scores, and an improvement score for each home team is generated.

[3] The requirement to combine the improvement points of all members of the same team in order to reward any individual(s) makes it clear that students are dependent upon the group for whatever rewards they may earn. Thus, students accept that their own success is ultimately linked to the extent of the success of every member of their group.

Jigsaw II from a Student's Perspective

To illustrate a Jigsaw II classroom, the following narrative reveals a typical high-school economics class through several days of Jigsaw II instruction. It is followed by a description of what teachers must do to implement Jigsaw II and sample instructional materials.

Monday. Pablo Martinez is a high-school senior taking economics this fall semester. His economics teacher, Ken Jackson, is using Jigsaw II. On Monday morning, Pablo enters Mr. Jackson's room wondering how he did on Friday's test. Mr. Jackson starts class, passes back Friday's test, and Pablo is relieved to see that he got 78 percent right and his usual grade of C. Pablo has a generally positive impression of Mr. Jackson, but he thinks economics is one of the tougher courses he has taken in high school.

Mr. Jackson announces that the next unit will focus on Gross National Product (GNP) and economic growth. Pablo is unimpressed. Mr. Jackson explains that this topic will be approached differently than other topics in the past. He explains that the class will be divided into learning teams, called home teams, and students will help one another learn the subject matter. Each of these teams will then break up into expert groups. Each expert group will specialize in different parts of the required subject matter and skills. After studying together as an expert group, members of each expert group will prepare a lesson to teach to members of their home teams. Then all students will return to their original home teams. After each home-team member teaches his or her teammates what he or she has learned in the expert group, everyone will take a test over all the subject matter and skills.

Mr. Jackson announces that there will be a test at the end of the unit. The test will be made of the content and skills described on the worksheets he will distribute to be studied by the home and expert groups. In addition, much of the knowledge stressed in the unit will be on the comprehensive test given at the end of the nine-week period.

Then Mr. Jackson mentions that teams whose members show high improvement in their test scores for this unit over the average score of their tests for the past two units will earn special prizes. Individual students will not get prizes outside of their team. Each student can earn improvement points for his or her team based upon how high the unit test scores are above their scores on past tests. The higher the score is above the average score for the previous units, the more improvement points one earns for his or her team. Because prizes only go to teams, every member of every team needs to work hard to help everyone learn the content and skills and do well on the unit test.

Pablo is not completely clear about how Jigsaw II is going to work, but it does sound different, and dividing up the work does have a good sound to it. He feels some skepticism about whether all students will really pull their fair share of the workload. However, it occurs to him that if he ends up in the right group, two or three students in this class will probably do most of the expert group work anyway. However, he also thinks about the fact that he will not get a prize unless every member of his home team learns a great deal and does well on the unit test. This is not something he has ever heard of before. "Time will tell," he thinks to himself.

Mr. Jackson proceeds to assign students to their heterogeneous home teams.[4] They are allowed five minutes to think up names for their groups. Almost any name is acceptable as long as it is not offensive. The five teams of five members each meet, and Pablo notices right away that he has had good luck; Keisha, a serious A student, is on his team. Frank, Debbie, and Christy make up the rest of the team. After a few minutes, Pablo's team chooses two "GNP" names. Mr. Jackson circulates by the group and vetoes "Gross Natural Processes," and the team settles on "Great Natural People."

Students form into five expert groups, *with one member of each home team in each expert group.* Each expert group is responsible for different material. One expert group will focus on a section of the textbook that shows how GNP can be used as a measure of the economy's performance and as a way to compare different economies. A second expert group, Pablo's, will focus on the section that explains the components of GNP and the events that affect these components. A third group will study the section on conditions needed for economic growth to occur. A fourth group will interview local businesspeople to find out what they think of current economic conditions and what needs to happen in the community to make their businesses more profitable. The fifth group is to find out about current economic conditions, causes of these conditions, and prospects for the future.

Mr. Jackson explains that each student must first ensure that all mem-

---

4 For this narrative, five-member groups are used. There can be three to five members in a group, with all groups for the same unit being as close to the same size as is possible.

bers of his or her expert group become experts in the information and abilities. Then, each expert must be prepared to teach these to his or her home-team members so that they master the same knowledge and abilities. Furthermore, Mr. Jackson remarks, after each expert is finished teaching, he or she needs to test all members of the home group to ensure that each has acquired the knowledge and abilities to an acceptable level. This review will get students ready for the individual test to be taken at the end of the unit.

Pablo's expert group, consisting of Karen, Antonio, Jim, Cassandra, and Pablo, now focuses on the components of GNP. According to Mr. Jackson's directions, the group chooses a discussion leader, Jim. Mr. Jackson circulates by the group and hands out five copies of the expert worksheet related to the group's topic. The expert sheet tells specifically what parts of the chapter Pablo's expert group must master and teach to those of the members' home groups. This worksheet also contains questions to focus on the key ideas in their area of responsibility. (See Figure 5-11 on page 126 for an example of a typical expert sheet.) Each student in the expert group takes one or two of the questions as a special responsibility.

All members of the group begin reading the textbook. Each pays special attention to information related to his or her questions.

The period is almost over.[5] Mr. Jackson has the students move their seats back into rows and emphasizes that students need to bring their textbooks to class every day until the unit is completed. He announces that all students are responsible for learning all the important information in the text, so they need to read the chapter by Thursday. He asks students to review their notes on the purposes and roles of each group and the responsibilities of each student in each group.

Tuesday. Mr. Jackson assigns areas of the room for the five expert groups to meet, and students move to those areas. He reemphasizes that the expert groups are to make sure that all students in the group are able to answer all the questions on their expert sheets. Pablo's expert group members look at each other. Jim asks who read the chapter last night.

---

5 The first few times the teacher uses Jigsaw II (or any cooperative learning strategy) a lot of class time will be used up explaining the purposes of the strategy and the tasks and responsibilities of individual students. After several such activities, very little class time will be needed for these explanatory purposes. Therefore, teachers should not be concerned that using Jigsaw activities will always require large amounts of class time for directions.

The group decides to look up the answers to its assigned questions individually. Pablo had read the part that answered his questions "What two factors influence the level of investment spending?" and "How does each operate?"

Jim calls time after ten minutes. He reminds the group that they all must comprehend the answers and be ready to teach the material to their home teams. Pablo wants to know how they are supposed to teach their home-team members. The answer is not clear yet, but their peers obviously must know the answers to the questions and correctly use this information when and where needed. Consequently, each member of the expert group presents the answers to his or her questions. All take notes on the answers. Karen thinks Antonio misunderstands part of his assignment and after some discussion, one of Antonio's answers is revised. When they finish, each expert group member has a set of clear answers. Mr. Jackson stops by several times and checks the answers, so Pablo feels pretty confident that the answers are correct.

Mr. Jackson asks each group to take five minutes to review all they have discussed during the period, to determine how this information interrelates, and to consider how this information could be used in their daily lives.

Mr. Jackson then describes some ways the expert groups might plan to teach their assignments to their home-team members. Each expert must be prepared to provide the answers to all the questions and directions on the expert group sheet. Where necessary, each should be prepared to clarify, expand upon, and apply the knowledge associated with the questions, as well as justify why particular answers were selected. A chart, diagram, or outline might help to highlight or summarize some of the ideas studied. Mr. Jackson asks students to think about ways to teach their expert knowledge and abilities. He also asks how they might go about testing their peers to determine whether they have mastered the material. Mr. Jackson says that they will work on these matters tomorrow. For homework, he asks each student to make a list of things he or she might want to do to teach his or her teammates and to test them. He then uses the last few minutes to discuss the importance of economic growth in the community.

Wednesday. Mr. Jackson starts class by announcing that the expert groups will plan how to teach their home teammates. The students move to their expert groups. Pablo, Jim, Antonio, Cassandra, and Karen look at one another and wonder where to begin. Jim suggests that they review the answers to the questions. He asks each member of the expert group to answer questions that he or she was not responsible for answering yesterday. After fifteen minutes, each student can answer all the questions without referring to notes.

After reviewing the questions and answers, the group still is not sure what to do, so Jim asks Mr. Jackson to come over. Mr. Jackson encourages the group by telling them that they are on track. He suggests that much of the content of their section could be summarized in a diagram, using a pie graph that illustrates the textbook's equation GNP = C (consumption) + I (investment) + G (government spending). They could then add some information to the diagram about factors affecting the various components of GNP. It takes about ten minutes to work out a diagram that looks decent; each member then copies it. In addition, the group takes steps to ensure that all members comprehend the definitions of consumption, investment, and government spending, since these meanings are critical to comprehending the chart.

Mr. Jackson emphasizes that the test for this unit will be based on the content and abilities all five expert groups have been studying. He also emphasizes that each home team's performance will depend on the individual performances of the team members. Consequently, each expert's efforts will have a major impact on his or her home team members' abilities to perform well on the test.

Thursday. Before school starts, Pablo reviews his presentation. Since he has to teach his expertise, he wants his teammates to believe he knows what he is talking about. As a direct result of his expert group involvement, he does know quite well what he is talking about.

Mr. Jackson starts the class by reviewing the procedures for the day. The students are assembled in their home groups.[6] Each expert will have eight to ten minutes to teach his or her subject to the rest of the team. Mr. Jackson lists on the chalkboard the order in which the expert lessons will be conducted. He will keep track of the time and progress of the presentations and tell the teams if they are rushing or going too slowly.

---

6 The teacher may want to have students start the period in their expert groups for five to ten minutes for any last-minute ideas they want to share or review as well as to allow students to encourage one another to do the best job possible in making all their home-group members as "expert" as they themselves have become. Remember, students are not necessarily "expert teachers" just because they have become experts in a small area of social studies knowledge and abilities.

Pablo and his Great Natural People teammates form their group.

Christy begins by reminding her groupmates that her responsibility is to enable each of them to become an expert in the knowledge and abilities she has been studying. She tells them that she will be checking each of them to determine whether he or she has learned what she is going to teach. Next, Christy shows her groupmates the questions and directions her expert group studied regarding the definition of GNP, how GNP can be used to measure the performance of the economy, and how it can be used to compare the economy over time or to compare different nations' economies. She carefully explains the answers to the questions. She also uses a graph of GNP statistics to show how the GNP of the United States has grown over the years and how that has translated into a higher standard of living. She displays a chart to show how the GNPs of various nations differ drastically. Before ending her segment, she directs her peers to close their texts and notebooks and asks different members to answer her expert-group questions. Some discussion to clarify a couple of the answers is necessary.[7]

Next, it is Pablo's turn. He presents the questions, explains the answers, and also uses the GNP pie graph diagram. Like Christy, he quizzes to make sure members comprehend the questions and answers. He helps one student who developed a misconception of an important concept.

Frank's expert group interviewed several businesspeople in town, including the owner of a frozen yogurt shop, the manager of a Mexican restaurant, the manager of an auto parts store, and a real estate agent about the effects of current economic conditions on their businesses. Among other things, Frank reports that business is off and profits are down at the yogurt shop and the Mexican restaurant. The restaurant manager's plans to build another restaurant across town have been postponed indefinitely. The real estate agent was especially gloomy because few people were willing to buy houses. In contrast, the auto parts business was doing very well as people fixed up their old cars rather than buy new ones. Pablo notices and comments on the connection between the consumption and investment components of GNP and information

---

[7] If members of the group do not retain the appropriate knowledge or cannot apply it correctly, then Christy would take additional time to work with these students. Remember, her responsibility is to ensure that each member becomes an expert; it is not just to cover the material or tell the answers her expert group found.

Frank shared from his interviews. Pablo is pleased with himself for this contribution.

Using a format similar to Christy's and Pablo's, Debbie explains the answers to her questions. Frank comments that the real estate agent mentioned some of the same conditions for economic growth that Debbie found in the textbook.

With five minutes remaining, Mr. Jackson asks the class to take four minutes to review the important information they studied during the period as well as consider how the information shared by one expert was related to that shared by another. With one minute left, Mr. Jackson congratulates the class on its good work. Students are told to get together in their home teams as they enter the classroom tomorrow.

Friday. With the students already in their home teams, Mr. Jackson directs them to spend a few minutes reviewing the information they shared and studied in their groups the day before. Since Debbie had not finished her teaching, she resumes by quizzing her teammates to make sure they comprehend and can use the knowledge. Doing an equally thorough job, Keisha presents her questions and answers and then quizzes her teammates.

Mr. Jackson ends the experts' lessons and convenes the class into a large group. Based on what he has heard during the experts' presentations and team discussions, he conducts a large-group discussion of GNP and economic growth.

Mr. Jackson announces a test for Monday. Each student's test score will be recorded and will count. Based on the students' test performances within each group, all high-performance teams will be rewarded. He emphasizes that each team's performance is dependent on each individual team member's test score contribution. Pablo leaves wondering how he will do on the test; he feels that he ought to do all right.

Sunday. Pablo has never called a classmate about homework before. But he wants to check with two of his home teammates to verify answers to three questions. He smiles. Maybe he also helped his two teammates and they will score higher on the test so that the whole team might get the prize Mr. Jackson promised.

Monday. As usual, Pablo gets to school about twenty minutes before homeroom. He knows that today is the test in economics class. He also remembers that he has not carefully reread the last section of the chapter on economic growth. Since his team's award depends on his performance, he takes fifteen minutes to reread the last section of the chapter that includes the information Debbie shared.

Later in the morning, Mr. Jackson calls the class to order. The students take the test. Pablo leaves class thinking that the test was not very hard. In the time remaining, students begin reading the next chapter.

Tuesday. Mr. Jackson passes back the test, and Pablo is pleased to see that he got 91 percent right and earned a B+. He also notices that he earned 30 improvement points and that his team averaged 28 improvement points. The class reviews and discusses the test.

Then, Mr. Jackson announces the performance of the home teams. Based on their improvement points, one team is complimented on its *good* performance. Three other teams are complimented on their *excellent* team results on the test. Mr. Jackson puts their team names and individual names on a bulletin board display honoring academic performance. Pablo's team, the Great Natural People, is asked to stand to be recognized because of its excellent performance. Mr. Jackson gives each member a short letter complimenting them on their academic performance. He asks them to show the letter to their parents.

Pablo smiles at the big deal Mr. Jackson is making of this. But why not? Pablo can stand a little good publicity at home. Mr. Jackson leads the class in a review of what behaviors in the small groups really helped make the groups a success and what behaviors interfered with this success. He urges students to work hard on the positive behaviors and equally hard at stopping any negative behaviors.

Mr. Jackson introduces the next unit.

How To Plan for and Implement the Jigsaw II Strategy

Planning a Unit That Incorporates the Jigsaw II Strategy

In order to teach a social studies unit using Jigsaw II, you must plan the overall unit prior to the first day of instruction. Once Jigsaw II goes into effect, the workload shifts significantly from the teacher to the students. During this planning, you need to take the following steps:

- Select clear and specific student outcome objectives.

- Select and locate appropriate reading materials that contain the must-learn content and skills.

- Prepare the appropriate number of expert sheets that will focus students' attention on the content and skills.

- Determine students' initial base scores.

- Assign students to home teams.

- Assign students to expert groups.

- Construct an outcome-aligned test or quiz over the unit.

Once the Jigsaw II student tasks are organized, decide which instructions, if any, you want to provide students in addition to what is required for Jigsaw II's two levels of group tasks. While the students are working in their Jigsaw II home teams and expert groups, you keep time, check on each group's progress and processing, and consult with students to facilitate the successful completion of their work. At the conclusion of the unit, you will score individual tests. Then you determine improvement points using the students' test or quiz scores, compute team scores, announce the team results, and provide appropriate public recognition for students' exemplary achievement.

Select and Locate Reading Materials. Jigsaw II activities typically involve students encountering all of the to-be-learned information by reading. Consequently, appropriate materials aligned with the objectives of the unit and the students' reading-skill levels should be located. All reading material should be easily accessible to all students. Furthermore, from the beginning, all students are usually assigned all the reading materials selected for the unit.[8]

One option is to stick to the textbook.[9] Various sections of a textbook chapter can be assigned to the expert groups. Pablo's economics class

---

[8] This point is made because of a misconception that students only have to read and study a portion of the material or only that part they need to become "expert" in.

[9] Note that the use of the textbook is an option, not a requirement.

activities illustrate a second option. Some expert groups can be given assignments that require little or no reading, such as the interview group in Pablo's class. Other expert groups can be assigned more difficult reading, such as library references or more challenging periodicals.

Prepare Expert Sheets. Expert sheets guide the work of the expert groups. Preparation of easily comprehended expert sheets is central to the Jigsaw II strategy. At the end of this chapter two sets of expert sheets (one for middle grades and one for high school) are provided as examples of what the teacher might use in a typical social studies classroom.

Each expert sheet should clearly state the page numbers of the textbook section an expert group must master. If nontext reading materials are used, expert sheets must clearly describe those materials and where they can be found. Each sheet includes key questions and directions to focus the experts' study on the key concepts, information, and abilities to be learned. If the teacher expects students to engage in analytical thinking, the questions should be phrased so that students have to engage in this kind of thinking to arrive at an acceptable answer. The questions or directions should be listed in such a way that they can be divided among the expert group members to facilitate division of labor. For example, if expert groups will consist of five members, then the number of questions should be some multiple of five.

Depending on the complexity of the assignments, the expert sheets might be duplicated for each expert group member, or they might be written on poster paper and put on the classroom walls. Preparation of expert sheets warrants considerable effort; otherwise, the students and you will spend valuable class time clarifying ambiguities, correcting errors, or improving questions. Ambiguous questions and directions frequently lead students to off-task behaviors.[10]

Expert sheets are the unique resources within Jigsaw II, the only materials that must be formally prepared to focus and guide student study and learning. The ten sample Jigsaw II expert sheets included in this chapter illustrate the kinds of specificity and format that are to be used in constructing these learning-task guides. (See Figures 5-5 through 5-14

---

[10] Should students get off-task because of ambiguous and inadequate questions and directions on the expert sheets they are given, the cooperative learning technique should not be blamed as the cause of this off-task behavior.

at the end of this chapter.) One set of five expert sheets is applicable to a middle grades United States history class; the other fits a senior high-school economics class much like Pablo's. The format of these expert sheets is generic and would have to be modified to fit the emphasis of your unit materials.

Determine Students' Initial Base Scores. Jigsaw II awards recognition for academic achievement based on current student test performance compared with past performance. Consequently, you must determine an initial base score for each student. You may give students a pretest or diagnostic test aligned with the unit objectives a few days before the start of the unit and use these test scores as a measure of students' base-line knowledge. If test scores from earlier in the course are available, average two or three recent test scores to determine a base score. Alternatively, if this is the first few weeks of the new school year, use last year's or term's social studies grade to determine a base score. For example, translate an A to 95 percent, an A- or B+ to 90 percent, a B to 85 percent, and so on. These two ways are outlined in Figure 5-1 on page 112.

As the school year progresses, students' base scores can be adjusted depending on their achievement on later unit tests.

Assign Students to Heterogeneous Home Teams. Each home team should be as heterogeneous as possible in academic ability or achievement. To accomplish this, first rank the students from high to low in terms of academic ability or achievement. Previous test scores in the course, last year's grades, standardized achievement test scores, writing samples, or observations in class are all acceptable grounds for ranking students.

Second, divide the students into teams so that each team is approximately equal in academic ability or achievement. For example, assume a class of thirty students with six teams of five students each. Start at the top of the ranked list of students and assign the top student to team A, the second-ranked student to team B, and so on to the sixth-ranked student to team F. Then assign the seventh-ranked student to team F also, then the eighth ranked student to team E, and so on back to team A. Figure 5-2 on page 113 illustrates how this might be done for a class of thirty-two students divided into eight groups of four members each.

Figure 5-1   *Two Methods of Computing a Student's Base Score*

A. Calculating base score using the student's final grade in the subject for the previous grading period.

Last Year's Grade	Initial Base Score
A	95
A–/B+	90
B	85
B–/C+	80
C	75
C–/D+	70
D	65
F	60

B. Calculating base score in terms of the student's grades over past quizzes. For example:

Mary's Three Test Scores

	90 (Quiz 1)
	78 (Quiz 2)
	84 (Quiz 3)
Total	252
Divided by	3
Mary's Base Score =	84

Third, check the tentative team assignments to ensure sex, race, and ethnic diversity. Juggle the assignments when any team diverges much from the general class distribution. If any unfortunate combinations of friends or antagonists result from the tentative assignments, change them! This process will produce teams of reasonably equivalent overall academic abilities and sex, race, and gender diversity.

Assign Students to Expert Groups. There are two major options in assigning students to expert groups. The first is to assign students so that the groups are heterogeneous in terms of academic achievement or ability. This can be done by assigning the first-ranked student in team A to

Figure 5-2 *Example of How To Rank Order Students and Then Assign Them to Jigsaw II Groups of Four for Initial Heterogeneous Groups Based on Academic Achievement*

	Rank Order	Team Name
Highest-Achieving Students	1	A
	2	B
	3	C
	4	D
	5	E
	6	F
	7	G
	8	H
Average-Achieving Students	9	H
	10	G
	11	F
	12	E
	13	D
	14	C
	15	B
	16	A
	17	A
	18	B
	19	C
	20	D
	21	E
	22	F
	23	G
	24	H
Low-Achieving Students	25	H
	26	G
	27	F
	28	E
	29	D
	30	C
	31	B
	32	A

expert group 1, the second-ranked student in team B to expert group 1, and so on. For expert group 2, assign the second-ranked student in team A, the third-ranked student in Team B, and so on. The second option is to group students so that the expert groups are homogeneous according to some criterion. Pablo's teacher used the second option. Most lower-reading-ability students were assigned to a group that interviewed businesspeople; the best readers were assigned periodical reading materials that were more difficult than the textbook. Other criteria could be used to assign students to expert groups.

Construct an Outcome-Aligned Test Over the Unit. As usual, you construct a test that assesses students' achievement of the unit objectives.[11] The test items should be consistent with the objectives and questions specified on the expert sheets.[12] Additional questions can be added to address other content objectives that were not part of the Jigsaw II activity but were emphasized in the group discussion and unit objectives.

Once Under Way, Monitor Student Work

Once the Jigsaw II activities begin, you move to the instructional background. However, your efforts are very important. By monitoring expert-group and home-team work, you can decide how much time to allot to various activities such as expert-group lesson planning and peer teaching. You can provide needed assistance or prompting. Even when groups are working productively, you can make observations or ask questions to raise additional ideas for consideration. Also, you can provide additional information, clarify difficult concepts, or amplify ideas students encounter in the reading materials as needed.

---

[11] Jigsaw II may be used to help students study an entire unit, part of a unit, or several units over an extended period of two, three, four, or more weeks. In other words, there is no required maximum length of time to use this strategy.

[12] Teachers involved in Outcomes-Based Education and Mastery Learning know that their unit tests are constructed before the unit begins, immediately after the specific student outcome objectives are determined. Consequently, the major focus for the expert sheets and learning tasks in the Jigsaw II groups is the knowledge and abilities needed to be successful on the tests.

Assess Students' Achievement To Establish and Reinforce the Notion of Individual Accountability

Students, as individuals, take a comprehensive unit test that includes items directly aligned with the unit outcome objectives and the expert sheets. Each student is given a single test score and grade to indicate the level of his or her achievement. This test and score reconfirm a critical principle of cooperative learning: each student is *individually accountable*, in the end, for what he or she was to have learned. This accountability ensures that students see that the purpose of these cooperative groups is to help everyone learn and succeed.

Determine Individual Student Improvement Points. Once the Jigsaw II activities are completed and students have been tested, determine the number of improvement points students have earned. Compare a student's test score with his or her base score and assign the improvement points. For example, if a student scores more than 10 points below the base score, assign zero improvement points. If a student scores 10 points to 1 point below the base score, post 10 improvement points. Similarly, if a student scores up to 10 points above the base score, award 20 improvement points. For more than 10 points above the base score or for a perfect score, assign 30 improvement points. Pablo's base score was an 80 because his average score over the past two unit tests was 80; his Jigsaw II unit test score was 91, 11 points above his base score. Consequently, he earned 30 improvement points. Note that improvement points are not the same as the number of score points between the base score and unit test score. The sheet shown in Figure 5-3 on page 116 can be used to record the base scores and improvement points of students in an entire class.

Compute Team Improvement Points and Determine Minimum Levels of Team Improvement for Awards. Team scores are simply the average of the team members' improvement points for the unit. (Figure 5-4 on page 117 can be used to record the improvement points for each team.) For example, assume that five team members earned the following improvement points: 0, 10, 20, 30, 30. The average for the team is 18. However, the overall level of team performance is modest. Students with an average team score of 25 or higher consistently scored well above their base scores.

Figure 5-3 *Example of a Blank Base Score and Improvement Points Sheet for Two Jigsaw II Units*

BASE SCORE AND IMPROVEMENT POINTS SHEET FOR ENTIRE CLASS

Course:_____ Period:_____

Student	Quiz No. _____			Quiz No. _____		
	Base Score	Quiz Score	Improvement Points	Base Score	Quiz Score	Improvement Points
1.						
2.						
3.						
4.						
5.						
6.						
7.						
8.						
9.						
10.						
11.						
12.						
13.						
14.						

Provide Appropriate Public Recognition. When test results are returned to the students, you should communicate their test scores, base scores, and number of improvement points. You should also announce the criteria for different levels of recognition. For example, a team average score of 15–19 could indicate *good* academic performance, 20–24 could indicate *excellent* performance, and 25 or more could indicate *outstanding* performance.

Recognition for different levels of performance can be provided in various ways. Mr. Jackson placed the students' names and their team name on a bulletin board display honoring academic achievement. Very high performance was also recognized by a letter of congratulations and praise. Another alternative is to prepare a class newsletter in which students and teams are praised for their work. Certificates could be produced to recognize team achievement. The exact nature of the recognition will depend on the age of the student. Nevertheless, students of all ages appreciate public recognition of their good work.

Figure 5-4   *Examples of Team Summary Sheets*

TEAM SUMMARY SHEET
(Individual and Team Improvement Points Per Jigsaw II Unit)

TEAM NAME: _____

TEAM MEMBERS	UNIT/WEEK								
	1	2	3	4	5	6	7	8	9
Kelly	20								
Carlo	30								
Justin	30								
Rachel	30								
Total Team Score	110								
Team Average	28								
Team Award This Unit/Week									

TEAM SUMMARY SHEET
(Individual and Team Improvement Points Per Jigsaw II Unit)

TEAM NAME: _____

TEAM MEMBERS	UNIT/WEEK								
	1	2	3	4	5	6	7	8	9
Kelly	20								
Carlo	30								
Justin	30								
Rachel	30								
Total Team Score	110								
Team Average	28								
Team Standing This Unit/Week	1								
Total Team Score to Date	110								
Team Standing by Team Total to Date	1								
Team Award for This Unit/Week									

A Checklist of Teacher Actions for Jigsaw II

Assume that you wanted to use Jigsaw II within your classroom. The list below provides an abbreviated set of steps you would want to follow.

In order to use Jigsaw II in my social studies classes, I need to do the following:

— I need to select a topic and objectives for my unit of instruction.

— I need to select and locate appropriate reading materials.

— I need to make a test over the unit of instruction.

— I need to prepare expert sheets.

— I need to determine my students' initial base scores.

— I need to assign my students to cooperative learning home teams.

— I need to assign my students to expert groups.

— I need to explain the Jigsaw II process to my students and organize them into home teams and expert groups.

— I need to monitor and facilitate my students' group work.

— I need to test my students' academic achievement and determine their individual scores as well as their improvement points.

— I need to compute team scores and determine each team's level of academic achievement.

— I need to provide appropriate public recognition and rewards for students' and teams' academic achievement.

Course: Middle Grades United States History
Unit Topic: European Exploration of the New World

Figure 5-5   *Example of a Typical Expert Sheet*

Expert Sheet 1: Europe in the Fifteenth Century

Read: Read Section 1 on pages 1–4.
Answer: Work with your expert group to find answers to these questions.

1. If you were a "common man" or "common woman" in Europe during the 1400s, what would a typical week in your life be like?

2. During the 1400s, what kinds of political leaders were common in Europe? How did these leaders keep their power?

3. In the 1400s, how were the majority of Europeans organized to produce the food, clothing, and other things they needed?

4. What are at least four particular ways the ideas and arts of the Renaissance affected Europeans' attitudes and beliefs about the world outside of Europe?

5. What are at least five ways that life in Europe in the 1400s was very different from our lives today?

Discuss: After each person has found the answers to his or her questions, discuss the answers to make sure everyone has the appropriate information. Then the group should verify that each member can explain the answers clearly. Take turns explaining the answers to one another. Write the answers out in complete sentences with one paragraph for each question.

Plan to Teach: Plan together how to teach the members of your home teams the knowledge you have gained from your reading and discussion. Remember, compared to your home teammates, you are experts on these questions. You are to help them learn what you know.

1. How will you share and explain the answers to the above questions?

2. What two things will you share with your home teammates concerning what you believe is good, bad, surprising, amazing, strange, or still important from this period for our lives today?

3. What specific thing might you show your home teammates that will help them understand the important information about these people at this time in history? For example, is there a painting, drawing, map, or graph you can locate or develop and then use?

4. In what order will you present this information to your teammates?

5. In what specific ways will you check to determine that each teammate comprehends and remembers the knowledge you will share?

Rehearse: Practice teaching your lesson in your expert group.

Figure 5-6   *A Second Example of a Typical Expert Sheet*

Expert Sheet 2: Trade Between Europe and Asia

Read: Read Section 2 on pages 5–9.

Answer: Work with your expert-group members to find the answers to the following questions.

1. What are at least four reasons why fifteenth-century Europeans were interested in trading with the Far East, particularly India and China?

2. What are at least two reasons why the Western European nations at this time wanted to find a water route to Asia when they already had a land route?

3. What contributions did Prince Henry the Navigator make that enabled merchants and explorers to find a water route around Africa to Asia?

4. What are two ways that Prince Henry's activities were similar to those involved in the exploration of space today?

Discuss: After each person has found the answers to his or her questions, discuss the answers to make sure everyone has the appropriate information. Then the group should verify that each member can explain the answers clearly. Take turns explaining the answers to one another. Write the answers out in complete sentences with one paragraph for each question.

Plan to Teach: Plan together how to teach the members of your home teams the knowledge you have gained from your reading and discussion. Remember, compared to your home teammates, you are experts on these questions. You are to help them learn what you know.

1. How will you share and then explain the answers to the above questions?

2. What two things will you share with your home teammates concerning what you believe is good, bad, surprising, amazing, strange, or still important from this period for our lives today?

3. What specific thing might you show your home teammates that will help them understand the important information about these people at this time in history? For example, is there a painting, drawing, map, or graph you can locate or develop and then use?

4. In what order will you present this information to your home teammates?

5. In what specific ways will you check to determine that each teammate comprehends and remembers the knowledge you will share?

Rehearse: Practice teaching your lesson in your expert group.

Figure 5-7   *A Third Example of a Typical Expert Sheet*

Expert Sheet 3: Columbus: Admiral of the Ocean Sea

Read: Read Section 3 on pages 10–14.

Answer: Work with your expert-group members to answer these questions.

1. What are two reasons Columbus used to justify sailing west to Asia rather than following Prince Henry's route south around Africa?

2. What reasons did Queen Isabella and King Ferdinand of Spain have for helping Columbus in his search for a western route to Asia?

3. When he reached land for the first time on his original voyage, what did Columbus actually find?

4. Of all the things Columbus did after reaching land on this first voyage, which three things are especially important to remember?

5. What are three of Columbus's important beliefs concerning his discoveries on this initial voyage?

Discuss: Discuss the answers to make sure everyone has the appropriate information. Then the group should verify that each member can explain the answers clearly. Take turns explaining the answers to one another. Write the answers out in complete sentences with one paragraph for each question.

Plan to Teach: Plan together how to teach the members of your home teams the knowledge you have gained from your reading and discussion. Remember, compared to your home teammates, you are experts on these questions. You can help them learn what you know.

1. How will you share and then explain the answers to the above questions?

2. What two things will you share with your home teammates concerning what you believe is good, bad, surprising, amazing, strange, or still important from this period for our lives today?

3. What specific thing might you show your home teammates that will help them understand the important information about these people at this time in history? For example, is there a painting, drawing, map, or graph you can locate or develop and then use?

4. In what order will you present this information to your home teammates?

5. In what specific ways will you check to determine that each teammate comprehends and remembers the knowledge you will share?

Rehearse: Practice teaching your lesson in your expert group.

Figure 5-8   *A Fourth Example of a Typical Expert Sheet*

Expert Sheet 4: Existing Native American Cultures

Read: Read Section 4 on pages 15–20.

Answer: Work with your expert-group members to find the answers to the following questions.

1. What words best describe the political, economic, and religious beliefs and systems of the Aztec and Inca civilizations?

2. What words would best describe the scientific and technological ideas and devices of the Aztec and Inca civilizations?

3. In the year 1500, in what specific locations in North America did large groups of Indians live?

4. At the time of Columbus's first voyage, what are at least three important ways the major Aztec and Inca Indian cultures differed from each other in their ways of life?

Discuss: After each person has found the answers to his or her questions, discuss the answers to make sure everyone has the appropriate information. Then the group should verify that each member can explain the answers clearly. Take turns explaining the answers to one another. Write the answers out in complete sentences with one paragraph for each question.

Plan to Teach: Plan together how to teach the members of your home teams the knowledge you have gained from your reading and discussion. Remember, compared to your home teammates, you are experts on these questions. You can help them learn what you know.

1. How will you share and then explain the answers to the above questions?

2. What two things will you share with your home teammates concerning what you believe is good, bad, surprising, amazing, strange, or still important from this period for our lives today?

3. What specific thing might you show your home teammates that will help them understand the important information about these people at this time in history? For example, is there a picture, drawing, map, or a graph you can locate or develop and then use?

4. In what order will you present this information to your home teammates?

5. In what specific ways will you check to determine that each teammate comprehends and remembers the knowledge you will share?

Rehearse: Practice teaching your lesson in your expert group.

Figure 5-9   *A Fifth Example of a Typical Expert Sheet*

Expert Sheet 5: The Conquistadors

Read: Read Section 5 on pages 20–24.

Answer: Work with your expert-group members to find the answers to the following questions.

1. What were the goals of Spanish conquistadors such as Cortez and Pizarro?

2. How did the Aztecs' religion and the beliefs of their leader, Montezuma, help Cortez to defeat the Aztecs?

3. What specific steps did Pizarro take in order to defeat the Incas?

4. What were at least three specific advantages the conquistadors had over the Native Americans living in Central and South America at this time?

5. From the perspective of the conquistadors, what contributions were they making to the lives of the Native Americans they conquered?

6. If you were an Aztec or Inca at this time, what would have been your view of these conquistadors?

7. If you were an Aztec or Inca at this time, in what specific ways would your views of the conquistadors have differed from the views of the conquistadors themselves?

Discuss: Take turns explaining the answers to one another. Write the answers out in complete sentences with one paragraph for each question.

Plan to Teach: Plan together how to teach the members of your home teams the knowledge you have gained from your reading and discussion.

1. How will you share and then explain the answers to the above questions?

2. What two things will you share with your home teammates concerning what you believe is good, bad, surprising, amazing, strange, or still important from this period for our lives today?

3. What specific thing might you show your home teammates that will help them understand the important information about these people at this time in history? For example, is there a picture, drawing, map, or graph you can locate or develop and then use?

4. In what order will you present this information to your home teammates?

5. In what specific ways will you check to determine that each teammate comprehends and remembers the knowledge you will share?

Rehearse: Practice teaching your lesson in your expert group.

Course: **High School Economics**
Unit Topic: **GNP and Economic Growth**

Figure 5-10　*Example of a Typical Expert Sheet*

Expert Sheet 1: Gross National Product (GNP)

Read: Read all of Chapter 9—"GNP and Economic Growth." Read and carefully study the information on pages 130–136.

Answer: Work with your expert-group members to find the answers to the following questions.

1. What is the definition of Gross National Product (GNP)?

2. What specific rules do economists use to decide what to include in computing a nation's GNP? What are six items economists would include in computing the GNP of a particular nation? What are six items they would not include in making this calculation?

3. How can GNP statistics be used to compare the economy of a nation in different years? Locate a table of GNP statistics for the United States (or any country) over a five-year period. In what ways were these GNP figures identical? Similar? Different? As a result of this comparison, what conclusions can you draw about changes in the GNP over this period?

4. How can GNP statistics be used to compare the economies of different nations? Locate a table of GNP statistics for a second country over the same five-year period. Use these two sets of numbers as the basis for comparing these nations' GNPs. As a result of this comparison, what conclusions can you draw about the economies of these two countries over this same time period?

5. What do GNP statistics indicate about life in a particular country? What can GNP statistics not reveal about life in a particular country?

Discuss: After each person has found the answers to his or her questions, discuss the answers to make sure everyone has the appropriate information. Then the group should verify that each member can explain the answers clearly. Take turns explaining the answers to one another. Write the answers out in complete sentences with one paragraph for each question.

Plan to Teach: Plan together how to teach the members of your home teams the information you have gained from your reading and discussion. Remember, compared to your home teammates, you are experts on these questions. You can help them learn what you know.

1. How will you share and then explain the answers to the above questions?

2. What two things will you share with your home teammates concerning what you believe is good, bad, surprising, or important about GNP for our lives today?

3. What specific thing might you show your home teammates that will help them understand the important information about the concept of GNP and the GNP of any particular nation? For example, is there a picture, drawing, map, or graphic you can locate or develop and then use?

4. In what order will you present this information to your home teammates?

5. In what specific ways will you check to determine that each teammate comprehends and remembers the knowledge you will share?

Rehearse: Practice teaching your lesson in your expert group.

Figure 5-11   *A Second Example of a Typical Expert Sheet*

Expert Sheet 2: GNP = C + I + G

Read: Read all of Chapter 9—"GNP and Economic Growth." Read and carefully study the information on pages 136–143.

Answer: Work with your expert group to find answers to these questions.

1. What are the three components of GNP? What are their relative sizes as parts of total GNP?

2. What specific kinds of events are likely to influence consumers to spend larger or smaller amounts of money? Describe one such event. Explain why it would lead consumers to change the amount they spend.

3. What two factors influence the level of investment spending? How does each operate?

4. What specific kinds of events are likely to influence government leaders to increase or decrease government spending? Describe one event that would influence government leaders to spend larger or smaller amounts of money. Why would this event lead these leaders to change the amount they spend?

5. At the present time, what is happening in the economy of the United States relative to these three GNP components?

Discuss: After each person has found the answers to his or her questions, discuss the answers to make sure everyone has the appropriate information. Then the group should verify that each member can explain the answers clearly. Take turns explaining the answers to one another. Write the answers out in complete sentences with one paragraph for each question.

Plan to Teach: Plan together how to teach the members of your home teams the information you have gained from your reading and discussion. Remember, compared to your home teammates, you are experts on these questions. You can help them learn what you know.

1. How will you share and explain the answers to the above questions?

2. What two things will you share with your teammates concerning what you believe is important about the GNP components for our lives today?

3. What specific thing might you show your teammates that will help them understand the key components of GNP? For example, is there a drawing, map, or graphic you can locate or develop and then use?

4. In what order will you present this information to your teammates? Specifically, how will you check to determine that each teammate comprehends and remembers the information you will share?

Rehearse: Practice teaching your lesson in your expert group.

Figure 5-12   *A Third Example of a Typical Expert Sheet*

Expert Sheet 3: Economic Growth

Read: Read Chapter 9, and study the information on pages 143–152.
Answer: Work with your expert-group members to answer these questions.

1. What is the definition of economic growth?

2. What three major factors determine the economy's ability to grow? Using examples not in the text, what are examples of each?

3. Under what conditions would a nation's total economic growth most likely lead to increasing standards of living for its people?

4. What are three productivity problems currently facing the U.S.?

5. In what ways are a nation's productivity and economic growth linked?

6. To what extent is it possible for a nation to grow economically without an increase in productivity?

Discuss: After each person has found the answers to his or her questions, discuss the answers to make sure everyone has the appropriate information. Then the group should verify that each member can explain the answers clearly. Take turns explaining the answers to one another. Write the answers out in complete sentences with one paragraph for each question.

Plan to Teach: Plan together how to teach the members of your home teams the information you have gained from your reading and discussion. Remember, compared to your home teammates, you are experts on these questions. You can help them learn what you know.

1. How will you share and then explain the answers to the questions?

2. What two things will you share with your home teammates concerning what you believe is good, bad, surprising, or important about economic growth and productivity for our lives?

3. What specific thing might you show your home teammates that will help them understand the important information about the economic activity of a nation or community at a particular moment? For example, is there a picture, drawing, map, or graphic you can locate or develop and then use?

4. In what order will you present this information to your home teammates?

5. In what specific ways will you check to determine that each teammate comprehends and remembers the knowledge you will share?

Rehearse: Practice teaching your lesson in your expert group.

Figure 5-13 *A Fourth Example of a Typical Expert Sheet*

Expert Sheet 4: Business Interviews

Read: Read Chapter 9—"GNP and Economic Growth."

Interview: Interview the following local businesspeople to learn about economic growth in our community and how national economic conditions have local effects.

Ms. Yolanda Higgs, owner, Yogurt for You (555-4763)

Mr. Barlow Rodriguez, manager, The Taco Terrace (555-8163)

Mr. Harry Fix, manager, Piedmont Auto Parts (555-1357)

Ms. Daisy Cantrell, agent, Tara Real Estate (555-7764)

You can use the following questions to get your interview started; however, have a conversation and find out all you can about economic growth in our community and about how national economic conditions have local effects.

1. What words would best describe how your business has been doing over the past year?

2. What specific kinds of events tend to make business activity and profits better and worse for your business?

3. What specific events have recently occurred to change your business activity or profits for the better or worse?

4. In order to make your business more profitable, what steps would you need to take with your business?

5. How do conditions in the economy in general affect your business?

6. How healthy do you expect the local economy to be in the next few months?

7. In order to make our community a more profitable place for you to do business, what could people do locally?

Discuss: After each person has completed his or her interviews, a summary of the responses to questions such as those above should be developed and written. Discuss the responses to make sure everyone has the appropriate information relevant to each question. Then the group should verify that each member can explain the answers clearly. Take turns explaining the responses to one another. Write the answers out in complete sentences with one or more paragraphs for each question.

Plan to Teach: Plan together how to teach the members of your home teams the information you have gained from your interviews. Remember, compared to your home teammates, you are experts on the local economy, especially as it relates to major economic concepts and principles the class has studied. You can help them learn what you know.

1. How will you share and then explain the answers to the questions you asked the businesspeople? How will you deal with the similarities and differences among their responses?

2. What two things will you share with your home teammates concerning what you believe is good, bad, surprising, or important concerning the local economy for our lives today?

3. What specific thing might you show your home teammates that will help them understand the important information concerning the local economy at this time? Is there a picture, drawing, map, or graphic you can locate or develop and then use?

4. What specific economic concepts and principles can you use to explain, clarify, or more adequately comprehend the points the businesspeople were making in their interviews?

5. To what extent should segments of the interviews be used to emphasize points the businesspeople were making in reference to the economy?

6. In what order will you present this information to your home teammates?

7. In what specific ways will you check to determine that each teammate comprehends and remembers the knowledge you will share?

Rehearse: Practice teaching your lesson in your expert group.

Figure 5-14 *A Fifth Example of a Typical Expert Sheet*

Expert Sheet 5: General Economic Conditions

Read: Read Chapter 9—"GNP and Economic Growth." Also, read articles placed on reserve for you in the school library that deal with current economic conditions in the state and nation. The articles come from a variety of periodicals including *Time, Newsweek, Business Week, U.S. News and World Report,* and the city and state sections of two major metropolitan newspapers.

Answer: Work with your expert-group members to find the answers to the following questions.

1. What is the current condition of the economy? What are the specific indicators of this condition?

2. What specific events most likely led to the current condition of the nation's economy?

3. What is the forecast for the economy's condition over the next few months? What specific indicators and expectations support this prediction?

4. What sorts of people attempt to predict the future of the economy? What are their qualifications to predict the economic future? To what extent do they agree?

5. What is known about consumers' beliefs concerning the current condition of the economy? Given that consumers hold these beliefs, what is likely to happen to our nation's economy in the near future?

6. What specific economic policies should the national and state governments pursue in the near future?

Discuss: After each person has found the answers to his or her questions, discuss the answers to make sure everyone has the appropriate information. The articles do not completely agree with one another, so you must decide how to interpret the views expressed in them. Then the group should verify that each member can explain the answers clearly. Take turns explaining the answers to one another. Write the answers out in complete sentences with one paragraph for each question.

Plan to Teach: Plan together how to teach the members of your home teams the information you have gained from your reading and discussion. Remember, compared to your home teammates, you are experts on these questions. You can help them learn what you know.

1. How will you share and then explain the answers to the above questions?

2. What two things will you share with your home teammates concerning what you believe is good, bad, surprising, or important concerning the growth of the nation's and state's economies for our lives today?

3. What specific thing might you show your home teammates that will help them understand the important information about likely economic growth at this time? For example, is there a picture, drawing, map, or a graphic you can locate or develop and then use?

4. In what order will you present this information to your home teammates?

5. In what specific ways will you check to determine that each teammate comprehends and remembers the knowledge and skills you will share?

Rehearse: Practice teaching your lesson in your expert group.

References

Mattingly, R. M., and R. L. VanSickle. 1991. Cooperative learning and achievement in social studies: Jigsaw II. *Social Education*, 55, 392-95.

Slavin, R. E. 1986. *Using student team learning*, 3rd ed. Baltimore: Center for Research on Elementary and Middle Schools, The Johns Hopkins University.

———. 1990. *Cooperative learning: Theory, research, and practice*. Englewood Cliffs, NJ: Prentice Hall.

6.

Jigsaw III = Jigsaw II + Cooperative Test Review: Applications to the Social Studies Classroom

JOHN E. STEINBRINK AND ROBERT J. STAHL

Social studies education can evolve from a traditional, teacher-centered, direct-instruction model to one in which students work and learn cooperatively in groups discussing, even debating, worthwhile content issues. Traditionally passive students who often are expected to learn content for its own sake can be transformed into active learners by appropriate cooperative learning groups and structures. To accomplish this transformation, students and teachers need to complete a number of rather specific tasks and meet a number of specific criteria or elements, such as working in heterogeneous groups and being individually accountable.

Overview of the Four-Level Jigsaw III Strategy

Jigsaw III is an expansion of the standard Jigsaw II strategy,[1] adding a cooperative test review team phase that is essentially a third responsibility for the home team. The four levels and six phases of Jigsaw III, illustrated in Figure 6-1 on page 134, are described in this chapter, followed by an extended classroom example that elaborates Jigsaw III's required steps and guidelines.

---

[1] The reader unfamiliar with the Jigsaw II strategy may wish to study Chapter 5, which describes this strategy in depth.

Figure 6-1　*Schematic of the Six Phases and Four Levels of the Jigsaw III Strategy*

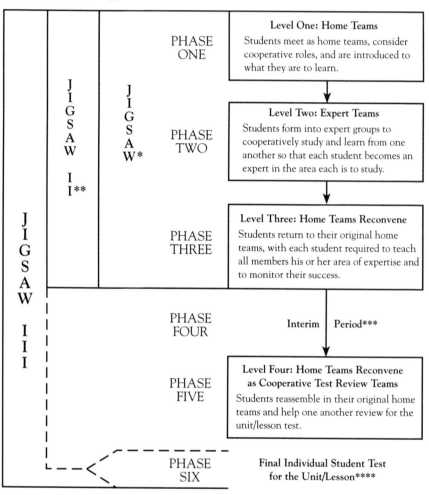

*Jigsaw may have "expert groups" meet or may have students split up work within their own group. Jigsaw does not require students to take individual tests that are then used to compute group scores, bonus points, and group rewards.

Level One: Home Teams
Students meet as home teams, consider cooperative roles, and are introduced to what they are to learn.

Level Two: Expert Teams
Students form into expert groups to cooperatively study and learn from one another so that each student becomes an expert in the area each is to study.

Level Three: Home Teams Reconvene
Students return to their original home teams, with each student required to teach all members his or her area of expertise and to monitor their success.

Level Four: Home Teams Reconvene as Cooperative Test Review Teams
Students reassemble in their original home teams and help one another review for the unit/lesson test.

Final Individual Student Test for the Unit/Lesson**

**Jigsaw may have "expert groups" meet or may have students split up work within their own group. Jigsaw does not require students to take individual tests that are then used to compute group scores, bonus points, and group rewards.

**Jigsaw II *requires that students take individual tests*, which are then used to compute group scores, bonus points, and group rewards. Jigsaw II usually has students taking tests almost immediately after students have returned to their home teams and shared their expertise. Thus "Phase Four" of Jigsaw II, which is "Phase Six" of Jigsaw III, typically follows "Phase Three" within a day or two if not at the end of the class period.

***In Jigsaw III, this interim period is usually a week to several weeks and may occur as a review of a major unit or term within which students take individual tests on particular shorter lessons using Jigsaw II or other strategies.

****What separates Jigsaw II and Jigsaw III from variations of Jigsaw is that *students must take individual tests* at the end for "individual accountability," and the scores are used to compute team scores, team bonus points, and team rewards.

All of the requirements for Jigsaw II, including arranging students into heterogeneous groups, determining base scores, determining improvement points, and providing for public recognition, are used in Jigsaw III. These requirements will not be repeated in depth here since they are described in the previous chapter on Jigsaw II.

Jigsaw II: The First Three Levels of Jigsaw III

Cooperative learning takes many forms. The Jigsaw and Jigsaw II strategies (e.g., Aronson et al., 1978; Kagan, 1985; Wood, 1987; Slavin, 1990) encourage individual responsibility by making each student an "expert" on one part of an instructional unit. During the typical Jigsaw II lesson, students usually read a common narrative such as a chapter or section of a chapter. They move from their *home base groups* (or *home teams*) to their respective *expert groups*, where they are to become experts on a subsection of that material.

After mastering the subsection in the expert group, student experts return to their home team to teach, coach, and tutor every member of their home team to become experts as well. This home-team task represents the third level (and third phase) of both the Jigsaw II and Jigsaw III strategies.

Afterwards, students may remain in their respective home teams or function as individual learners and as members of yet other groups for one or more days during the unit. In some units they may go several days to weeks after returning from their expert groups without meeting again in their home teams. This period of time between the home-group meetings immediately after the expert-group meetings is the *fourth phase of the six-phase Jigsaw III strategy*.

Cooperative Test Review: The Fourth Level of Jigsaw III

Cooperative test review involves reconvening cooperative learning home teams and providing them with review tasks that focus on the specific concepts and skills to be evaluated in a chapter or unit test (Jones and Steinbrink, 1988). Test review teams have *different goals and tasks* from the standard content- and skill-learning home teams.

Cooperative test review groups are formed by having students *reconvene into their heterogeneous home teams* to, among other things:

a) locate and re-review responses to questions in the textbook

b) re-review the content of the expert sheets

c) clarify concepts and skills through discussion

d) coach each home-team member to answer specific items.

Test review teams focus on increased individual mastery and "remastery" of targeted content and skills, and increased individual test achievement *after* the formal instructional sessions have ended and one or two days prior to a major test for the unit. These cooperative test review team tasks also provide critical additional help for minority and disadvantaged students who are commonly more group oriented and interactive than their middle-class, white peers (Reeves, 1988). Working as members of cooperative test review teams constitutes the fourth level (and fifth phase) of the Jigsaw III strategy.

Postinstruction cooperative test review teams consistently generate test mean-score gains on chapter and unit tests of more than ten points over traditional test-review approaches (Jones and Steinbrink, 1988, 1989). A majority of the gain usually has occurred in the test scores of students who previously scored in the lower half of the class (Jones and Johnson, 1990). Appropriate cooperative review has significantly increased class mean scores while compacting grade distributions, increasing grade average, and reducing marginal grades and student failure.

The sixth phase of Jigsaw III includes individual student test-taking tasks and the provision for feedback and rewards associated with acceptable levels of performance on the tests.

Collaborative Skills: Essential Behaviors in Jigsaw III Groups

Cooperative learning depends on appropriate use of such social skills as shared leadership, effective communication, trust building, and conflict management. Although numerous collaborative skills can be identified, five specific collaborative skills are especially appropriate for Jigsaw II and III activities. These key skills should be described in detail to stu-

Figure 6-2   *Example of a Collaborative Skills Checklist*

Collaborative Skills Checklist			
Students in Teams	Always	Seldom	Never
Share materials			
Encourage all members to participate			
Summarize the material aloud			
Criticize ideas without criticizing people			
Integrate different ideas into single positions			

dents and then practiced during home-team and expert-group sessions. Figure 6-2 provides a checklist that may be used to assess the collaboration behaviors of an entire group or of individuals within each group. Both students and the teacher may use the checklist.

Planning and Implementing a Jigsaw III Strategy

Preparation for Jigsaw III Cooperative Group Tasks

Research on complex cooperative learning instruction reveals that on-task interaction is critical for effective group learning (Slavin, 1990). This interaction is most likely to occur when students are provided with clear details as to what they are to learn and how they are to learn it. The critical elements to ensure on-task team work include (a) reading and study organizers designed as expert sheets; (b) a clear set of directions; (c) outcome-aligned text and reference material; (d) as necessary, appropriate supplemental materials such as maps, globes, and data tables; and (e) test review instructions and possibly review materials.[2]

---

[2] Elements (a) through (d) are also needed for the three-level Jigsaw II strategy.

The social studies teacher should follow these seven easy steps to construct Jigsaw III cooperative group materials:

1. *Select one or more academic outcome objectives.*

2. *Select a chapter or unit that can be completed in five to ten instructional days.* While the selection may include publisher-furnished text and chapter-review study items, teachers may develop their own instructional materials or use nontextbook sources.

3. *Locate, write, or develop expert sheets.* Each expert sheet provides a list of questions or tasks to direct students to important information and concepts in each paragraph. To reflect the major content and concepts in the reading material, we suggest approximately one question for each paragraph. Textbook chapters generally are divided into three, four, or five subsections. The key to dividing a chapter to prepare expert sheets is to have an equal number of items for each expert group, providing equal workloads for all groups. Expert sheets typically require one class period to discuss and complete. Tasks that require maximum interaction and discussion among all group members result in greater learning gains than study tasks that allow one student to dominate and the other group members to merely copy or listen (Cohen, Lotan, & Leechor, 1989). An example of an expert sheet based on a high school geography text is provided in Figure 6-3 on page 139. An example of an elementary social studies expert sheet appears on page 149.

4. *Locate and, as necessary, gather supplementary materials to support each expert group.* Work with the librarian and other resource people to assemble relevant learning materials such as maps, graphs, books, and artifacts.

5. *Construct or locate the final exam for the unit or lesson,* taking special care to ensure that the focus of student learning and expert-sheet tasks is directly aligned with information, concepts, and skills to be assessed on this exam.

6. *Determine and, as necessary, locate rewards to be distributed to teams that have earned recognition* for their high levels of achievement as determined by your improvement points reward structure.

7. *Prepare team summary sheets and other forms that are used to compute individual base scores, improvement points, etc. as per Jigsaw II.*

Figure 6-3   *Example Expert Sheet at the Secondary Level*

EXPERT SHEET

Japan and Korea Today: Chapter 13

Expert Group I

1. The Regions of Japan pp. 285–287, 306–309
(Attach answers on a separate sheet.)

1. Locate and be able to name the four large islands of Japan on the map on page 285. Locate Tokyo and the Inland Sea.

2. Describe the landforms of Japan. Where do most of the Japanese people live?

3. Describe Japan's climate by comparing it to the eastern United States. In what ways are these two regions alike in climate? How are they different? What is a typhoon?

4. On the map on page 307, locate the three major subregions of Japan.

5. What is the settlement pattern on Hokkaido?

6. What are the two major sources of wealth on Hokkaido?

7. What are the climate and settlement patterns of northern Honshu?

8. What are five characteristics of the Japanese heartland?

9. What are at least five important facts that describe Tokyo?

10. Locate Nagoya, Japan's second largest city, on both maps on pages 285 and 287. Locate Osaka and Kobe. What words would best describe the hinterland that surrounds Osaka and Kobe?

Forming Jigsaw III Cooperative Learning Groups

In Jigsaw III, heterogeneous grouping is crucial to support the social studies goals of integration, participation, and interaction. Four principles for forming these heterogeneous groups are:[3]

1. *Know your students.* Since each home team and expert group should have students from a variety of backgrounds and characteristics, the best students, best leaders, and least reliable students should be assigned to different groups.

2. *Form heterogeneous groups.* Ensure that the membership of the groups is heterogeneously mixed according to academic and skill levels as well as ethnic, gender, socioeconomic, and racial characteristics. One by-product of maximally mixed socioethnic, gender, skill, and ability grouping is that the groups tend to complete their tasks at approximately the same time (Platte, 1991).

3. *Keep the groups as small as possible.* Groups tend to range from two to six, depending on the task. Larger groups have a greater range of abilities, expertise, and skills. However, the larger the group, the less opportunity and time each individual has to participate. Remember, however, the number and size of groups depend on the nature of the activity rather than the class size (Wong and Wong, 1991). For example, every home team requires at least as many members as there are expert sheets.

4. *Promote interdependence by assigning complementary group roles to students.* In Jigsaw III, both home and expert groups require two functional roles: group leader and materials manager. Other students can be assigned such collaborative skill roles as encourager or observer. All students are recorders because they are responsible for taking notes so that they can teach their expertise and master the material in home teams (see Figure 6-4 on page 141).

---

[3] Again, refer to Jigsaw II for many of the details on how to accomplish this task. Chapter 5 and the work of Slavin (1990) provide ample details on steps to follow.

Steps in the Six-Phase, Four-Level Cooperative Learning Process

Getting Started

1. *Explain the students' tasks in the group activity*, then describe the general procedures in the lesson. The teacher announces to students that they are to

   - be productive members of a home team and an expert group.

   - become experts on one section of the material.

   - teach their home-team members to be experts on the same material.

   - learn the targeted knowledge and skills so that they will do well on the chapter and unit tests.

Phase One/Level One: Home Teams Convene

2. *Arrange students in home teams and designate individuals to fulfill certain roles*; for example, group leader and materials manager.

3. *Describe the roles that students are to perform within the group.*

Figure 6-4   *Descriptions of Some Important Group Roles*

GROUP ROLES

Functional Roles

Group Leader: Convenes the group, keeps the group on task, and talks to the teacher.

Materials Manager: Distributes and collects materials. Cleans up after task completion.

Collaborative Roles

Encourager: Reinforces members' contributions. Encourages everyone to speak up in the group.

Observer: Monitors how well the group collaborates. Reports to the whole class or teacher.

---

4. *Introduce the unit to the class.* The unit overview is a set-induction activity to cue prior knowledge, provide cognitive linkage, and generate excitement.

5. *Allow students to review targeted learning tasks for the lesson* as well as roles in the groups and expectations for all members of the group during all later phases of the lesson.

Phase Two/Level Two: Expert Groups Convene

6. *Form heterogeneous expert groups and distribute the expert sheets.* The "Procedures for Expert Groups" transparency (Figure 6-5) should be displayed, followed by a short discussion to ensure students comprehend its requirements.[4]

7. *Allow students sufficient time to complete their expert-group tasks.* All students in each group are to become experts in the areas included on the group's expert sheet.

8. *Circulate among the groups and answer questions* during the expert-group session, which normally takes about one class period. Remember, the groups should discuss any content or process problems among the entire group. The teacher should interact only with the group leader.

Figure 6-5   *"Procedures for Expert Groups" Transparency Master*

PROCEDURES FOR EXPERT GROUPS

1. You will be a member of an expert group.

2. You will discuss each item on the expert sheet with all the members of your expert group.

3. You will agree on the best and most accurate response.

4. You will write down the answer to each item on a separate sheet of paper and be able to explain it to your expert group.

5. You will only meet in expert groups once per chapter or unit.

6. You will have _____ minutes to complete the task today.

---

[4] Figures 6-2, 6-4, and 6-5 may be used with Jigsaw II groups such as those described in Chapter 5.

9. *Assist students to prepare to teach what they now have learned to members of their respective home teams.*

Phase Three/Level Three: Home Teams Reassemble

10. *Direct student experts to return to their home teams.* Experts teach the material from the expert sheets to home-team members. Home-team members listen to, study, discuss, and learn all the concepts and answers on each expert sheet. For inexperienced students, the "Procedures for Home Teams" transparency (Figure 6-6) should be displayed to help them understand their functions in the group.

11. *Conduct a whole-class summary of the material.* This discussion clarifies content answers, minimizing the possibility that an incorrect response has been presented in the small groups.

12. *Debrief the collaborative skills by asking each group to analyze how well its members worked together.*[5] Assessing how well the members cooperated and how they could improve are vital tasks in making cooperative learning groups work well. This debriefing is important for many reasons, one of which is that it reminds students that the teacher is concerned that they learn to use appropriate cooperative

Figure 6-6   *"Procedures for Home Teams After the Expert Groups Have Met" Transparency Master*

PROCEDURES FOR HOME TEAMS AFTER THE EXPERT GROUPS HAVE MET

1. Find your home-team leader and meet in home teams.

2. Be certain that every expert group is represented by at least one person.

3. Teach the content of your expert sheet to all members of your home team.

4. You should understand and record the responses to each item on all the expert sheets.

5. You will have _____ minutes to work together and learn the information and abilities on all expert sheets.

---

5 This debriefing activity is commonly referred to as *processing.*

group behaviors. The questions asked need to be very specific as to what students are to reflect upon and describe as group behaviors. A selected list of typical questions is provided below.

- To what extent did everyone in your group participate as needed?

- In what ways did members of your group share what they found?

- In what ways did your group stay on task?

- What specific things did members do to stay on task?

- What specific behaviors worked the most to enable your group to be successful?

- What problems occurred in your group to limit its success?

Phase Four: Interim Period

13. *Continue with the rest of the lesson and unit,* which may or may not involve instructional strategies other than those in steps 1–12.

Phase Five/Level Four: Home Teams Reconvene as Cooperative Test Review Teams

14. *Reconvene home teams to serve as cooperative test review teams one or more days prior to the test.* Every student reviews and, as needed, remasters the information, concepts, and skills to be assessed on the unit test. All the materials already studied, especially the items included on all the expert sheets, are to be emphasized in this review. Home-team leaders are to arrange for group members to tutor and coach weak students so that they too will learn the social studies knowledge and skills needed to score well on the test.

Phase Six: Post-Home-Group Activities Including Individual Test Taking and Feedback

15. *Test students using test items aligned with those on the expert sheets and student outcome objectives.*

16. *Assess students' test performance and compute appropriate improvement points.*

17. *Reward publicly individual students and groups on the basis of their*

test performance improvement and adherence to appropriate coopera-
tive group behaviors.

The above steps provide a detailed outline of the essential steps needed to properly execute the Jigsaw III strategy. A later section illustrates what these steps would most likely look like within actual classroom settings. An example of an elementary school geography lesson focusing on the United States is provided. Before we move to the example, we would like to suggest an additional area in which students may earn recognition and awards.

Recognition of Work of Expert Groups' Members

In all versions of Jigsaw, improvement points are computed and awards are distributed based upon the home-team members collectively meeting certain levels of improvement. For instance, the team members might need to average 25 improvement points in order to earn recognition for their achievement over their base scores. However, the contributions and achievements of the expert teams are traditionally ignored when the recognition awards are distributed. Given this, students within their respective expert groups are never able to attain recognition for their work in these groups.

To remedy this lack of attention and to provide an additional incentive for expert groups to do the very best job possible, Stahl has recently used the team summary sheets (see Chapter 5, page 117) to record the improvement of students within their expert groups. A team summary sheet is completed for each expert group in the same way it is completed for each home team. Recognition and awards also are provided in a manner similar to that for home-team accomplishments.

Initial work with the recognition of expert-group improvements has been very positive. Students who may not have earned recognition in their home teams may get recognition because the improvement points of their expert groups met a criterion level. A number of students liked the challenge of trying to be part of two teams that earned recognition.

This addition to the tradition of recognizing only home-group improvement is too new to say much more at this time. We encourage teachers to try recognizing expert groups' improvement and to let us know what success they have with it.

Application of the Steps of the Jigsaw III Strategy Within the Classroom: A Practical Example

An Elementary School Lesson: Focus on Physical Geography

This lesson uses the Jigsaw III strategy to facilitate student learning relative to the physical geography of the United States.[6] While the focus of this example lesson is the content and skills featured in the chapter, one major task of the teacher is to integrate the five fundamental themes of geography into the discussions and learning requirements. The lesson may take three or four class periods with additional time devoted to supplementary activities, as the teacher desires.

Objectives

- To describe and use correctly a number of collaborative skills

- To comprehend and apply the five fundamental themes of geography

- To define *temperature, climate, elevation,* and *precipitation*

- To describe factors that affect climate, and to describe how climate affects how people live in particular regions

- To locate Boston, Des Moines, San Francisco, and Phoenix on a map

Materials Needed

- Three distinct expert sheets (one copy for each student, with each sheet color-coded)[7]

- Physical map of the United States that is accessible to every student

- Textbook and/or other reference materials with information on the physical geography of the United States

---

[6] This elementary level lesson was developed from *Regions Near and Far.* B. K. Beyer et al. New York: Macmillan, 1990.

[7] The expert sheet for this example lesson was developed from Chapter 2, "Our Country's Land," in Beyer, et al., op. cit. pp. 50-55.

Instructional Steps

To illustrate the steps, imagine that we are visiting the fourth-grade classroom of Ms. Stein.

Phase One/Level One: Home Teams Convene

1. After completing all the preinstruction planning steps, Ms. Stein assigns her students to heterogeneous home teams of three. She appoints a group leader and a materials manager for each group.

2. She then allows these groups some time to form, to organize themselves as a functional home group, and to begin viewing themselves as a group. Students also spend some time reviewing their home-team role requirements.

3. Ms. Stein introduces the lesson, describes the learning tasks, and supplies a motivational activity. Sitting in their home teams at this time, students are instructed to look around and name something that does not originally come from the earth. For example, she asks, "In what ways did this chair or that map or that book come from the earth?" After students realize that everything in one way or other is a product of the earth, Ms. Stein directs them to name two manufactured items in the classroom. She then asks them to describe in general terms how each object came from the earth. A plastic chair, for example, was originally petroleum in the earth that was extracted, refined, molded into plastic, and manufactured into a chair.

4. Ms. Stein focuses the students' attention on two fundamental themes of geography.

   - *Human-environment interactions:* everything we are and have comes from the earth.

   - *Movement:* everything we have, both manufactured and natural, comes to us through some type of movement— such as pipelines, electric lines, railroads, trucks, and weather fronts.

Phase Two/Level Two: Expert Groups Convene

5. Students are directed to form their expert groups and are reminded to take their textbooks to the expert-group session. A group leader and a materials manager for each expert group are then appointed by Ms. Stein. An encourager and an observer are also appointed.

6. She asks students to review the transparency "Procedures for Expert Groups" (see Figure 6-5 on page 142).

7. Ms. Stein now provides each student in the three expert groups with a color-coded expert sheet.[8] Everyone in Expert Group 1 is given the green Group I expert sheet; students in Expert Group 2 receive the yellow Group II expert sheet (see Figure 6-7 on page 149), and so on.

8. Ms. Stein explains that following the expert-group sessions, each student will rejoin his or her home team. Expert group members are told they will eventually be responsible for teaching their expert-sheet material to the home team. The tasks of the expert groups are to meet together, locate answers in their references, discuss, synthesize, and write down their agreed-upon responses on their expert sheets. Each group is given approximately 20 minutes to discuss the material and complete its expert sheets. She reminds them to take good notes on a separate sheet of paper so that they can be a well-prepared expert in their home team.

Phase Three/Level Three: Home Teams Reconvene

9. Once the expert sheets are completed and all group members have become experts on their respective sections, Ms. Stein directs students to return to their home teams. Every home team now has at least one representative from each of the three expert groups.

10. Ms. Stein distributes the remaining expert sheets so that every student has three separate expert sheets, including two which she or he has not previously seen. To help her students at this time, she places the "Procedures for Home Teams" transparency (Figure 6-6) on the overhead. After careful review of its contents, she is ready to proceed.

11. At this point, each student's task is to teach the ten items on his or her respective expert sheet to all other members of his or her home team. Students take careful notes on the two expert sheets that they have not seen before this session. This home-team task takes approximately 25 minutes.

12. Upon completion of the home-team cooperative teaching-learning session, Ms. Stein helps students debrief the collaborative skills used or not used in the two group settings.

---

[8] If the number of students in expert groups exceeds six or seven, the teacher may want to subdivide into smaller groups.

Figure 6-7   *Example of an Expert Sheet at the Elementary Level*

EXPERT SHEET

Our Country's Land: Chapter 2

Expert Group II

2. Our Country's Climate pp. 46–49
(Attach answers on a separate sheet.)

1. Review page 25 in Chapter One. What is the major difference between weather and climate?

2. Define *temperature*.

3. Give three reasons why regions have different temperatures.

4. Define *elevation*.

5. How would distance from an ocean affect the climate of a place?

6. Locate Boston and Des Moines on the map (page 47) and study the graph on page 48. How does the ocean affect the temperature in Boston? What connection does the ocean have with the temperature of Boston for each of the four seasons?

7. What are names and definitions of the four forms of precipitation?

8. Look at the diagram on page 49. What are the four stages of the precipitation process?

9. What are three factors that affect climate?

10. What type(s) of climate region do farmers prefer? Give two reasons why farmers prefer this climate.

Among the specific questions Ms. Stein asks are:

- To what extent did everyone in your group actively participate?
- To what extent did everyone in your group take notes?
- In what ways did group members criticize ideas rather than criticize people?
- How close was your home team to reaching a consensus?
- What did members do to ensure that everyone in their group learned the content and skills?

13. Ms. Stein then helps her students to summarize the content of the chapter in a large-group session. They use a map of the United States to review the major physical features. This large-group review, which can be as detailed or as simple as she deems appropriate, clarifies any content disputes from the earlier sessions.

14. She reviews the two fundamental themes of geography infused earlier (human-environment interactions and movement) within the context of the chapter. Among her questions are the following:

Theme: Human-Environment Interactions

- How do specific landforms affect human life-styles?
- What are two specific examples that illustrate how particular landforms may affect human lifestyles?

  (Sample answers: People who live near the tops of mountains have limited crop options. People who live on coastal plains typically have increased crop options.)
- How do climate systems affect population patterns?
- How does the presence of useful minerals affect population patterns?

Theme: Movement

- How do specific landforms influence transportation patterns?
- How are transportation systems influenced by mineral deposits? By climate?

15. Once students have answered her questions, Ms. Stein introduces the new geography themes of location, place, and region.

- She asks students to describe their community as a place. "What makes our community a unique place?"

- She asks students to describe their community in terms of location and region. Her students reported that they lived in a city near the Gulf Coast (location).

Phase Four: Interim Period

16. The class continues through the unit as Ms. Stein uses a number of other teaching strategies to help students gain the knowledge and abilities targeted as outcome objectives.

Phase Five/Level Four: Home Teams Reconvene as Cooperative Test Review Teams

17. One week later and the day before a major test on the unit, Ms. Stein reassembles students within their heterogeneous home teams to prepare themselves to function as *cooperative review teams*. As usual, each review/home team has a group leader (appointed by the teacher) and a materials manager. Each of these test-review teams is to ensure that all individual members master the knowledge and skills represented on all the expert sheets.

18. She assigns the home teams to locate, answer, and discuss review sections within the chapter and the review questions at the end of the chapter. Working in home teams, students locate the review items, discuss the content, and record an agreed-upon response for unfamiliar questions. At the end of the session, every student appears prepared to score well on the unit test. This session takes about twenty minutes.

19. As an *optional activity*, Ms. Stein organizes the home teams into "families" and plays "family feud" (or some other whole-class review game). This review game provides slow learners with additional opportunities to learn the material while being motivational for nearly everyone. She makes sure that this review game does not take more than twenty minutes. This review-game activity, which becomes noisy, emotional, and motivational, is popular with students and receives positive reports from parents.

Phase Six: Postgroup Activities, Including Test Taking and Feedback

20. On the next day, Ms. Stein administers the individual unit test that generates individual grades.

21. When students receive their test grades, she publicly celebrates the high achievement of the qualified high-achieving home teams. She focuses on the average team-improvement scores that are the highest, rather than calling attention to the lowest groups. She gives bonus points as needed.

This concludes an elementary classroom example of Jigsaw III in action.[8]

Additional Hints and Suggestions for Making Jigsaw III Work for You

Here are some suggestions developed by teachers who use the Jigsaw III strategy.

- Expect to spend about two hours per chapter in writing expert sheets. It will likely take longer the first few times you attempt to construct worthwhile, precise, and highly specific expert-group study guides.

- When possible, write specific items for expert sheets that include maps, charts, diagrams, etc.

- Provide co-expert roles for absentees or marginal learners. For instance, a marginal student might be paired with a reliable student so that each expert group is represented in home teams. This means that some home teams and some expert groups may have extra members.

- Encourage students to carry out enrichment activities. Work with the librarian to locate materials for brief reports. Limit each enrichment report to five minutes. Encourage students to rehearse their reports before their oral presentations. Require them to include at least one map, diagram, poster, artifact, or book.

- Encourage home teams to stay together outside the social studies classroom and to work together on other school assignments.

---

8 Examples of middle and high school Jigsaw III classrooms, such as that just described, along with sample expert sheets, are available from the authors.

References

Aronson, E., N. Blaney, C. Stephen, J. Sikes, and M. Snapp. 1978. *The jigsaw classroom.* Beverly Hills, CA: Sage.

Cohen, E. G., and R. Lotan, with C. Leechor. 1989. Can classrooms learn? *Sociology of Education,* 62, 75-94.

Jones, R. M., and L. C. Johnson. 1990. Improving at-risk student scores. *Southwest Journal of Educational Research Into Practice,* 3, 13-17.

Jones, R. M., and J. E. Steinbrink. 1988. Concept learning strategies: Using cooperative groups in science and social studies. *Southwest Journal of Educational Research Into Practice,* 2, 43-49.

————. 1989. Using cooperative groups in science teaching. *School Science and Mathematics,* 89(7): 541-51.

Kagan, S. 1985. *Cooperative learning. Resources for teachers.* Riverside, CA: University of California, Department of Psychology.

Platte, S. A. 1991. Cooperative learning: A practical application strategy. *Social Education,* 35(2): 326-28.

Reeves, M. S. 1988. Self-interest and the common weal: Focusing on the bottom half. *Education Week,* (April 27), 18.

Slavin, R. E. 1990. *Cooperative learning: Theory, research, and practice.* Englewood Cliffs, NJ: Prentice Hall.

Wong, H. K., and R. T. Wong. 1991. How to get your students to work cooperatively. In *The first days of school,* 245-66. Sunnyvale, CA: Harry K. Wong Publications.

Wood, K. 1987. Fostering cooperative learning in middle and secondary level classrooms. *Journal of Reading,* 31(2): 10-19.

7.

Student Teams-Achievement Divisions (STAD): Applications to the Social Studies Classroom

QUINTON G. PRIEST

Student Teams-Achievement Divisions (STAD) is an excellent Team-Assisted Instruction (TAI) framework for teachers new to cooperative learning (Slavin, 1988, 1990). STAD follows a seven-step process that emphasizes individual accountability and self-improvement and that also earns points for the entire cooperative learning team. STAD can be used to teach any set of content or abilities in which questions with one right answer can be posed. This chapter provides an overview of, and guidelines for using, the STAD cooperative learning strategy in the social studies classroom.

Three advantages to using STAD in the classroom are: (1) all students have an equal opportunity to receive rewards after each lesson; (2) each student has an equal chance to earn top grades (e.g., student performances are compared with their own past performances, giving weak and strong students alike an opportunity to earn high grades); and (3) group-based rewards are used to motivate achievement among students (Kagan, 1989). Within the teams, every student contributes to his or her own success and that of the team only by improving his or her own base scores on outcome-aligned quizzes (Slavin, 1988).

Student Teams-Achievement Divisions (STAD)

If you have not used cooperative learning in the classroom, it is best to spend some time with students describing the behavioral expectations in cooperative learning. Stress how cooperative learning groups differ from traditional group work. How much time is spent helping students acquire details about *working as and in cooperative groups* depends on how often cooperative learning has already been used in your classroom. Minimally, this help includes modeling the formation of and the purposes of student groups, describing positive and dysfunctional roles and behaviors, and reviewing the meaning of *interdependence* and *individual accountability* and their relation to grades and rewards. The teacher should discuss his or her role in monitoring group and individual behavior. Because *team building* and *class building* are essential to the success of cooperative learning, time should also be taken during closure to review consciously the students' accomplishments in these areas.

Seven Major Components of the STAD Strategy

From the teacher's perspective, STAD has seven major components: (1) clear student outcome objectives; (2) preinstruction preparation; (3) ensuring that students encounter must-learn content; (4) cooperative learning STAD teams; (5) individual quizzes; (6) individual improvement scores; and (7) team recognition. The requirements of each component are provided below.

1. *Clear Student Outcome Objectives.* This decision requires the teacher to decide exactly what information students are to learn and what students need to be able to do with this content at the end of the unit of study. Words like *understanding, realize, comprehend, aware,* and *appreciate* are not found in these statements. Instead, the objectives might expect students to write a paraphrased definition of the concept of city-state, apply the legends on a map to interpret a section of a map, explain why a new scenario is or is not an example of the concept of imperialism, etc. Whereas the easiest objectives require students merely to recall facts, STAD and the other team approaches allow numbers of other abilities whereby students complete application and other

analytical thinking processes to generate acceptable answers. The presentations and all test items are to be directly aligned with these outcome objectives. These objectives concern what students are to know and do at the end of the unit rather than describe what content will be covered and which activities will be completed during the unit.

2. *Preinstruction Preparation.* This set of decisions involves setting up the membership of the cooperative learning groups, determining base scores, and selecting and preparing study guides, worksheets, and outcome-aligned quizzes. It also involves determining how students will be informed as to the structure and steps in the STAD strategy, locating reference materials, and preparing minilectures as needed, as well as selecting rewards for teams that meet the standards for high achievement.

3. *Student Encounter with Outcome-Aligned Content.* The teacher can use a variety of ways to ensure that students have contact with the outcome-aligned content. These include direct instruction, a lecture-discussion, a video, a guest speaker, or an audiovisual presentation. The teacher's initial task is to focus the presentation directly on the content aligned with the student outcomes targeted for the STAD unit. Students are told that they must pay attention to the content in the presentation(s) and materials in order to do well on the quizzes, and that their quiz scores will determine their team scores and rewards.

4. *Cooperative Learning STAD Teams.* STAD teams usually comprise four students who are selected to represent a cross section of the class in terms of academic achievement, sex, and race or ethnicity. Because the major tasks of the team are to help members master the content and to do well on the quiz, the team, *working as a team to benefit the individual members and working as a whole,* is an important feature of STAD. Both teacher and students must emphasize that team members do their best for the team, and that the team does its best to help each member to learn the content targeted. For instance, if students are expected to learn to apply the attributes of the concept of terrorism to distinguish examples from nonexamples of terrorist acts, then the team must work together so that every student can correctly apply these attributes to make these decisions. Students are given about the same amount of time

in their cooperative groups as was taken to encounter the to-be-learned content.

The team provides the peer support for academic effort that is important for successful learning. STAD teams also provide the mutual concern and respect that are necessary for successful inter-group relations, self-esteem, and peer acceptance.

5. *Individual Quiz.* After the content has been encountered using the resources provided, which may cover one or two periods (equal time is usually provided for teams to practice), students take individual quizzes. At this point, to ensure that students are held individually accountable for what they were to have learned, every student is individually assessed for knowing the material and doing well on the quiz.

6. *Individual Improvement Scores.* The individual improvement scores are the incentive for each student to set successively higher performance goals. A student contributes points to his or her team only when his or her quiz performance shows improvement over past performance(s). Each student's improvement score is calculated from a base score that is the student's average performance on similar quizzes during one or more prior units. The total number of improvement points each student earns is based on how much the student's quiz score exceeds his or her base score. The collective improvement points for all members of the team become the basis of the team score.

7. *Public Team Recognition and Rewards.* Teams earn certificates or privileges only when their average team scores exceed a certain number of points. The higher the average team score above the criterion level, the more points the team can earn. All teams can earn the highest number of points possible. Team scores also may be used as part of the individual grades for the unit.

These seven components along with complementary guidelines and suggestions are expanded upon in the next section.

Planning and Implementing a STAD Strategy and Unit

The STAD strategy allows each student to progress at his or her own rate and be part of a team, having peers who care about and encourage his or her academic progress. STAD's simple structure can be used with almost any curriculum content. STAD can serve as a first step in developing the cooperative and communicative skills needed in the more complex, multistructural strategies. STAD is also very useful after any number of other cooperative learning strategies have been used.

One STAD unit on maps from my world geography course will be used in this chapter as a practical demonstration of how the STAD strategy may work in any social studies classroom. For the sake of brevity, we'll assume that the necessary earlier discussion of cooperative learning and student roles and expectations has been completed. Before the example unit begins, students will have cooperatively completed two prerequisite units emphasizing map elements (e.g., title, orientation, legend, and scale) and a review and elaboration of the earth's grid system.

Preinstruction Planning

This unit is designed to teach the principles of map projection.[1] To ensure that instruction is consistent with expectations for students, the following decisions are made:

Time needed to present must-learn content: 1–2 class periods.

Academic student outcome objectives: At the end of this unit, students will be able to:

- describe the differences and similarities between a globe and several map projections (on an individual quiz).

- state the characteristics, functions, and advantages of four different map projections (on an individual quiz).

- apply the principle of the primacy of location on any projection (on an individual quiz).

Materials needed: Lesson plan, transparencies of various map projections, a globe, some string, a marking pen for transparencies, and wall maps (optional).

Anticipatory set is planned: Pointing to maps on the wall, ask students why there are so many types of map projections since they all seem to show the same information.

---

[1] Figure 7-6 on page 187 provides a skeleton lesson plan form for STAD and Teams-Games-Tournament (TGT) lessons.

<u>Prior reading assignment(s):</u> The section on map projections in the text is to be read prior to beginning the unit.[2] In addition, students are selected for their heterogeneous groups according to the guidelines for heterogeneity already discussed. Worksheets are prepared along with the quiz. The forms to record individual and team improvement points are also prepared (see Figures 7-2 and 7-4 on pages 161 and 164).

Preparing Materials

You may easily make your own curriculum materials or adapt current materials to the STAD structure. For student use, simply make a worksheet, a worksheet answer sheet, and a quiz. Each unit usually takes three to five days to complete, although a unit can take much longer. In this example I will use a one-week STAD unit. You need to prepare one copy of the Team Summary Sheet (see Figure 7-4 on page 164) for each four students and one copy of a Base Score and Improvement Points Sheet (see Figure 7-2 on page 161) for every two units that will use STAD (Slavin, 1988).[3]

Determining Initial Base Score for Each Student

Initial base scores represent either individual student average scores on past quizzes or the team base score (total of base scores divided by the number of team members). If you have not given three or more quizzes so far in the new unit, use the students' final grades from the previous grading term—or last year's final grade if this is the beginning of the new school year (see Figure 7-1 on page 160). Base scores are recorded on the Base Score and Improvement Points Sheet in Figure 7-2 on page 161.[4] (This task can be completed before or after students have been assigned to their teams.)

Assigning Students to Teams

Heterogeneous teams, or as close to heterogeneity as is possible, should be selected for STAD units and any other group activity that will

---

2 The majority of the reading for STAD units is usually assigned and completed before starting a unit. STAD units that continue over many weeks will of course require homework and reading assignments throughout the duration of the unit.

3 8 1/2" x 11" sheets of all figures described in Chapters 5, 6, 7, 8, and 9 are available from Robert J. Stahl, Secondary Education, Arizona State University, Tempe, AZ 85287-1911.

4 Figure 7-2 provides three sets of data. At this point only the scores for the Base Scores column can be recorded. Where to obtain the data for the Quiz Scores and Improvement Points columns will be discussed later in this chapter.

Figure 7-1   *Two Methods of Computing a Student's Base Score*

A. Calculating base score using the student's final grade in the subject for the previous grading period.

Last Year's Grade	Initial Base Score
A	95
A–/B+	90
B	85
B–/C+	80
C	75
C–/D+	70
D	65
F	60

B. Calculating base score in terms of the student's grades over past quizzes. For example:

Mary's Three Test Scores

90 (Quiz 1)
78 (Quiz 2)
84 (Quiz 3)

Total	252
Divided by	3
Mary's Base Score =	84

take more than a couple of days. Because of the racial, ethnic, gender, and ability mix, heterogeneous teams provide greater opportunity for multi-characteristic peer tutoring and support, as well as class building than do traditional homogeneous groups, especially when teams are together for four or five weeks.

A four-student STAD team ideally has two boys and two girls and a balance of students from different cultures or races (e.g., two Anglo students, one African American and one Hispanic student). Each team should have one high-ability, two average-ability, and one low-ability student. The closest approximation to the ideal is your goal for each unit.

One very useful method for assigning students to teams follows.

1. *Decide on the number of teams.* If the class is divisible by 4 you can implement this decision very quickly. If the division is uneven you will have a remainder of 1, 2, or 3. You can then opt for a mix of 4- and 5-member teams.

Figure 7-2 *Base Score and Improvement Points Sheet with One Quiz Score Recorded and Improvement Points Computed for One STAD Unit*

BASE SCORE AND IMPROVEMENT POINTS SHEET FOR ENTIRE CLASS

Course: Geography   Period: 4th

Student	9/10/92 Quiz No. Map Projections			Quiz No. _____		
	Base Score	Quiz Score	Improvement Points	Base Score	Quiz Score	Improvement Points
1. Avery	90	94	20			
Fumika	90	100	40			
Shannon	87	95	20			
Aaron	85	89	20			
5. Sachiko	84	90	20			
Sara	84	88	20			
Larissa	82	90	20			
Adam	78	65	10			
Katie	77	89	30			
10. Alfredo	75	80	20			
James	75	75	10			
Zane	74	86	30			
Carissa	73	78	20			
Joaquin	66	79	30			
15. Taro	64	71	20			
Kara	63	74	30			
Liza	62	70	20			

2. *Rank students.* Rank students from highest to lowest, based on past performance. Test scores are very useful to work with, as are grades. With a class of eight teams, rank-order your list, and using letters A through H, assign each student a letter in order from top to bottom. When you get to H, continue lettering in the opposite order until you reach A; again continue, this time beginning with A. The fourth and final set will consist of students listed H to A. Each team will consist of those students with the same letter. The teams will be close to being academically heterogeneous. Students not assigned at this point (i.e., those in excess of multiples of four) can now be assigned to teams based on your judgment. You may then want to make parallel adjustments to achieve a cross-gender and/or cross-ethnic balance. Figure 7-3 on page 163 illustrates how this chart might be set up for a 32-member class. In all cases you want to achieve the right mix of at least one high student, two medium students, and one low student based on previous performances.

3. *Assign students to teams.* Here, you have three primary criteria to meet: (a) each team should be composed of students whose performance levels range from low to high; (b) the average performance level of all the teams should be about equal; and (c) each team needs to be as heterogeneous as is possible according to gender, race, and ethnicity.

4. *Reassigning students to ensure heterogeneity.* Once this initial grouping is completed, the membership of the groups is then checked for the greatest possible heterogeneous mix. In reassigning students, efforts should be made to match the students being moved between teams as closely to their initial ranking as possible.

5. *Complete the Team Summary Sheets.* Make one copy of a Team Summary Sheet for each team and fill in the names of the students on each team (see Figure 7-4 on page 164).

Figure 7-3 *Example of How To Rank Order Students and Then Assign Them to STAD Groups of Four for Initial Heterogeneous Groups Based on Academic Achievement**

	Rank Order	Team Name
Highest-achieving students	1	A
	2	B
	3	C
	4	D
	5	E
	6	F
	7	G
	8	H
Average-achieving students	9	H
	10	G
	11	F
	12	E
	13	D
	14	C
	15	B
	16	A
	17	A
	18	B
	19	C
	20	D
	21	E
	22	F
	23	G
	24	H
Low-achieving students	25	H
	26	G
	27	F
	28	E
	29	D
	30	C
	31	B
	32	A

* Once this initial heterogeneous grouping is established, students then may need to be reassigned to new groups in order to achieve gender, race, and ethnic heterogeneity.

Figure 7-4 *Example of Two Team Summary Sheets As They May Be Completed for One or More STAD Units/Lessons*

TEAM SUMMARY SHEET
(Individual and team improvement points per STAD unit)

TEAM NAME: Terminators

	UNIT/WEEK								
TEAM MEMBERS	1	2	3	4	5	6	7	8	9
Avery	20								
Zane	30								
Carissa	20								
Kara	20								
Total team score	90								
Team average	23								
Team award for this unit/week									

TEAM SUMMARY SHEET
(Individual and team improvement points per STAD unit)

TEAM NAME: Terminators

	UNIT/WEEK								
TEAM MEMBERS	1	2	3	4	5	6	7	8	9
Avery	20								
Zane	30								
Carissa	20								
Kara	20								
Total team score	90								
Team average	23								
Team standing this unit/week	2								
Total team score to date	90								
Team standing by team total to date	2								
Team award for this unit/week									

Implementing Classroom Activities To Complete the STAD Strategy

Forming the STAD Cooperative Learning Groups/Teams

The STAD teams should already have been formed on paper before beginning the presentation part of the unit.

Once I complete the team assignment process, I conduct a classroom activity that lets students know who their teammates are. For this unit I cut eight maps into fourths, putting one part of a map on each student's desk. The four parts of a single map go to the four students who will be members of the same group. This manner of informing students as to who their teammates are is not required. More traditional ways of informing them may be used. I find that such activities as I use serve the additional purpose of providing an anticipatory set for the content of the upcoming unit.

STAD teams are then formed so that students are conscious of their potential roles, who their peers will be, and what they must pay attention to in order to contribute to the team's success.

Opening and Focusing the Initial Group Meeting

When the teams meet for the first time as cooperative learning groups, the teacher establishes team expectations and adopts certain classroom management techniques. Proper focus and handling of the first team as a team session cannot be stressed enough. It is far easier to begin the process right than to go back and undo bad habits.

Team Name and Logo[5]

Allow the teams time to come up with their own names and logos. Any name or logo is good as long as it is not demeaning to others, in bad taste, or gang related. The teams may even engage in a get-acquainted activity to build team spirit.

---

5 This task may be completed in the class period before the unit begins.

Assign and Review Individual Roles Within the Group[6]

At this time teams should assign their members task roles, individual functions that are required to carry out the group's tasks. Among the roles students are to carry out are initiator, information seeker, elaboration seeker, coordinator, encourager, and summarizer (labels for these roles will vary according to the author).[7] Obviously, not all roles can be filled in a four-member team, and those roles that are assigned will not be accomplished perfectly on the first try. This is just a start.

The teacher should plan to discuss the behaviors of each task role assigned. Making the assessment of task roles a part of the teacher's monitoring activity will stress these roles' importance to students. (This task may be completed before or after teams have agreed upon a team name and logo.)

Structuring the Teams' Cooperative Learning Tasks

After the teams are established, guidelines to complete their major tasks are provided, along with an explanation as to what it means to work *in teams* and *as a team*. On the chalkboard or overhead projector, rules such as the following may be discussed with the class. (Alternative ones created by you or students may be used.)

1. Students have the responsibility to make sure that their teammates have learned the material. No one is finished until all teammates have mastered the content and abilities.

2. Ask all teammates for help before asking the teacher. (This is necessary because students will often try to pull you back into a whole-class structure by demanding individual attention.)

3. If the problem cannot be solved by the team, then a signal must be made to indicate that help is needed.[8]

---

[6] This task is especially important when students have not had extensive experience working in structured cooperative groups. Once they have become pros with these roles and groups, there is no need to review these roles at the start of a unit.

[7] Any good book on cooperative learning will elaborate these roles: e.g., Johnson, Johnson & Holubec (1988), Slavin (1988, 1990), and Stahl and VanSickle (1992).

[8] One method is to have all team members raise their hands. Another is to have a signaling device, such as a colored card, that is displayed for the purpose of indicating that help is needed. To avoid disrupting other teams and creating dead time, the teacher announces that team signals will be answered as quickly as possible.

4. Respect the responsibilities inherent in each member's perform-ance of his or her task role.

5. Teammates always talk to one another in "quiet voices."

Teaching and Encountering the To-Be-Learned Content

Opening the Unit and Starting the Presentation

Students first need to be informed as to exactly what they are to learn and why this content is important for them to learn. While they know they will be tested on this information, I provide many other reasons for their learning this content. The expected outcomes of the example unit are for students to demonstrate the differences between a globe and a map projection and to describe the uses of several of the most common map projections.

I begin by asking a student to indicate on a wall map the most direct route between two places (e.g., Seattle, Washington, and Cairo, Egypt) by stretching a string between the two locations. Another student is asked to do the same thing on a globe. I then direct a third student to draw the line formed by the string on the globe on the wall map. The line will form an arc whose apex is above the Arctic Circle and will appear not to be the shortest distance at all! We spend some time brain-storming the reasons for this puzzle. The solution is that the line on the globe is a "great circle." This activity is concluded by my explanation of great circles and of how distortion occurs in every attempt to project a round feature on a flat surface.

Arranging for Students to Encounter the Must-Learn Content

The teacher must stick close to the content objectives that will be included on the test. Meanings and application, not memorization, are to be emphasized. In this unit, using visual aids and many examples I physically demonstrate targeted concepts and abilities. I assess my stu-dents' comprehension by asking questions at strategic points. After nearly all students respond to the questions, either I or the students explain why an answer is correct or incorrect. To maintain momentum on learning the content we move to the next concept as soon as stu-dents have comprehended and can correctly apply the current concept.

Six specific guidelines that should be followed closely in teaching and arranging for the important content are as follows:

- Review briefly any prerequisite content or skills.

- Select and emphasize content and skills directly aligned with the targeted student outcomes.

- Stress and check frequently for student comprehension, paraphrasing, and use of content rather than mere memorization.

- Provide clear examples and models while checking to determine that students comprehend what these are examples of and why they are examples of targeted concepts, ideas, etc.

- Ask students to state their reasons for their answers.

- Maintain momentum by eliminating interruptions and moving smoothly and rapidly through the presentations and demonstrations, but be careful not to move so fast that the content is just being covered rather than taught.[9]

Returning to the map-projection unit, handouts are provided to accompany my lecture, along with explanations, transparencies, and the material found in the textbook. These represent the content that is to be mastered. I also include learning tasks in which students have to comprehend and see applications of the important content aligned with the outcome objectives.

I build on students' experiences of great circles to discuss map projections in general and to demonstrate and explain the value of various projections. The four projections stressed are the azimuthal polar, the Mercator, the Robinson, and the Gall-Peters. Each has a specific function that students need to remember when they use maps in the future.[10] Students are taught the five basic elements of meridians as they appear on a globe. They then compare their very different appearances on a projection. I stress what these differences mean for distortion of a projection. They also are taught the *principle of the primacy of location* on any projection (i.e., any element may be distorted to a given standard except

---

[9] Adapted from Good, Grouws & Ehmeier (1983). These also apply to the Teams-Games-Tournament (TGT) strategy that follows in the next chapter.

[10] A good source for this information is *Choosing a world map: Attributes, distortions, classes, aspects*. American Cartographic Association (1988).

location with respect to the grid system) and the importance of equal-area projections for mapping geographic distribution (e.g., Robinson and Gall-Peters).

Teachers should not give long homework assignments at this point. As mentioned before, extensive reading assignments should be given before the teaching phase in STAD.

Checking for Understanding and Providing Initial Guided Practice

As part of my presentation, I stop periodically to have students answer some fact questions and work appropriate examples. To check for understanding, I ask a question and after three or more seconds of wait-time silence, I call on students at random. This makes all students prepare themselves to answer.

Cooperative Learning STAD Team Study

Time for cooperative learning team work: 1-2 class periods.
Collaborative skills to be emphasized during the groups: Functioning; formulating.
Method of monitoring group interaction: Teacher visiting each team with checklist (provided as Figure 7-5 on page 170).
Group size: 4.
Special materials: Worksheet and worksheet answer sheet, atlases, globe(s), compasses.

The teacher now proceeds to structure the group activity. The teacher stresses that the major tasks of team members are to master the content provided and to help all their teammates master the content.

Either before or immediately after the groups' task structure is stated, the teacher needs to:

- have group members move their desks or move to tables to directly face one another.

- hand out the worksheets that serve as study guides around the must-learn content and skills.

- inform students that the worksheets are to guide their study and are not simply to be filled out and then ignored.

Figure 7-5 *Sample of a Teacher's Monitoring Sheet for Describing and Assessing Student Interaction Behaviors with Their Cooperative Learning Groups*

MONITORING SHEET

Unit/Lesson:_____ Date: _____

Boxes are marked whenever the particular behavior is observed. On the back, make notes of interesting exchanges not covered by categories. Try to collect one or more good things that a group says to share with students during closure.

TEAM NAME	NAMES OF TEAM MEMBERS				
COLLABORATIVE SKILLS 1. Forming					
2. Functioning					
3. Formulating					
4. Functioning					
TASK ROLES 1. Contributes ideas					
2. Summarizes					
3. Encourages others					
4. Initiates group activities					
5. Coordinates group activities					

- inform all students that they are responsible for all the content and skills targeted for learning, which means they all need to do the reading and work at answering all the questions on the worksheets.

- suggest that group members share their answers and the reasons for their answers with other members of their group.

- use their answer sheets to check their answers.[11]

- have students quiz one another and give one another feedback about the quality of their answers.

- have students try to answer any questions in their groups before asking the teacher for an answer.

- have students praise one another's correct answers as well as correct inadequate answers (Slavin, 1988).

Providing Extended, Highly Structured Guided Practice

There are at least three options students may use to complete their group learning tasks. One is that at the start of the group task, each team is given four copies of the worksheet and two copies of the answer sheet. However, with each student having a worksheet and then passing the answer sheet to a peer, the tendency is for each student to work individually with little helping of, or help from, team members. A second way is to give each group two worksheets and two answer sheets, thereby forcing students to work in pairs. However, sometimes students form into dyads or triads and never work together as a group of four.

One effective way to structure this activity to ensure on-task interaction is as follows:

1. All team members place their pencils in the middle of the table.

2. A student reads the first problem.

3. All students brainstorm the answer, using all resources available (task roles come into play here).

---

[11]Rather than giving the answer sheets to each group at the beginning, the teacher may wait for several minutes before distributing them to ensure that students work through the reading materials, review their notes, and complete the worksheets on their own rather than merely copying the correct answers on the worksheets immediately after the answer sheets are distributed.

4. The group coordinator checks to see that all comprehend and agree with the answer.

5. When everyone agrees, all students pick up their pencils and write the answer on the worksheet.

6. The next person takes the next problem on the worksheet and the procedure repeats.

It is important that students understand they are to explain *how* they arrived at the answer, rather than just stating it. The worksheets are for studying and mastering the material, not merely for filling out and handing in. When a team has finished the worksheet, the teacher provides the answer sheet so that members can check the accuracy of their work. Teammates should discuss and correct any wrong answers, rotating among themselves explaining why the right answers were right and why and how wrong answers need to be revised.

Returning to the map-projections example, the worksheet consists of a number of exercises designed to demonstrate by doing the content objectives targeted for the unit. For instance, students are given a number of blank maps based on various projections. On the Mercator and the Robinson projections, students indicate the linear distance between any two points, say a thousand miles apart at the Equator, the Tropic of Cancer, 80 degrees north latitude, and at the Arctic Circle. They represent these distances on the blank maps at the appropriate places. This involves research in the atlas and the use of scale. They compare the square miles of the United States and Africa with their relative sizes on the two projections. The group discusses what this exercise tells them about such factors as distortion, maps, and projections. They then decide which map would be best used for depicting area distribution of cropland (e.g., the great amount of distortion would rule out the Mercator).

Monitoring Group Interaction and On-Task Work

While the students are working in teams, circulate and monitor the teams. A clipboard with one or more sheets of paper can be carried from group to group. The paper(s) should list the team names, the names of the team members and their task roles, and the targeted collaborative skills (see Figure 7-5 on page 170). Make a check or tally mark under each student's name whenever you observe the task role being carried out, writing comments and any students' statements that you overhear. Students should be made aware that you are not grading them but rather using a tool to help them improve their team's efforts. These evaluation forms will be used during closure when the students reflect upon their group's activity (Johnson, Johnson, and Holubec, 1988).

Closure of Instruction for the Unit

Once the teacher senses that the students have mastered the content ("mastered" and not merely "covered"), he or she brings the instructional phase of this strategy to a close. Students leave the class period expecting individual quizzes the next day over the content and skills stressed in the lesson.

Testing Using Individual Quizzes

<u>Time for the test</u>: 1/2–1 class period.
<u>Type of test</u>: Individual quizzes aligned directly with student outcomes and studied content.
<u>Material needed</u>: One quiz per student.

Students are reminded that the purpose of the quiz is to show what they have learned as individuals. The teacher distributes the quiz and provides sufficient time for all to complete it, and students work on the quiz individually. The quizzes need to be scored and team scores calculated in time for the next class.

For the map-projection unit, I give the students a quiz that includes new map manipulations similar to the ones they did in their groups and a multiple-choice portion to test their concept acquisition.

Determining Individual and Team Scores

In order to make a strong connection between doing well and receiving recognition, it is important to compute the scores before the next class and announce team scores. In order to carry out this segment of the STAD strategy, the teacher needs to take a number of steps including the crucial ones that follow.

A. <u>Computing individual improvement points</u>. Students earn points for their teams based on the degree to which their quiz scores exceed their base scores. The charts on page 174 are examples of how these scores may be computed.

Quiz Score	Improvement Points
more than 10 points below base score	0
between 10 points below and the base score	10
1 to 10 points above base score	20
more than 10 points above base score	30
perfect paper (regardless of base score)	40

An alternative way that these scores may be computed follows.

Quiz Score	Improvement Points
1 or more points below base score	0
base score is matched	0
1 to 10 points above base score	equal to the increase
more than 10 points above base score	10
perfect paper (regardless of base score)	15

Improvement points are easily computed in a few minutes. Figure 7-2 on page 161 shows how to record improvement points using the first example.

As these examples suggest, the points awarded for improvement points can vary just as long as more points are awarded for the greater increases over one's base score. It is also important that students are well aware of the point scale that will be used so that they know *far in advance* what they have to do to earn the most points for themselves and their teams.

The use of base scores and improvement points makes it possible for all students to earn the maximum number of points for their teams. Because student scores are compared to their personal past performance, improvement is really a matter of personal effort and improvement within a team setting. This scoring system allows for improvement and a sense of accomplishment at all levels of skill and ability. It is also a positive incentive for all students to strive for maximum personal improvement.

B. Computing team scores. Computing team improvement points is relatively simple. List the students' base scores, quiz scores, and improvement points on a Base Score and Improvement Points Sheet (see Figure 7-2 on page 161). Then these improvement points are transferred to a Team Summary Sheet (see Figure 7-4 on page 164) so that a team-average improvement score can be computed. For example, if students on one team earned 20, 30, 20, and 20 improvement points, respectively, they earned 90 improvement points for their team. Averaging the individual improvement points yields a team score of 23 (22.5) points (see Figure 7-4). *Team scores are based on improvement points* rather than on raw quiz scores.

Public Team Recognition and Rewards

Time for team recognition and reward announcement: 10 minutes of class time.
Main teacher tasks: Computing individual improvement scores and team scores, awarding certificates or other team awards. Setting up class newspaper, bulletin board, or other means of publicly announcing all the team scores.

You should create an award/reward structure that best suits your needs and teaching style. I generally give three awards at three levels: teams whose average improvement points exceed 30 points receive the Outstanding Team Award; teams whose average meets or exceed 25 points receive the Powerhouse Team Award; and teams that meet or exceed 20 points receive the Little Giants Award.

To help students have a target to shoot for, a chart like the one that follows may be put in a highly visible area of the room throughout the entire unit.

Average Improvement Points for a Team	Award Category
20	Little Giants
25	Powerhouse Team
30	Outstanding Team

Of course these numbers and award names may be changed to suit the teacher's needs and the students in the class. However, the minimum number of points needed to earn high recognition should be kept high enough to serve as an added incentive for students to work together as a team to ensure every student has mastered the content and skills.

Each award category gives the recipient corresponding rewards. In my classroom, all members of recognized teams receive a homework pass, redeemable for one homework assignment in designated categories, or some other valued award (e.g., the Powerhouse Team members are given two coupons redeemable at the school store). In my case, awards are given during the all-school Friday assembly, and students are congratulated by the headmaster at that time. Finally, the team awards and names of team members are listed on the class bulletin board and kept there for the quarter. Each teacher's imagination and creativity can suggest many more ways that teams can be recognized for their accomplishments. Special badges, a student-created newsletter, or extra credit toward the quarter grade are options that have been successful.[12]

Unit Closure and Structured Reflection

Adequate closure following the use of the STAD strategy consists of going over the quizzes with students for academic content and reviewing the point system on which their team scores were calculated.

Students may have gone along with your initial explanation of STAD teams not fully understanding it but trusting that somehow it would all work out. Now they have before them their first set of graded quizzes together with their Team Summary Sheets containing their base scores, quiz scores, improvement points, and team scores.

This is a good time to again explain the improvement point system. In your explanation, emphasize the following:

- The improvement point system's primary purpose is to establish a minimum score based on individual past performance. The target is to exceed the minimum score. In this way, everyone has an equal chance to be successful when she or he does her or his best academically.

- Everyone's score on his or her team is important because everyone's improvement earns his or her team improvement points.

---

[12]Slavin (1988) provides a number of excellent examples of class newsletters to announce team scores.

- The improvement point system is a very fair method of grading, because each student is really only competing with himself or herself and not with the class average (Slavin, 1988).

Structured Reflection

Basically, structured reflection is the teacher and students reconsidering and assessing the group sessions, describing which actions were helpful or counterproductive, and making decisions about which behaviors and attitudes to continue and which ones to change (see, for example, Johnson, Johnson, and Holubec, 1988; Kagan 1989; Roy, Chapter 2, this book). The teacher shares what he or she discovered about the groups' processes while monitoring their activities. Generally I make a transparency of the monitoring sheet and any comments that I overheard and wrote down on the back. I find that it is very constructive to focus on positive behaviors during my input and allow the students to criticize themselves. I close by having each group come up with one thing that the team needs to focus on the next time they meet and one thing that each group member did to help the team reach its goals.

Keeping the STAD Strategy and Program Fresh[13]

I have found it necessary to make periodic adjustments to the base scores and the teams when STAD is regularly employed as a teaching strategy. It is also necessary to restate the objectives of STAD, at least after the first quizzes are returned. This reinforces the group structure and member roles as a means to maximize achievement among students. I have also found doing things in the following areas very useful in helping to maintain the effectiveness of STAD in my classroom.

Recomputing Base Scores. As students improve it will be necessary to recompute their average quiz scores on all quizzes and assign them new base scores.

Changing Team Membership/Forming New Teams. After a period of time, five or six weeks, reassign students to new teams. This gives students the opportunity to work with other classmates and keeps the program fresh.

---

[13]These ideas also may be used for the Teams-Games-Tournament (TGT) strategy in Chapter 8.

A word of caution, however. The class is in trouble if you come in one day and announce, "Tomorrow we are forming new teams." After four or five weeks, students will have built up relationships and attachments that they do not easily break. Following such sudden breakups of long-existing teams, the teacher may find resistance to forming new teams and perhaps negative behavior in the new team situation. The teacher needs a parting activity to make team re-formation a very positive experience. Two ways I have done this follow suggestions by Kagan (1989):

1. The teammates write a final team statement: "What we have learned together."

2. Students introduce one another to the class with the idea that "One thing you will like about working with _____ is . . . ."

Another possibility is to have a group reunion after a few weeks. Group reunions can serve as a kind of support group for students to help them adjust to new working styles and group personalities.

Epilogue to the STAD Strategy

My students learn a great deal of content within their STAD groups, many achieving far more than when they work alone. Overall, my students' grades are much higher with no reduction in standards. What is equally important is that students are excited about learning, feel more successful in social studies, voluntarily stay on-task longer, and practice a number of the social participation skills that are valued by the social studies community. I spend very little time on disciplining students and more time helping them learn and praising them for their achievements.

Many teachers believe that the STAD strategy is a very complicated and time-consuming cooperative learning strategy. In addition, social studies teachers rarely use STAD because the examples of this strategy in nearly every book and workshop on STAD use math and science content. *STAD is not a difficult strategy to use.* STAD can be used from middle-elementary level through twelfth-grade classrooms with excellent academic and affective results.

The next chapter describes the Teams-Games-Tournament (TGT) strategy. TGT is identical to STAD in every way except that a games-tournament activity replaces the STAD individual quizzes.

Applications of STAD: Practical Classroom Examples

Sample sets of materials and guidelines for completing a STAD unit for middle-level and/or high-school geography follow.

Sample Application #1: Contours and Vertical Exaggeration

Focus of Study: Contours and topographic (relief) maps
Level of Difficulty: Middle school/high school
Courses/Units: Geography/world geography

Student Outcome Objectives
1. The student will comprehend definitions of basic topographic terminology and apply these definitions to describe and interpret a topographic map.

2. The student will correctly convert a given map scale into either of the other two scales.

3. The student will correctly read a topographic map and describe the physical features a given map represents.

4. The student will apply guidelines relative to vertical exaggeration to interpret a topographic map.

Providing Students Access to the To-Be-Learned Content
1. Demonstrate the concept of cross section using a large mountain-shaped rock in a pan of water. Mark the waterline at intervals of one inch.

2. Explain that contour lines show elevation on a map in much the same manner as in our rock demonstration. By connecting all points that are the same height, with respect to a datum plane, a map can show relief.

3. Show the class how to read the contour lines (see A. on page 180: "Eight general rules about topographic maps") using an overhead projector and transparency of a section of a topographic map. Be certain to stress the basic terminology and information given in B. on page 181: "Five basic terms."

4. Demonstrate vertical exaggeration and how to determine it on a

topographic map. Explain that knowing vertical exaggeration is important because it gives you accurate horizontal distances on a map.

STAD Materials for This Unit

1. Sections of a topographic map enlarged on the copier and with their main physical features labeled A through H.

2. Worksheet and worksheet answer sheet "Student Exercises for Contours and Vertical Exaggeration" is given to each student or two per team (see page 182).

Getting Groups Started

Organize the class into four-member student teams and explain that the goal is to exceed the teams' base scores based on individual quiz scores.

Quiz

The quiz consists of the same worksheet with a different but similar topographic map section attached. You may have to alter the quiz somewhat, depending on your choice of a second map section. In general try to find map sections similar to the ones used in the group activity.

Here are a few samples of the questions I have used with this unit.

1. What is the purpose of a topographic map?

2. On a map, what is meant by the term *scale*? By what methods may scales be expressed?

3. What is the name of the quadrangle you have before you?

4. What is the date of the survey? Is it a revised map?

5. Approximately how many miles is your map in width?

Teaching Aids

A. Eight general rules about topographic maps.

Contour lines are lines known to cartographers as *isopleths* or isolines. Together with the *contour interval*, contour lines observe the following rules:

1. All points on any one contour line have the same elevation.

2. Normally, contours cannot cross, intersect, or touch one another. Exceptions are necessary in the case of vertical cliffs (which appear as coincident contours) and overhanging slopes (in which the lower contours collide with a higher contour).

3. A contour line never splits into two or more lines.

4. A contour line that closes within the limits of a map generally indicates a hilltop or ridgetop.

5. A hachured contour line indicates a closed depression. The short dashes (hachures) always point into the depression. Note that ordinary valleys with rivers flowing through them are not closed depressions.

6. Contour lines point "up-valley" when crossing a stream channel.

7. Variation in the horizontal spacing between contours on any one map is determined by variations in slope steepness. Therefore:

   a. contour lines that are uniformly spaced indicate a uniform (constant) slope.

   b. closely spaced contour lines indicate a steep slope, relatively.

   c. widely spaced contour lines indicate a gentle slope, relatively.

8. By observing rules 7a–c, one can identify different slope forms on a contour map, such as concave, convex, and straight slopes.

B. Five basic terms

   Contour (or **contour line**): a map line that connects points of equal elevation.

   Elevation: the vertical distance (or height) above a datum plane, commonly mean sea level.

   Contour interval: the difference in elevation between two adjacent contour lines of different elevations. Normally the contour interval is constant on any given map, but there are exceptions.

   Bench mark: a point of known elevation and location, usually indicated on the topographic (contour) map by the letters BM, with the elevation given to the nearest foot.

Relief: for any given area, the difference in elevation between the highest elevations (e.g., bottom of valleys). Depending on the area size being considered, the terms *local relief, general relief,* or *maximum relief* are sometimes used.

Student Exercises for Contours and Vertical Exaggeration

A. Contour Lines

On the next page is a diagram with contour lines that show the topography and drainage pattern of an area. Consult with your teammates and use the diagram to answer the following questions.

1. What is a contour interval?

2. What is the contour interval (in feet) of the attached map?

3. Give the elevation of each of the following points shown on the map. Note that some must have single, exact values, whereas others can only be estimates (or approximations) but within a specific range of values. In the latter case, upper and lower limits may be given as answers, or single answers must be indicated as approximations. (Hint: It is important to note whether the asked-for point is *on a contour* or *between two contours.*)

A. _____	E. _____
B. _____	F. _____
C. _____	G. _____
D. _____	H. _____

4. Topographic maps also contain information about an area's drainage pattern and the direction of stream flow. Places G and H are located on the banks of the same stream or river. Which one is downstream of the other? What is the evidence for this?

B. Map Features

1. What is a contour interval? What is the contour interval (in feet) of the attached map?

2. What is a bench mark? What symbol is used to indicate a bench mark?

3. What is the name of the quadrangle you have before you?

4. What is the date of the survey? Is it a revised map?

5. Approximately how many miles in width is your map?

6. What quadrangles join your map on the north?

7. What agency of the government published the map?

8. What colors are used on the map and what does each represent?

9. Draw and describe the meaning of ten symbols on your map.

C. Vertical Exaggeration

Using a sheet of lined notebook paper, work out graphically a cross section, or profile, of the ups and downs on the map.

1. Convert the graphic scale on the map to a verbal scale.

2. Express the degree of vertical exaggeration of your cross section profile. [Note: If the map were on a scale of 1 inch representing 1/8 of a mile, which means 660 feet of ground to 1 inch of paper, or 165 feet of ground to 1/4 inch of paper, then, with a contour interval of 10 feet, we are using 1/4 inch to represent only 10 feet in our vertical measurement as against 165 feet of horizontal measurements. This is an exaggeration of 16 1/2 times (ordinarily the vertical scale should exaggerate the horizontal from 5 to 10 times).]

3. Describe in writing the area depicted on the map as if you were standing in the area and describing it to a friend by phone.

Sample Application #2: *Land Ordinance and Township Survey*

Focus of Study: Township survey system
Level of Difficulty: Middle school/high school
Courses/Units: World geography/United States history

Student Outcome Objectives:

1. The student will describe the origins and purpose of the township survey system used in the western United States.

2. The student will explain the township system using a map.

3. The student will describe the historical significance of the Land Ordinance of 1785 and the Northwest Ordinance of 1787.

Providing Students Access to the To-Be-Learned Content

Through teacher lectures, explanations, and use of transparencies, the content emphasized will be the origins, purposes, and historical significance of the land ordinances and the township survey system used in the western United States. Key vocabulary, including definitions, guidelines, and details needed for plotting and interpreting township-survey maps must be included and demonstrated. If possible, transparencies made from township maps of one's local community are excellent to use for this demonstration.

STAD Materials for This Unit

1. Use any good history-book description of the Land Ordinance of 1785 and the Northwest Ordinance of 1787 to get information for the presentation. Students may also be asked to read about these two ordinances in their textbooks. Thomas D. Clark's *Frontier America: The Story of the Westward Movement* (1959) and the "Special Section on the Northwest Ordinance of 1787" in *Magazine of History*, 1987, 2 (4, Fall): 8-19, may also be used.

2. Worksheet, "Land Ordinances and Township Survey in the United States" and worksheet answer sheet. Give one worksheet to each student or two per team. Provide two answer sheets per team.

Getting Groups Started

Organize students into four-member teams and explain to them that the purpose of working in groups is to succeed on the quiz and to earn improvement points that will be applied toward team points. Distribute the worksheet and have students work to answer the questions and learn the content and skills.

Quiz

The quiz consists of activities identical to those provided on the worksheet except using different figures representing different land areas from those in the worksheet figures. In general try to find map sections similar to the ones used in the group activity. Additional quiz items are included from a list of questions that should be added relative to the origins, purposes, and historical significance of the two land ordinances and definitions of key terms relative to the township survey system.

Land Ordinance and Township Survey in the United States

Read: "Experimenting with Self-Government," pp. 156-166 in your textbook. Pay special attention to the information on pp. 159-163.
Answer: Work with your teammates to answer the following questions. All information is based on the standard survey of the United States west of the Appalachian Mountains.

A. Thinking and Writing Together

1. What were the purposes of the Land Ordinance of 1785? In what ways did it solve the problem of making new lands into territories and of paying for education?

2. What are the basic elements of the township survey system?

3. In your own words, what was the Northwest Ordinance of 1787? What did it say? How did it solve a problem that the British could not and that led to the War for Independence?

4. In your own words, what is a township? What are the important features of the township survey system?

5. What are at least three positive results of the land ordinances' township survey system on your life today?

B. Township Surveying

Work within your group to complete the following tasks. To answer some problems you will need an atlas (e.g., *Goode's Atlas*, 18th edition).

Figure 1

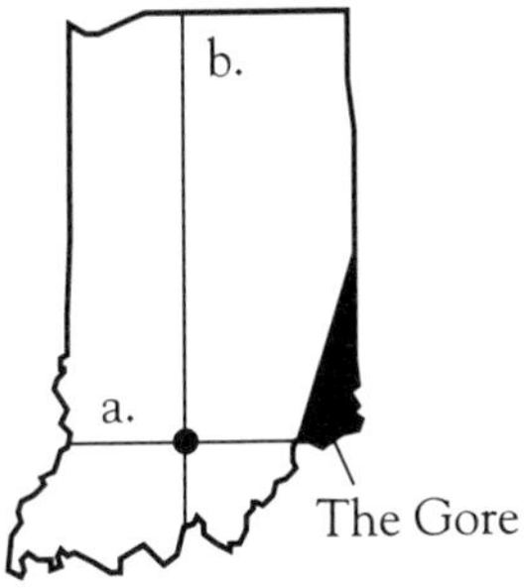

b.

a.

The Gore

1. What are the correct names of the intersecting lines indicated in Figure 1?

   a. _____

   b. _____

Figure 2

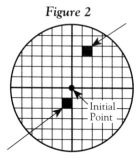

Initial Point

Figure 3

6	5	4	3	2	1
7	8	9	10	11	12
18	17	16	15	14	13
19	20	21	22		24
30	29	28	27	26	25
31	32	33	34	35	36

Figure 4

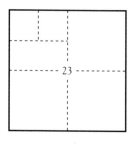

23

2. The shaded townships in Figure 2 have specific designations with respect to their location east, west, north, and south of the lines you named in Question 1. Using the township-range system, what are their specific locations?

   a. _____

   b. _____

3. The darkened square in the township in Figure 3 is called a section. What is the specific number of acres in a section?_____

4. In Figure 3, which specific section is set aside for public education? _____

5. In Figure 3, what are the names of the north-south and east-west lines?

   a. _____

   b. _____

6. Draw the northwest quarter-quarter section on Figure 4 and label it A. (Be careful, as each subsection will be given its own compass orientation corresponding to the compass orientation of the entire section.)

7. Draw the northeast quarter section on Figure 4 and label it.

8. If I were to divide the quarter-quarter section in Question 6 in half (into eighth-eighth sections), what would be the total number of acres in each section? _____

9. What will be the total number of acres in the south half-section? _____

10. What will be the total number of acres in the southeast quarter of the southeast quarter (quarter-quarter section)? _____

Figure 7-6 *Example of a Unit/Lesson Plan Adapted for a Cooperative Learning Strategy*

UNIT/LESSON PLAN

Course:_____   Grade level:_____

Subject/focus of learning:_____   Dates of unit/lesson:_____

Academic student outcome objectives:

a) _____

b) _____

c) _____

d) _____

Collaborative skill(s) to be emphasized: 1)_____   2)_____   3)_____

Social, collaborative skills and behavior desired (What I will look for/What I need to hear): _____

Method of monitoring student group interaction: _____

Monitoring forms necessary: _____

Group size: _____ students   Method of assignment: _____

Materials needed: _____

How I will explain the following to students:

　　Positive interdependence/structure: _____

　　Individual accountability: _____

Time needed to present to-be-learned content and abilities: _____

Time needed for student cooperative learning group tasks: _____

Anticipatory set to be used: _____

Type of individual outcome-aligned test/quiz: _____

_____

Criteria for success: _____

Rewards to be provided/distributed: _____

Academic comments/notes: _____

Group processing comments/notes: _____

Focus of structured reflection/closure: _____

References

Good, T. L., D. Grouws, and H. Ehmeier. 1983. *Active mathematics teaching*. New York: Longman.

Johnson, D. W., R. T. Johnson, and E. J. Holubec. 1988. *Cooperation in the classroom*, rev. ed. Edina, MN: Interaction Books.

Kagan, S. 1989. *Cooperative learning: Resources for teachers*. San Juan Capistrano, CA: Resources for Teachers.

Slavin, R. E. 1988. *Student team learning: An overview and practical guide*, 2nd ed. Washington, DC: National Educational Association.

———. 1990. *Cooperative learning: Theory, research, and practice*. Englewood Cliffs, NJ: Prentice Hall.

Stahl, R. J., and R. L. VanSickle. 1992. *Cooperative learning in the social studies classroom: An invitation to social study*. Washington, DC: National Council for the Social Studies.

8.

Teams-Games-Tournament (TGT): Applications to the Social Studies Classroom

QUINTON G. PRIEST AND ROBERT J. STAHL

Like Student Teams-Achievement Divisions (STAD), Teams-Games-Tournaments (TGT) is an excellent cooperative learning strategy for learning social studies content. Three benefits of using TGT are: (1) each student has an equal chance to earn top grades; (2) all students have an equal opportunity to receive rewards after each lesson; and (3) group-based rewards are used to motivate achievement among students (Kagan, 1989; Slavin, 1988, 1990). TGT can be used to teach any set of content or abilities in which questions with one right answer can be posed. The objective is mastery of and the ability to use specific academic content. This chapter provides an overview of the TGT strategy and guidelines to follow in order to use this strategy in the social studies classroom.

TGT and STAD are the same in every respect but two. Instead of the STAD quizzes and the individual improvement score system, TGT uses games and tournament; and instead of the STAD groups preparing students to do well on individual quizzes, TGT groups prepare for doing well during the games/tournament. *Consequently, in TGT the teams are given the alternative task of preparing their members to compete successfully in a tournament.* Students on different teams who attain similar academic ranking represent their team in tournament competitions to bring points back to their team. A bumping system assures students that they will be competing with others who are their academic equals; also it offers all students an equal chance to improve their academic standing. Following are the two components that make TGT unique.

Games. Games are designed to test students' knowledge gained from class resources and team practice.[1] *Each team sends its representatives to appropriate game tables*—typically, four students sit at each game table.[2] In Quinton Priest's geography unit, one game strategy consists of giving students a set of colored index cards with a number written on one side of each card and a set of questions printed on a separate sheet of paper, with each question corresponding to a number on the index cards. For another unit, Priest uses index cards with questions printed on one side for students to answer, or cards that have blank maps with numbers to indicated targeted countries, capitals, physical features, or other content that students are to name. A student picks a number card and attempts to answer the question corresponding to the number he or she has drawn, or draws a question card and answers the question. Other students may challenge the student's answer.

Tournaments. The tournament is the umbrella structure in which the individual games take place. The tournament, held in place of the quiz in STAD, is held at the end of the presentation-team study sequence. In the same way that STAD improvement points allow students at all levels to contribute maximally to their team score based on their academic achievement to date, TGT tournaments allow students to contribute maximally to their team score through game competition *among academic equals*.

A tournament may consist of one or more completed games at each table. It is not uncommon for the tournament at one table to consist of two games while students at another table complete three or four games. It is not important that the same number of games be played at each table during the same tournament.

For the first tournament, students move from their respective study teams to game tables according to their base scores for quizzes up to that

---

[1] A game consists of one round during which students answer questions keyed to a stack of game cards. For instance, if 24 cards are used, the game or round is over once students at a particular table have tried to answer the 24 questions keyed to these cards. Depending upon the students at the table and the number of cards, students might complete two, three, or four games or rounds in a class period.

[2] Usually four students, one each from four different teams, sit to compete at the same table during each tournament. However, game tables may consist of two, three, or five students, again each student representing a different team. This chapter uses four-member game tables, which we have found to be practical and effective.

Figure 8-1 *Realignment of Students from Heterogeneous Team Groupings to Homogeneous Game-Tournament Groupings So That Students of Near-Equal Abilities Challenge One Another During the Tournament Round(s)*

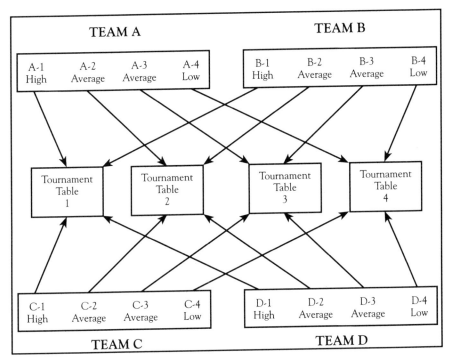

point. The top students in four teams sit together at one table, the second-highest-ability students in the same four teams sit at a second table, the third-highest-ability go to a third table, and the lowest-ability students in each of the same four groups compete against one another at a fourth table. Through this and other methods of assignment of students to game tables, the tournaments allow the teacher to combine heterogeneous groups with homogeneous-in-achievement game competition. A schematic of how this distribution can take place is provided in Figure 8-1.

At the end of a tournament, students may be "bumped up" to the next higher level, stay at the same level, or be "bumped down" to the next lower level, based on their best performance during that tournament. For example, the winner at each table progresses to the next higher level, the second-place scorer stays at the same table, and the third-place scorer moves to the next lowest table. Students are thus constantly moved up or down until they attain their achieved level of competence. (Details on the "bumping" process are provided later in this chapter).

Planning and Implementing a TGT Strategy and Structure

From the teacher's perspective, TGT has six major components: (1) clear student outcome objectives; (2) preinstruction preparation; (3) class presentations; (4) cooperative learning TGT teams; (5) games-tournament; and (6) team recognition and rewards. The details for 1, 2, 3, and 6 were provided in Chapter 7 on STAD and will not be repeated in depth here. Components 4 and 5, which are unique to TGT, are described here in detail.

Planning and Preparing Materials

This is almost the same as for STAD. The difference is that instead of preparing a quiz, the teacher prepares for the games and tournament. The same lesson-plan format as used for STAD may be used here (see Figure 7-6 in Chapter 7).

Materials needed: Lesson plan, worksheets, and study guides along with answer sheets; reference materials, lecture notes, transparencies, and so forth as needed to complement the presentation(s); and game cards and game sheets needed to provide questions or problems for students during the tournament. The game cards and answer sheets are the same as a quiz and quiz answer sheet in STAD.

Arrangements for student encounter with outcome-aligned content: Same options as for STAD.

Team formation and cooperative learning tasks: Same options as for STAD with the addition of preparation for the games-tournament activities. (See Figures 7-1 and 7-3 in Chapter 7 for computing student base scores and distributing students to appropriate groups.)

Special TGT materials needed for the games-tournament: The teacher usually makes a set of cards numbered 1 to 24, 28, or 32 for each tournament table. These cards may be made from colored index cards. All tables get the same number of cards and the same set of questions. The card sets and questions for TGT tables stress the must-learn content students studied in their groups. There are no trick questions. Other than these cards and question sheets, the social studies curriculum content, references, and materials are the same as for STAD. Remember that for TGT the teacher does not write and grade quizzes.

Public team recognition and rewards: Same options as for STAD and Jigsaw II and III.

Form Cooperative Learning TGT Groups/Teams

Use the same options as for STAD and Jigsaw II and III. Heterogeneity in ability as well as gender, race, and ethnic background is the goal. Again, form the study teams before the beginning of instruction for the unit. Role expectations and objectives of the group tasks are reviewed. This overview and review are especially important during the first three times that TGT is used.

Teaching and Providing Students Access to the To-Be-Learned Content and Abilities

TGT is an alternative to the STAD structure. Both were designed to teach a single unit of academic social studies content for which there is a single answer to each question posed.

Time for encountering the to-be-learned content: 1–2 class periods if a single unit or chapter is to be completed. (When the TGT tournament is to be used as a review activity as part of another teaching strategy, including just before a STAD or Jigsaw quiz, the presentation of content may occur over many days.)

Encountering the need-to-learn content: Same options as in STAD.

Team study: Usually 1–2 days. Students work in cooperative learning groups to master the content as in STAD and to prepare their members for the TGT games-tournament.

The tournament itself: Usually 1 class period. Students form a circle with their desks and play one or more academic games (rounds) at three-, four-, or five-member tournament tables.

After organizing the teams and providing the targeted content information, move to the team-study phase. Students need to be told the length of time that they will be working in teams. They also need to know that at the end of that time, each team will send representatives to tournament tables to compete in academic games to earn points for their teams. The teams, not the tournament tables, that exceed certain levels of achievement points will receive recognition and rewards.

TGT Cooperative Learning Team Study

TGT is usually used for a team study that is to be completed in a single unit, or about one week. When TGT is used to review a single chapter or unit in the text, the team study requires review sheets made for that purpose and that focus on the content targeted in the chapter or textbook unit. (A set of study guides similar to those found for the Jigsaw II and III and STAD strategies may be used, providing all students cooperate to learn all the content in the study guides used.)

Time for cooperative learning group tasks: 1–2 class periods.

Focus of TGT group activities: Students study the content and complete the worksheets in their teams, help ensure everyone has mastered the content, and prepare for the games-tournament.

Materials needed: Outcome-aligned worksheets or review sheets and answer sheets for either every two or every four students in each group. (See the earlier sections on team study for STAD, pages 169-177.)

The TGT Games-Tournament

Time for tournament: Usually 1 class period.

Main activity: Academic competition at three-, four-, or five-member tournament tables. Students complete as many games as they can in the time allowed.

Materials needed: Tournament Table Assignment Sheet (see Figure 8-2 on page 195); TGT Game Score Card (see Figure 8-3 on page 199); TGT Team Summary Sheets (see Figure 8-5 on page 203); numbered cards or question/answer cards; a question sheet; and an answer sheet.

Assigning Students to Initial Games-Tournament Tables

A Tournament Table Assignment Sheet similar to the sheet used to form teams is made up (for example, see Figures 8-1 and 8-2). Tables of four students each are assembled. Initially rank order the students as you did to form teams. If there are four-member study teams, then four-student game tables would be assembled. Since you placed students in their TGT cooperative learning groups according to their rank order (i.e., each team had a high and low achiever and two midlevel achievers), a

Figure 8-2   *Tournament Table Assignment Sheet: Example Completed with the Table Assignments for the First Three TGT Units*

Tournament Table Assignment Sheet*

Student:	Team:	Unit/Game Number									
		1	2	3	4	5	6	7	8	9	10
Shaman	Pazzaz	4	3	3							
Avery	Terminators	③	④	5							
Fumika	Ninjas	④	⑤	5							
Aaron	Bulls	4	4	3							
Carol	Pazzaz	5	5	4							
Zane	Terminators	5	4	4							
Sara	Ninjas	⑤	5	5							
Kane	Bulls	3	③	4							
Alfredo	Ninjas	1	①	2							
Adam	Pazzaz	②	3	2							
Carissa	Terminators	2	1	1							
James	Bulls	4	4	4							
Liza	Bulls	1	1	1							
Joaquin	Pazzaz	3	②	3							
Kara	Terminators	2	2	1							
Taro	Ninjas	①	2	2							

Key:

__ indicates high score at that table.

O indicates low score at that table.

No mark indicates a middle score at that table.

Table assignment for next tournament

Table assignment and results of most recent tournament

*Numbers in columns represent the table numbers.

representative from each TGT team will likely be included at each of the one high, two middle, and one low tables. In other words, each game table will be roughly homogeneous in academic achievement. Figures

8-1 and 8-2 illustrate graphically and in tabular form how these groups may be assembled. (If three- or five-member TGT cooperative learning teams are formed, then the game tables will have three or five players each. Due to class size, some study groups and tournament tables may have an extra student. See Figure 8-6 on pages 205 and 206.)

The Games-Tournament

At the beginning of the tournament, have students sit with their teammates. In this way, as the tournament-table assignments are announced, the students can offer encouragement and support for their teammates as they go off to their respective game tables. Tournament-table assignments should be announced in such a manner that the tables are not easily identified as "top" and "bottom" tables. After the tournament-table assignments have been announced, have students in each tournament group rearrange their desks into a circle. As a general rule, each table will have the number of cards that is equal to multiples of the number of students at the table. For instance, when four-person game tables are used, then there should be 24, 28, 32, or other multiple of 4 cards at the table. We have found that for four-person game competition, 24 or 28 cards would be the most that students should be asked to handle for a particular tournament. The question sheet and a separate answer sheet is provided for each table.[3]

Once everyone is settled and the game rules are reviewed, begin the table games within the tournament.

Game Roles, Guidelines, and Structure[4]

Reader

1. Shuffles the stack of cards and lays the deck facedown on the table.

---

[3] An equivalent to a separate answer sheet is a set of index cards numbered to have the correct answer for that numbered question written on the back. This way the student who checks the answer given by a student to a question cannot look at the answers to other questions as he or she verifies the answer given to the question just considered.

[4] These roles and guidelines may be given to students on a handout and discussed with them at the beginning of the unit and just prior to having students break from their TGT teams to their respective tournament game tables. In this way all students have a "rule book" with them throughout the unit and tournament.

2. Picks a numbered card and locates the corresponding question on the question sheet.[5]

3. Reads out loud the question on the question sheet or game card.

4. Offers an answer.*

5. Can guess at an answer with no penalty.

First Challenger (student to the left of the reader)

1. Considers the reader's answer and passes when he or she thinks that answer was correct.*

2. Can challenge the proposed answer by the reader when he or she thinks the answer is incorrect.*

3. When a challenge occurs, he or she must suggest a correct answer.*

Second Challenger

1. Considers the reader's answer and first challenger's decision and passes when he or she thinks that an answer given by one of these two was correct.*

2. Can challenge the reader's response when the first challenger passes and when he or she wants to challenge the reader's answer.*

3. Can challenge the first challenger's answer when he or she thinks the challenged answer as given is incorrect.*

4. When a challenge occurs, he or she must suggest a correct answer.

Third Challenger (when four-member game tables are used)

1. Considers the reader's answer and the first and second challengers' decisions and passes when he or she thinks that an answer given by one of these two was correct.*

---

5 An alternative is to have the numbers correspond to answers with the students required to ask a question that will elicit that answer just as on "Jeopardy." In this case, the reader has the answer sheet, and the person who checks will use the question sheet. A variation of this is to have students go one game, starting with questions to be answered and then completing game two with the answers, which require students to generate correct questions.

* Indicates where specific time limits might be set for the student to make an appropriate statement. This is especially helpful toward the end of the playing time when a student might delay a decision to benefit his or her standing in the game.

2. Can challenge the reader's response when the first and second challengers pass and when he or she wants to challenge the reader's answer.*

3. Can challenge the first or second challenger's answer when he or she thinks the challenged answer as given is incorrect.*

4. When a challenge occurs, he or she must suggest a correct answer.*

When all have challenged or passed for each card, the last challenger checks the answer sheet. Whoever was right keeps the card for that question. If the *reader* was wrong, there is no penalty, but if any *challenger* was wrong, each student who proposed an incorrect response for that card must put a previously won card, if any, *back in the deck*. The card does not go to a student at the table. Students cannot go "in the hole." These cards may be inserted randomly back into the deck or may be set aside until the next game. We suggest that they should be returned to the deck. Students earn one point for each card they win.

To start the first game, students either draw numbered cards or write a number from 1 to 10 to determine the first reader. The game cards are shuffled and placed on the table. Play then proceeds clockwise from the first reader. The first reader draws one card off the top of the stack. If numbered cards are used, the card's number corresponds to the numbered question on the question sheet. For instance, if the card is number 16, the reader looks on the list for the question that corresponds to number 16. The reader reads the question aloud (as well as the possible answers if the questions are in a multiple-choice format). If question cards are used, the reader reads the question written on the card. The game then proceeds according to the guidelines above.[6] A game is complete when all the cards in the deck are distributed among the students at that table

For the second round or game, the first challenger becomes the reader and all other roles shift to the left one position: the second challenger becomes the first challenger and so forth until the last reader becomes the last challenger for the new game. A variation of this procedure is to require students to shift roles after a certain number of cards have been

---

[6] Again, an interesting variation is the answer-card option in which the list includes an answer and the students must come up with a question that elicits that answer. This makes the tournament a "Jeopardy" tournament.

answered within the same game. For instance, if four-member groups are used and there are 28 cards, then roles are shifted after the first 7 cards are answered by the first reader, the next 7 by the second reader, and so forth. This procedure allows every student at each table to have an equal chance of being a reader during each game.

Following these rules, when a group finishes all the cards before the time is up, it reshuffles the same game cards, records the number of cards each student earned for that game, shifts roles, and continues for the remaining time. In fact, some tournament tables always seem to play more games than others. From the beginning, students should be encouraged to complete at least two rounds within the period and to start a third or fourth round when time remains in the period.

Play continues for the period of time determined by the teacher, until the deck is exhausted, or until the period ends. The tournament usually runs for one class period. You should plan ten minutes at the end of each class period for the students to add up their scores and enter them on the game score cards. When time is called to end the tournament, tables at which all members have not had an equal number of turns at being a reader should continue until that has occurred. At the end of the game, players record the number of cards they won on the Game Score Card (Figure 8-3). Students then add up the scores for all games (game 1, game 2, etc.) to compute the day's total points. The game score cards are collected at the end of each day of tournament play.

Figure 8-3 *A TGT Game Score Card. (One sheet is placed on each game table.)*

TGT GAME SCORE CARD

Unit/Lesson: _____Geography_____   Date: ___Oct. 8___

Table No. ___4_____

Player	Team	Game 1	Game 2	Game 3	Day's Total	Tournament Points
Avery	Terminators	6	9		15	30
Aaron	Bulls	12	6		18	60
Nancy	Pazzaz	9	7		16	40
Connie	Ninjas	3	8		11	20

Monitoring the Games at Each Table

The teacher moves from table to table while the tournament is under way to answer questions and to be sure that everyone understands how to play the game. Students are encouraged to move as rapidly as possible between rounds and to complete as many games as possible. At tables where the readers are getting every answer correct for two rounds, students may be given enrichment materials, be asked to go through another round or two except this time the correct answer is an explanation as to how they arrived at their answer, or be asked to switch to the "Jeopardy" format and continue another game.

Computing Scores from the Tournament Play at Each Game Table

At the end of tournament play, students calculate their total tournament points.[7] (See right column in Figure 8-3, page 199.) Whereas individual game scores are recorded at the end of each game, total tournament points for each individual are computed only once. Once the total number of cards each student earned for all the games for the tournament is calculated, then game points are assigned to each student based upon his or her ranking among the students at that table. In my class, at a four-student table with no ties, the top scorer (the one with the most cards won) receives 60 points, the second-highest scorer 40 points, the third-highest scorer 30 points, and the lowest scorer earns 20 points. The maximum number of tournament points a player can earn for a single tournament is 60, regardless of the number of games that are played at that table during that tournament.[8] Figure 8-4 on pages 201 and 202 can be used to help determine the number of game points to assign for rankings within five-, four-, three-, and two-student tournament tables. Figure 8-4 is invaluable for situations in which two or more students are tied. When all tournament points have been calculated, the game score cards are collected.

---

[7] For young children, the teacher should collect these sheets once the individual points have been recorded by the students themselves.

[8] Slavin (1988) assigns students scores of from 1 to 6. We have found that many students like "bigger" numbers since these high numbers seem like many more points are being earned even though in reality they mean the same as the smaller numbers (6 rather than 60) within the TGT structure. To reduce the possible points to lower numbers, merely drop the "0" from the end of each number in Figure 8-4.

Figure 8-4   *Computation of Tournament Points for TGT**

For a Five-Player Game

Player	No ties	Tie for top	2-way tie for middle	3-way tie for middle	Tie for low
Top scorer	60	50	60	60	60
High middle scorer	40	50	35	30	40
Middle scorer	30	30	35	30	30
Low middle scorer	20	20	20	30	15
Low scorer	10	10	10	10	15

For a Five-Player Game, cont.

Player	3-way tie for top	4-way tie for top	5-way tie	3-way tie for low
Top scorer	40	35	30	60
High middle scorer	40	35	30	40
Middle scorer	40	35	30	20
Low middle scorer	20	35	30	20
Low scorer	10	10	30	20

For a Five-Player Game, cont.

Player	2-way tie for low middle	4-way tie for low	Tie for low and high
Top scorer	60	60	50
High middle scorer	40	25	50
Middle scorer	25	25	30
Low middle scorer	25	25	15
Low scorer	10	25	15

---

* Lower points may be devised by merely dropping the "0" after each number and converting numbers with a "5" (e.g., 45) into a decimal (e.g., 4.5).

Figure 8-4 *(cont.)*

For a Four-Player Game

Player	No ties	Tie for top	Tie for middle	Tie for low
Top scorer	60	50	60	60
High middle scorer	40	50	40	40
Low middle scorer	30	30	40	30
Low scorer	20	20	20	30

For a Four-Player Game, cont.

Player	3-way tie for top	3-way tie for low	4-way tie	Tie for low and high
Top scorer	50	60	40	50
High middle scorer	50	30	40	50
Low middle scorer	50	30	40	30
Low scorer	20	30	40	30

For a Three-Player Game

Player	No ties	Tie for top	Tie for low	3-way tie
Top scorer	60	50	60	40
Middle scorer	40	50	30	40
Low scorer	20	20	30	40

For a Two-Player Game

Player	No ties	Tied
Top scorer	60	40
Low scorer	20	40

Public Team Recognition and Rewards

It will be necessary now to compute total team scores and team rankings and proceed with team recognition. If we have used TGT for test review (see "Using TGT with Other Cooperative Learning Strategies" on page 208), we usually do the team recognition after my students have taken the unit test. In that way the students have an activity to relieve the anxiety over how they might have performed on the test.

Computing Team Scores. Check the tournament points on the game summary sheets to be certain that there are no errors. Then transfer each student's tournament points to the TGT Team Summary Sheet (see Figure 8-5).

Figure 8-5   *TGT Team Summary Sheet: Example with Record of Individual Points Earned for the Team for Four Tournaments*

TGT TEAM SUMMARY SHEET

TEAM NAME: _Neurons_

	Tournament								
TEAM MEMBERS	1	2	3	4	5	6	7	8	9
Steve S.	40	60	20	60					
Nancy N.	40	30	60	60					
Juan	40	30	40	50					
Millie	50	30	10	40					
Total team score	170	150	130	210					
*Prorated team score	170	150	130	210					
Team average	43	38	33	53					
Team standing this unit/week	2	4	4	2					
Total team score to date	170	320	450	660					
Team standing by team total to date	2	3	4	3					
Team award for this unit/week									

* Where prorated score as per Figure 8-6 would be placed.

If all teams have exactly the same number of students, then the raw total scores for the team are used. Because some teams may have more or fewer members than others, Slavin (1988) has proposed a system of pro-rating total team scores when teams of two, three, or five are used in addition to four-member groups. Using Figure 8-6 on pages 205-206, group total scores can be adjusted or prorated to equalize those groups' points with a four-member group score. Prorating scores ensures equity among all groups and offsets problems caused by an unequal number of members in the original study groups. Another use of Figure 8-6 comes into play when group members are absent during the tournament and the remaining members are left to earn all the points for their team. Figure 8-5 allows for recording of transformed scores should prorated scores be needed.

Usually the total team scores are used to rank the teams participating in the tournament. Some teachers prefer using the team average score to rank the teams.

Determining Team Performance and Awards

In Quinton Priest's classes, team awards are based on average team scores. Teams that average 50 points receive the Outstanding Team Award; teams that average 45 points receive the Powerhouse Team Award; and teams that average 40 points receive the Little Giants Award. If total team points are used and the group study teams had four members each, then each of the above averages would be multiplied by four to get the number of total team points for each award. Teachers may set any level for the awards. We suggest that the minimum level be at least an average of 35 (or 3.5) points.

Certificates and team rewards may also be the same as in STAD. End-of-each-tournament newsletters, such as that provided in Figure 8-7 on page 210, have been found to be highly effective in motivating students within their groups and during the tournament rounds. Here again, the teacher creates an award/reward structure that best suits the particular class and teaching style. It is important to recognize team effort—not individual effort—at this stage, although individual scores may be posted along with team scores. Individual achievement for grading purposes is determined by individual tests and reflected in quarterly grade reports. However, once STAD and TGT catch on and are used regularly, scores on individual unit tests increase as do final grades for the term.

Figure 8-6 Form To Prorate Student Scores To Equalize Team Total Scores When Teams Have Unequal Numbers of Players Competing During the TGT Games and Tournament*

4-member team total score	5-member team prorated score	3-member team prorated score	2-member team prorated score
40			80
50			100
60		80	120
70		90	140
80		110	160
90		120	180
100	80	130	200
110	90	150	220
120	100	160	240
130	110	170	260
140	120	190	280
150	120	200	300
160	130	210	320
170	140	230	340
180	140	240	360
190	150	250	380
200	160	270	400

Note 1: To read this table, if, for instance, a 5-member team earned a total of 160 points during a tournament and all the other teams consisted of 4 players, then 160 points would be prorated to 200 points to equalize its achievements with those in 4-member groups. If a 3-member team earned 150 team points for a tournament, this score would be equivalent to a score of 110 for a 4-member group. This prorated score is then included in the TGT Team Summary Sheet and is used to calculate team rankings, awards, etc. In this way teams are not penalized for having more or fewer students than the majority of teams in same tournament.

Note 2: This table was generated around the scoring system that we favor, which uses higher numbers of points. For instance, we would award 60 points where Slavin awards 6 points for the same accomplishments during a tournament. So a 4-member team earning a total of 210 points in our system would earn 21 points in Slavin's system. Merely eliminating the right-hand "0" in the above numbers conforms to Slavin's system. Some teachers prefer the lower numbers to simplify the mathematics involved in the computations.

* Adapted from Appendix 1 in Slavin (1988). This table is also used when teams have unequal participation due to absences on the day of the tournament.

Figure 8-6   (*cont.*)

4-member team total score	5-member team prorated score	3-member team prorated score	2-member team prorated score
210	170	280	
220	180	290	
230	180	310	
240	190	320	
250	200	330	
260	210	350	
270	220	360	
280	220	370	
290	230	400	
300	240	400	
310	250		
320	260		
330	260		
340	270		
350	280		
360	290		
370	300		
380	300		
390	310		
400	320		
410	330		
420	340		
430	350		
440	350		
450	360		
460	370		
470	380		
480	380		
490	390		
500	400		

Unit Closure and Structured Reflection

This has the same focus and purpose as STAD. The section in Chapter 7 should be consulted.

Bumping, or Reassigning Students to Game Tables for Future Tournaments

It is usually necessary to reassign students to new tournament tables for the next tournament. To "bump" students, use the following procedure:

1. Decide on a mark or symbol to indicate high and low students (e.g., circle high student scores and draw boxes around low student scores). Then mark one high and one low student on each game score card. If there are ties for high or low, break the tie by tossing a coin; there should be only one high and one low student from each team.

2. For the next tournament, bump all high students up to the next table and all low students down to the next lower table; the third student stays at his or her original table. For example, if Carissa at table 4 was the high scorer and James the low scorer, changing Carissa's table number from 4 to 3 and increasing James's from 4 to 5 effectively bumps them to the next higher and lower table respectively. The only exception to this will be the high scorer at table 1; since table 1 is the high table, that person will remain at table 1. The same is true for the low scorer at the lowest table; he or she cannot go down, so that student stays at the lowest table.

3. Count the students assigned to each table for the next tournament. There should be the same numbers as for the previous tournament. Make changes in table assignments if there are some discrepancies due to absenteeism or computing problems.

Applications of TGT: Practical Classroom Examples

The identical sets of materials and guidelines for middle-level and/or high-school geography and United States history provided at the end of the STAD chapter may also be used for a TGT strategy. Your task would be to make up the game cards or question sheets for the TGT games-tournament rather than making up an individual quiz as for STAD. The teacher could make up both a quiz and game cards and run a TGT games-tournament as a motivator or review prior to the STAD individual quiz.

Using TGT with Other Cooperative Learning Strategies

TGT can also be used as a culminating activity to prepare students for any unit or chapter test regardless of whether a cooperative learning strategy was used. In this usage, Quinton Priest has used TGT as the end activity of a series of related Jigsaw II or III or STAD units, sometimes using it as a review activity prior to a major unit test. In this instance, students are selected for tournament tables in the same manner, according to their original class standings and without regard to which teams exceeded their base scores in the STAD units. Whichever way you use TGT, for a single unit or for test review, tournaments generate high interest and enthusiasm among students.[9]

Grading

A word about grading TGT units: term grades should be based on students' actual quiz scores. Improvement points, tournament points, and team scores are for the purpose of class recognition. However, you may want to use the team scores for extra credit or to assess effort grades if your school records them. TGT does not generally produce scores that can be converted to individual grades for a unit. If you want to use TGT as an academic extra-credit activity, you may want to follow a tournament with a quiz over the material. This gives the student two means of taking points back to his or her team, and it gives you a better idea of student progress than the tournament games scores alone.

---

[9] A variation of reassembling the home team as a Test Review Team in Jigsaw III would be to use a tournament as the review activity.

Epilogue to the TGT Strategy and Structure

To review, TGT may be used to teach any subject area where questions with one right answer can be posed and the emphasis is mastery of targeted content and skills. In the classroom, TGT engenders a regular cycle of activities consisting of (1) *setting clear student outcome objectives*—describes precisely what students need to learn and be able to do at the end of the unit; (2) *planning and preparation*—includes selecting outcome objectives and getting materials ready for use once instruction begins; (3) *teaching and ensuring students encounter the academic content to be learned*; (4) *providing team study time and tasks*—allows students to work on worksheets in their teams to master the content and the ability to use it; (5) *managing and engaging students in team games and tournaments*—allows students to answer questions in gamelike conditions that earn bonus points for their team; and (6) *providing public team recognition and rewards*—means that team scores are computed based on team members' tournament points, and some form of team recognition is awarded.

As with STAD, many teachers believe that the TGT strategy is a very complicated and time-consuming cooperative learning strategy. As we have described above, TGT can occur and can be a very effective strategy in mid-elementary through twelfth-grade classrooms with excellent academic and affective results. Like all cooperative learning strategies, the more TGT is used, the more efficient students will become in their group roles and on-task activities.

Figure 8-7 *Sample Newsletter That May Be Generated for TGT Results*

TOURNAMENT TALES

Tournament Week No. 4   February 28

Space Cadets Not "Spacey" in Latest Tournament!

The Space Cadets were in near-perfect form this week in winning the tournament with a total of 220 points. Felipe, Lara, and Quinton all scored 60 points while Mary was close behind with her 40 points. Their success brings them into second place in the Left-Hemisphere Division of the Brain League.

Right behind the Space Cadets were the Neurons, who earned 210 points. Steve S. and Nancy N. were the top point scorers with 60 points each for this team. Their points moved the Neurons closer to first place in the Left-Hemisphere Division, but they are much closer to first place in total points than before this tournament.

Meanwhile, the Absent Minds, of the Right-Hemisphere Division, came in third for the tournament. The strongest finishers on their team were Alonzo and Clarissa, who scored 60 points each, and Bob and Marilyn, who contributed 40 points. Other table winners with 60 points were Elizabeth of the Long-Term Memories and Reid of the Restless Ones.

TOURNAMENT RESULTS FOR THIS WEEK

First Place—Space Cadets		Second Place—Neurons		Third Place—Absent Minds	
Felipe	60	Steve S.	60	Alonzo	60
Lara	60	Nancy N.	60	Clarissa	60
Quinton	60	Juan	50	Bob	40
Mary	40	Millie	40	Marilyn	40
	220		210	Ed	20
					220/180

Long-Term Memories		Restless Ones		Never Say Nevers		Terminator -4s	
Elizabeth	60	Reid	60	Tanya	40	Jackie	50
Jere	40	Nancy S.	30	Jose	40	Skip	30
Alfredo	40	Julio	20	Julio	20	Vickie	20
Karri	20	Bill	20	Terri	20	Steven A.	20
	160	Candy	20		120		120
			150/120				

BRAIN LEAGUE SEASON STANDINGS TO DATE

Left-Hemisphere Division		Right-Hemisphere Division	
Team	Season Score	Team	Season Score
Never Say Nevers	760	Restless Ones	730
Space Cadets	720	Absent Minds	650
Neurons	660	Long-Term Memories	580
Terminator-4s	610		

References

Kagan, S. 1989. *Cooperative learning: Resources for teachers*. San Juan Capistrano, CA: Resources for Teachers.

Slavin, R. E. 1988. *Student team learning: An overview and practical guide*, 2nd ed. Washington, DC: National Educational Association.

9.

Achieving Cooperative Learning Through Structured Individual-Then-Group Decision-Making Episodes

ROBERT J. STAHL

As these chapters have revealed, by structuring the tasks students must complete, a number of ways exist to arrange for cooperative learning to occur among students. This chapter describes a unique approach wherein students typically study need-to-learn content by working through specially constructed, content-based short-story episodes that require the use of a specific decision-making strategy. When constructed according to specific guidelines, these short-story episodes require students first to consider and rehearse important content as individuals and in a group and then re-rehearse the content as they make both individual and small-group decisions using a particular decision-making strategy.

In working with well-constructed episodes, students' tasks are structured to complete cooperative learning and decision tasks as they progress through stories contrived around the content that is to be learned. Using this structure, students are actively involved in learning the content during problem-solving activities in which outcome-aligned worksheets are frequently disguised within the context of a story and the problem they must resolve. To complete each episode, students make a set of structured individual decisions before moving on to making a small-group consensus decision. The group-consensus task is merely a device to get students to rehearse the important subject-matter *content* contained in the episode within the *context* of a problem-solving situation. Consequently, it is not important *what* decisions students make as individuals or as a group since *the decision structure is only a contrived situation and task to ensure that students attend in meaningful ways to the content, concepts, and abilities they are to learn.* What is important is that students complete the several decision tasks, since these ensure rehearsal of the content that is to be comprehended, made relevant, and retained.

Because much of the rest of this chapter will deal with the design of these cooperative learning episodes, including detailed descriptions of four decision strategies these episodes could incorporate, the reader is encouraged to take time now to read the sample episodes, "Big Bad John" and "Letter for Florence," at the end of this chapter, to get a sense of what students are to be given as the resource materials for this cooperative learning strategy.[1] Social studies teachers should also notice how adequately constructed episodes include clear directions as to how students need to proceed to complete the multiple tasks required and that these directions are built into the flow of the story as an integral part of the story. In this way, once students are given the episode materials, they can operate by themselves and as members of a small-group decision team without constantly asking questions concerning what they have to do next.

Origins of the Strategy and Research Findings from Classroom Studies

In studies that tested the effects of an earlier version of the model for the sample episode, students who used the episodes were found to have significantly higher content retention and affective scores than those who studied the content using lecture, textbook, and discussion methods (Hunt, 1981; Stahl, 1981, 1979). Since these formal studies, the original model, as developed by Doyle Casteel and Robert Stahl (1975) and upon which the content-centered episodes used in these studies were built, was refined (Casteel and Stahl, 1989). These refinements enable designers of learning episodes to increase the clarity and

---

[1] Robert J. and Nancy N. Stahl have recently completed a manuscript of 30 episodes relevant for helping students consider science-technology-society issues, entitled "Science and Society: Up Close and Personal." In addition, Robert J. Stahl et al. have completed 45 activities focusing on world and American history. For information on both sets of these episodes, contact the author.

depth of the particular decision-making strategy into the episodes themselves to enable students to remain on-task with that strategy as an integral part of completing the short-story episode tasks.

Meanwhile, Stahl (1987, 1990) modified the Casteel-Stahl model to make it more consistent with the requirements of cooperative learning. Stahl's modifications call for students to stop at particular places in the story episodes and review selected content as a group to ensure that everyone has comprehended this content and story context to that point. He requires a larger number of predecision activity sheets to be completed prior to the final individual and group decisions to ensure that students consciously and systematically reconsider the important academic information once again before they make their decisions. In addition, he requires these episodes to be used within the context of such cooperative learning elements as clear academic-outcome objectives, heterogeneous grouping, interdependency, and individual accountability. Both the refined and modified versions of the original Casteel-Stahl model are highly suitable for an effective learning of academic content, the attainment of positive affective consequences, and the systematic rehearsal of transferable decision strategies.

Focus of This Chapter

This chapter provides an overview of the components that are to be included in the short-story episodes within this cooperative group strategy. These components represent decision steps that the designers must complete in order to structure student thinking, task behaviors, and decisions in appropriate ways. Before these components are provided, four specific decision-making strategies that may be incorporated into these episodes and that students will be required to use will be described.

Four Explicit Decision-Making Strategies

A critical component of the instructional materials and student tasks in this cooperative learning strategy is the decision-making strategy that students must eventually complete as individuals and then as members of their group as a group. Each episode contains the must-learn content and one must-use decision strategy. This section describes four highly valued and transferable decision strategies that students may use as a means to rehearse and often apply the must-learn content.

The Rank-Order Decision Strategy

All too often students are given classroom activities that direct them to rank order a set of options, even though there is no real reason for them to do so except to follow the directions. In such instances, students pay attention to their first and second and last rankings and little attention to the options in between. Since typically the rankings between the first and last options are of no actual importance, students spend little time and effort in considering the rankings they assign to these in-between options. In this cooperative group approach, students are not asked to rank order just for the sake of ranking a set of options.

In this version of the rank-order strategy, students are provided from five to nine homogeneous options that they are to place in priority from most preferred, to the next most preferred, and so on until their final ranking is the most preferred of the last two remaining options.[2] In other words, this rank-order strategy usually involves students always selecting the most preferred choice from all remaining options. For instance, one may have won a free round-trip vacation for two to one of three spots on a space-available contract. The couple decide to go during the week of July Fourth. They are to rank order the three locations, Hawaii, Tahiti, and the Virgin Islands, from their first choice to third. If their first choice is available, they will go to that location. However, if their first choice is not available during that week, their second location will be checked. If available, then they go there; if unavailable, they will get their third-ranked location.

To help ensure that this continuous prioritization will be the case, these episodes frequently inform students that their first-ranked choice may not be available, may not work, or may not be entirely successful; hence their second-ranked option will be considered. The same situation could occur with their second choice, so their third choice will be considered. Movement to the next-ranked option is a possibility for all

---

[2] In the lower elementary grades, these options may be from three to five. Even among upper-level students, rank ordering of from 9 to 12 options should be limited, since rarely is the ranking of these many options a requirement to handle problems in everyday life.

options ranked. Constructing a rank-order decision in this way empha-sizes the importance of each ranking from beginning to end. This is a very different structure from what one typically encounters in rank-order activities.

The scenario created for the rank-order strategy must make it clear why the options provided are the only ones that can be considered; why the options must be rank ordered; and why students may not get their first, second, third, and so on ranked options even after they've made their personal and group decisions. In addition, all the options provided must be as homogeneous as possible so that students must rank among equally desirable or undesirable options within the context of the situa-tion they are to resolve or handle.

The Forced-Choice Decision Strategy

For this strategy, students are provided from three to five homoge-neous and mutually exclusive options from which they are to select the most preferred one. Furthermore, once they make their choice, they immediately lose all access to the other options they had considered. In other words, they are forced to make a decision from among a set of equally attractive or unattractive options knowing all along that once they make their decision, they lose those options not selected. For instance, suppose you entered three contests, each offering a free vaca-tion for two to a different spot. Suppose you won all three free vacations, one to Hawaii, one to Tahiti, and one to the Virgin Islands. However, failing to read the fine print, you did not notice that all three are for the exact same week with no substitutions or changes in date possible. In this case, you enter a forced-choice situation, selecting among three desirable places to go with no changes possible, and a selection of one automatically makes impossible the other two options in the situation.

To help ensure a forced-choice situation is the case, episodes includ-ing this strategy inform students that their first choice automatically makes the remaining options unavailable at the present and all future times. Structuring the decision strategy in this way ensures that students consider all the options carefully, since they get what they select but lose the others. In this way they consider what they gain and lose with each option and what they will lose when they lose access to all the nonse-lected options. In addition, they must make this decision considering the context of the problem as presented and the limitations restricting their access to all the options.

In most classroom activities students are given situations and directed to make a forced-choice decision as though their decision does not limit them from gaining access to the nonselected options. For instance, if you could go to all three vacation spots, you are not in a forced-choice situation since you lose nothing by your selection. When the selection among options has little negative consequence, students tend to spend little time and effort in considering the many things to be gained and lost by each option. In this cooperative group approach, students are quite aware that their selection automatically rules out access to the remaining options.

The scenario created for the forced-choice strategy must make it clear why the options provided are the only ones that can be considered, why only one option can be selected, and why the person(s) in the story cannot gain access to any of the nonselected options once he or she has made a personal and later a group decision. In addition, all the options provided must be as homogeneous as possible so that students must choose among equally desirable or undesirable options within the context of the situation they are to resolve or handle.

The Negotiation Decision Strategy

All too often students are given a situation and directed to rank order a long list of options because the teacher has no other strategy for helping students sort through an extended listing of alternatives. In these cases as mentioned above with rank ordering, students pay attention to their rankings of the first and second and last rankings and pay little attention to their rankings of the options in between.

There is, however, a very viable decision strategy that can be used instead of rank ordering options. This strategy, called the negotiation strategy, emphasizes elements of prioritizing options by groups, compromise, and the giving and taking of options to arrive at the most acceptable "package deal" possible given the situation. For this strategy, students are provided nine or more options that they are to place into three categories or groups. One category consists of options the individual *most wants to keep or obtain*; a second category consists of options the individual is *most willing to give up* or not obtain *in order to secure the first category of options*; and a third category includes options that may still be possible to secure at a later time. In essence, students have to sort through the options and decide which ones they most want to secure as well as those they are willing to forfeit forever in order to attain their most preferred options. Thus they must engage in personal and some-times social negotiation-compromise activities as they arrive at their three categories or groupings of options.

For instance, suppose you won nine contests in January and the equally valuable prizes are good until December 31 of that same year. In addition, you cannot transfer any prize to another person or group. Suppose you are just about ready to pick up all these prizes when your tax accountant calls and informs you that to collect all these prizes would put you in a tax situation from which you would never recover. You are asked to select the three you most want and do not want to give up under any circumstances and the three you are willing to forfeit to help ensure that you get the three you most want. The remaining three prizes will be considered after the tax liability is known from the first three options. Within the week you must write to the companies. If this is not done, your accountant says you may be forced to pay taxes on all the prizes even if you refuse them at a later date. In essence, to gain the three you most want you must decide which three prizes you are most willing to give up. Note how this decision requires a person to "negoti-ate" within oneself as to what is most preferred and what one is willing to surrender to gain those priorities.

To ensure this classification of options occurs, negotiation-strategy episodes usually provide nine or more homogeneous, mutually exclusive options and inform students that they must organize the options into three very distinct classes or groupings: one group contains options most wanted; one contains options most willing to surrender to secure the first group of options; and a third group contains the rest of the options that may be obtainable. In essence, students know that they will lose the last group but will gain the priority group of options. Constructing a decision in this way emphasizes the importance of each option in relation to every other option, which is a critical feature of both negotiating and compromising. This decision structure enables students to practice very important abilities needed within social settings where compromise, negotiation, and give-and-take decision formation are important.

The scenario created for the negotiation strategy must make it clear why the options provided are the only ones that can be considered, why the options must be clustered into three equal groupings, and why the person (or group) will lose even more if he or she fails to make selections into these three groupings. In addition, all the options provided must be as homogeneous as possible so that students must make their decisions among equally desirable or undesirable options within the context of the situation they are to resolve or handle.

The Invention Decision Strategy

For this strategy, students are provided from none to three or four options as possible choices they could make and are directed to make the best possible decision within the context. They are to consider the suggested options but are *free to invent any other options that they expect will work*. In essence, they are given an open-ended decision situation where they are to "invent" the best possible decision given the context and constraints available.

To help ensure that an invention situation is the case, episodes including this strategy inform students that a decision needs to be made and that they are to make the best decision possible. None to four options may be suggested as possible, but students are free to abandon, combine, or add to these as they see fit. Before students make a final choice, however, they are asked to consider consequences, advantages/disadvantages, or benefits/costs of at least four options they have considered. This ensures that they have considered one or more implications of at least four options to prevent their rushing in to make a quick, superficial decision. Structuring the decision strategy in this way ensures that students systematically consider at least four options carefully before making their final decision and consider what they gain and lose with each option. In addition, they must make their invented decision considering the context of the problem and the limitations restricting all options.

In the typical classroom activity, students are given situations and directed to make a free-choice decision, as though their decision is not limited by any constraints. For instance, a class of eleventh-grade American history students was observed discussing what they would have done if they had been with General George A. Custer at the Little Big Horn. As Custer, they would have set up Gatling guns along the top of the ridge. Using such guns, Custer's troops would not have been annihilated. The teacher praised the students for their creative and critical thinking even though Custer's troops had no Gatling guns to fire. The students would have been better served had they been asked to invent options given the limitations and constraints that existed at the time and in that place for Custer and his troops.

In real-life situations, students must make choices within the context and constraints available and invent choices that are viable within those circumstances. When the invented choices have little connection to context and constraints, students tend to invent options that are unrealistic, not bound by known or probable limitations or restrictions, and not likely to be viable were the students in that situation themselves. Structured free-response episodes help students acquire and refine this decision strategy because they must consciously consider possible options within the contexts and limitations of the situation.

The learning episodes requiring the use of these four strategies take the form of a story that is carefully structured and includes a decision strategy as an integral part of the story. More details concerning the structure of these episodes are provided in the next section.

Critical Components of the Individual-Then-Group Episodes Required for This Cooperative Learning Strategy

Cooperative-learning episodes that incorporate the four decision strategies described contain the seven major components given below. Teachers may use episodes already containing these components or may use the descriptions below to guide their construction of episodes for their own content, topics, and student needs.

1. *A problem-solving situation in story form that includes sufficient background information for comprehension of the context in which a number of options are to be considered and a decision made.* This component presents *in story form* a problem-solving situation or dilemma in which an individual or a group is required to resolve the problem by using one decision strategy. As the plot unfolds, each short story makes it explicit who the individual or the group is that is involved and what the problem is that needs to be resolved. This story provides a clear narrative within which students consider a

situation, a set of options, and the must-learn academic content. The story enables students to develop a perspective that would likely be taken by one or more characters in the story and provides students with a context in which to academically examine the context, content, concepts, and options. It enables them to construct a situation in which deciding among the options is a meaningful activity and has implications beyond the decision task itself. When developed fully, the story context enables students to engage in role-taking experiences and to consider areas where the particular decision strategy may be used in real-life situations.

This story also includes one or more important constraints and limitations that the individuals in the story must consider as they attempt to deal with the situation. These limitations may involve time, resources, space, lack of sufficient information, political or economic implications, and so forth. These constraints help students to see that quite often individuals in different times, places, and cultures are *not free* to make just any choices they want but must make choices under certain constraints and limitations that reduce their absolute freedom of choice. These constraints also enable students to more quickly take the roles of the persons in the story, since they tend to take students out of their present-day perspectives and move them toward the perspectives of individual(s) in the story.

2. *A quantity of must-learn information aligned directly with the student academic outcomes for the unit.* This component ensures that each episode includes outcome-aligned, must-learn information that students are to master and retain well beyond the end of the unit. Since these episodes typically replace or supplement traditional ways to give students access to the identical must-learn content (i.e., textbook, worksheets, lecture), they must include the subject matter students would be expected to acquire through other means. In addition, the plot and demands of the story must have students consciously considering and reconsidering this content as they move toward making a decision.

3. *A list of options to be considered.* In every episode, students make their decisions among a set of options. In three of the four decision strategies mentioned here, all the options are provided to students; these cannot be changed, added to, or replaced. The individuals within the context of the story are "stuck" with the options they

are given. In these instances, all the options are to be *homogeneous* in that they are all possible policies, actions, criteria, laws, and consequences, and are about equal in their attractiveness, desirability, possible effectiveness, and unattractiveness. For example, all the options are ones the individuals in the story really want or really don't want rather than options that represent some desirable and some undesirable choices. These options also are mutually exclusive in that each represents a unique alternative so that two or more cannot be combined to form a new option.

The invention decision strategy may provide one or more options but requires students to invent more than one possible option on their own before they make their final decision about how to resolve the problem or handle a situation.

4. *A set of clear instructions built in as an integral part of the story to inform students how and why they are to proceed to make their decisions.* Each episode builds in a set of guidelines showing students how to proceed through the activity, make their individual decisions, and move toward their group consensus decision. These instructions should be such that once students get started in their groups, the story plot and details in the story and materials instruct them how to proceed to complete the entire episode. When structured as required, the teacher's primary classroom task is to monitor the groups rather than spend time giving procedural directions or instructions.

5. *A set of predecision activities and/or Predecision Sheets to be completed first by each individual student and then by the group.* One or more Predecision Sheets are provided to structure the predecision tasks students are to complete. These sheets also inform students about what they are to record as public evidence of their predecision considerations and choices. These predecision tasks have students consciously consider and reconsider the critical information, conceptions, and abilities they are to learn.

Typically, one or two of these sheets are completed first by each student and then cooperatively by students in their groups *as a group* as they progress toward their consensus final decision. (Samples of these sheets are provided with the example episodes at the end of this chapter.) Teachers should study these sheets for the detailed directions they provide students. The more explicit the directions on each, the greater the number of students who will proceed on-task from sheet to sheet without having to ask the teacher questions about what to do next.

In other instances, students may be asked to take time to review particular parts of the story they have read to that point and to work with members of their group to check that all members comprehend the targeted data and context before moving on to the next part of the episode. In still other episodes, students are asked to complete these reflection and discussion tasks prior to completing one or more written Predecision Sheets.

6. *A set of final Decision Sheets to be completed, first by each individual student and then by the group.* Usually one Decision Sheet is provided for students to record their final individual choices, with a second sheet provided for the final group decision. (Samples of these sheets are provided with the example episodes at the end of this chapter.) These sheets provide explicit directions on what students need to report as public evidence of their preferences, reasons, and priorities. The teacher is reminded that the decisions themselves are rarely important for their own sake. These Decision Sheets provide closure for the story being considered, allow practice for the decision strategy required to complete the episode, and allow for systematic reconsideration of much of the information targeted for students to learn from the activity.

7. *A set of questions as discussion starters to focus inquiry and learning.* These questions are useful for at least three reasons. First, they help students review what they have just studied and considered as part of the academic content and context of the episode. Second, they enable students to assign meaning and find connections between what they considered and did in their groups to other data, to themselves, and to present, past, or future times, places, situations, and people. Third, they enable students to compare the perspectives and decisions made in reference to the individuals in the episode and those they may have made themselves in the same or similar situations. If the questions are limited to primarily the must-learn content included in the episode, then a fourth role for these questions, as test review questions, is fulfilled. As a general

rule, a minimum of from five to ten questions are asked of students within a whole-class setting after all groups have made their final decisions and shared them with the class.

The above components should make it clear that the episodes that make up the central resource of this cooperative learning strategy are highly structured, academically-oriented short stories that require cooperative learning prior to and during the decision-making process.[3]

Ensuring That Cooperative Learning Requirements Are Met

Learning episodes designed according to the above go a long way toward ensuring that the required elements for cooperative learning are met. However, other elements are met only as the teacher arranges for and ensures that the following are completed:

1. *Positive interdependence.* To meet this requirement, teachers must use episodes requiring that students (a) stop at appropriate moments to review the context, content, and situation within which all are to operate for that particular episode; (b) work together *as the group in the episode* to attain a group decision; and (c) complete each activity as individuals before the group meets to provide group reactions and clarifications followed by movement *as a group* to attain a group decision. For instance, in "Big Bad John," the group of barons cannot reach a group decision until each baron has made an individual decision, which in turn cannot be made until both the individuals and the group have worked together to consider the content, context, and options in a systematic way.

2. *Face-to-face interaction.* Students are to arrange themselves so that from the beginning to the end of their work through an episode, they are positioned and postured so that they are facing one another.

---

[3] A manuscript providing extensive details for creating episodes, including guidelines for constructing short stories that work within any subject area and at all grade levels, is being finalized.

3. *Individual accountability.* Students must eventually be formally tested on the extent to which each has learned the targeted academic content embedded in the episode. From "Big Bad John," students would be expected to provide a number of details about the setting of the signing of the Magna Carta and at least six of its clauses. This element is enhanced when the teacher makes it clear in introducing the activity that students are to learn this information as they complete their episode-related tasks. The teacher may want to compute average scores per team and recognize teams for their collective achievement, as suggested for Jigsaw II and III and STAD. However, this is a preferred but not required option.

4. *Heterogeneous groups.* As possible, teachers should organize the three-, four-, or five-member groups so that students are mixed as heterogeneously as possible according to academic abilities, ethnic backgrounds, race, socio-economic levels, and gender.

5. *Social interaction abilities.* To complete the episode tasks, students have to work together as members of the group described in the story. As students work through these activities they tend to engage in such interaction abilities as leadership, compromise, negotiation, and clarifying in order to complete their tasks. At the same time they tend to become tolerant of diverse viewpoints, to consider others' thoughts and feelings in depth, and to seek more support and clarification of others' positions. Students of very different academic or ethnic backgrounds, race, or gender often deal with critical issues or dilemmas in ways rarely found in other instructional strategies. For instance, after a prolonged discussion within an episode concerning Truman's decision to drop the atomic bomb, three students who made up one group announced that they had difficulty making up their minds as they realized they were "a group made up of a Native American, an African American, and a Hispanic deciding whether an Anglo should drop an unknown weapon likely to kill a huge number of Asians." The three shared how they had resorted to a number of different approaches to work toward a final decision as a group, especially when the task demanded that a consensus be achieved in both what to do and why that decision was the best choice at that time.

6. *Group debriefing.* Students spend time after the episode has been completed to reflect systematically on how they worked together as a team to consider the critical content, to help one another comprehend the context, content, and decision strategy, and to progress toward a final consensus decision. They also consider how they worked to maintain positive behaviors and attitudes to enable each individual and the entire team as a group to be successful. To achieve this, the teacher provides a structured reflection task and sufficient time after groups share their responses so that this debriefing occurs by design rather than by chance.

These six factors are not built into the episodes per se and thus depend upon the teacher to arrange for their completion.

A Classroom Scenario

What does this strategy look like in the classroom?

This section addresses this question in the form of a classroom scenario to illustrate what would occur in a typical social studies classroom where this strategy and a relevant episode are used. Our teacher, Ms. Jane Nance, is concerned that her students comprehend a number of ideas associated with the Magna Carta and consider the implications of these ideas on real-life situations and decisions in England in the early thirteenth century. She feels that her students need to have a strong sense of what the individual demands of the barons meant in terms of restricting the power of King John. She wants her students to reflect upon the meaning of these demands and of their possible consequences on the king's power, the power and roles of the barons, and the common person.

To help her accomplish her goals, Ms. Nance locates a structured resource entitled "Big Bad John" that contains nine of these demands in the form of a short-story episode (see this episode at the end of this chapter). She notices that these demands are listed within a context that provides details of this period in English history and that requires students to consider each demand on its own merits. She will start the unit by providing supplementary information about this period and its characteristics. Later, ideas relative to the English political system and the monarch will be investigated.

Following the introduction of the unit, Ms. Nance provides an overview of the feudal system in England at the beginning of the thirteenth century, with special emphasis on the power and actions of King John. She points out some features of the English way of life, stressing the conditions of the common person and barons under this king. Students are informed that they are to learn the details surrounding the signing of the Magna Carta, or Great Charter, as well as a number of the restrictions and rights this charter included.

After a few questions that clarify certain points of this background information, she assigns students into heterogeneous groups of five members. Students are asked to think of themselves as barons living in England in the year 1215. Students are asked to take a few minutes to review their notes on this period, especially those that refer to the prevailing powers and concept of the king of England and the roles of the barons within the political system. Ms. Nance allows her students six minutes to transport themselves back in time to the England of the days of King John and King Richard the Lion-Hearted.

Each student is then handed a copy of "Big Bad John." Ms. Nance directs students to read the story and to fill in the information requested. She tells them to answer each sheet by themselves as much as they can. Then the entire group will work together to share their responses, clarify ideas presented, and help ensure that all group members comprehend the information and have completed information on the forms provided. Students are to make individual decisions first before interacting as a group. Students are not to complete a new form or worksheet until the entire group has worked together on the previous sheet. Finally, she directs them that they are to reach their final group decision by consensus and not by majority vote. In response to two questions, she describes what it means to reach a decision by consensus. For this activity, she decides not to select group leaders but to allow the groups to take on their own leadership patterns.

To emphasize the importance of the students' participation and study, she announces that many of the important details of the Magna Carta that are to be learned are included in the activity the students are about to complete. The class of "medieval English barons" is then directed to begin reading the story and complete the forms included.

Students read the story, some pausing along the way to ask a group member the meaning of a particular word or to get more information about the rights of a king or baron during this era. As they get to a Predecision Sheet, each student writes information as directed, frequently turning back to the story to find details he or she wants to include. The students in each group wait until everyone is done or about done.

Then each group reviews what was written by each individual and works on clarifying, correcting, eliminating, and adding to what each member wrote. More than one student in each group again goes to the teacher-given notes or to the story to confirm a response or get information to support a decision they have made. Ms. Nance is not surprised that nearly every student is on-task. She smiles as some students refer to each other as Baron Jim, Duchess Rosanne, or Sir Gonzales to better fit the roles they are to take during this activity. One student even talks about what he had heard about King John during his recent journey on a crusade while another mentions the need to return to her manor for fear the lowly peasants might escape into the pest-infested city of London.

As the class period comes to an end, Ms. Nance reviews certain ideas about the political system of England in 1215 that students were ignoring in their discussions. Their homework assignment is to complete their personal choices and fill in the Decision Sheets.

The students proceed on with the episode. Their personal decisions in the context of the story as to the three demands they most want and the three demands they are most willing to give up are made. They have individually determined the reasons for their choices and the possible gains and losses for each choice.

Students arrive the next day and move into their groups of barons from the previous day. As directed, they spend five minutes reviewing the situation they found themselves in at Runnymede and what their task is as a group.

Now the groups spend time trying to reach a consensus as to what three demands they most want and what three demands they are most willing to give up. A lot of time is taken by individuals giving reasons for one choice over another. These reasons frequently concern possible consequences they desire or want to avoid. Ms. Nance has to remind one group that they have lost track of the era in which they are living. "They didn't have computers in 1215," she whispers to a student. In another group she hears four barons threaten to invade the manor of a fifth baron should he join forces with King John after the Charter is signed.

After twenty minutes, the groups are directed to stop their discussions. (Ms. Nance is quite aware that the final decisions are not as important here as is the opportunity for students to reconsider the important content as they move toward making their decisions in the public forum of their group discussion.)

Each group takes a minute or two to announce to the class what decisions it made and why they made the choices they made. The groups also mention how their group operated toward making a final decision. Facts and notions about the political system of England at the time are clarified or corrected. Students respond to ten questions Ms. Nance selects to guide their reflection of the situation they have studied. Ms. Nance follows this discussion with new information to supplement the information that was in the episode. Students are told that all nine of the demands or rules they considered were actually included and that John did eventually put his seal on the agreement. However, this document virtually ignored about 75 percent of the population.

She decides not to review the decision-making strategy students used during this episode or the positive and negative behaviors that students used during their work in their respective groups. She expects to do this after students complete each of the next four episodes planned for the unit. Over the next three days, Ms. Nance asks four or five questions each day concerning the Magna Carta and other details relative to the political system of England at the time.

At the end of the unit, the students take individual academic tests aligned with the outcome objectives targeted for this unit.[4]

The story just completed is a frequent scene in classrooms where these episodes are used. Once the students are organized into groups and begin the reading of the episode, the teacher moves into the role of monitoring and assisting student progress through the steps described explicitly within the story. Of course, what occurs before and following each episode may vary in length of time or depth of information, thus allowing for individual teacher differences, the needs of the students, and the content being studied.

Furthermore, with appropriate guidance, teachers like Ms. Nance are able to construct their own episodes to meet their unique needs.

---

[4] Earlier chapters provide details concerning how a teacher may also assign bonus points for individual and group achievement as a result of student involvement in these episodes.

Questions Regarding the Use of This Strategy and Relevant Episodes

What Areas of Student Learning Outcomes Are Appropriate for This Strategy?

From personal observations and extensive feedback from teachers who have used episodes based on this approach, appropriately structured episodes are likely to lead to the following positive results:

- increased comprehension of academic content and social studies events

- increased retention of content-specific information

- increased voluntary participation in academic tasks by slow learners and minority students

- improved attitudes about the value of the social studies course

- improved abilities to work with others within a group setting

- increased time spent on-task to complete these academic episodes in contrast to time students spend on reading textbook selections on the same topic

- increased interest in the subject matter and in participating in class activities and study

- improved self-image of students as students

- increased on-task academic talk among students in small groups

This list is not complete. One note to support the effects of these episodes is that teachers in the high schools in Tempe, Arizona, who participated in the experimental study in which earlier versions of this episode format were used still use those episodes as well as many others developed by the author since then.

In What Subject Areas May This Approach and Relevant Episodes Be Used?

This approach and its accompanying episodes are applicable to all content areas in the social studies, behavioral sciences, and the humanities as well as to integrated social studies topics and issues. This approach is particularly appropriate in situations in which the content can be arranged within short-story formats to facilitate active student involvement and small-group work.

At What Levels of Schooling May This Strategy and Related Episodes Be Used?

These small-group decision episodes may be used from primary grades through graduate-level university classes and within in-service staff development environments. Of course, such factors as the complexity of the topic chosen, the students' reading abilities, and the time available will affect how well students will complete an episode in any particular course at a given grade level.

What Amount of Class Time Is Needed to Complete an Episode?

Major factors that affect the length of time needed for successful completion of an episode for this strategy include: (a) the breadth or difficulty of the content selected to be learned; (b) the length of the story to be read; (c) the number of Predecision and Decision Sheets that must be completed and discussed; (d) the amount of time students need to complete their discussions; and (e) the number of students in each group. An episode could extend from as brief a time as one class period to three to five days. Even when the teacher is very familiar with this strategy and students are accomplished in the use of these episodes, the amount of time students may need on a particular episode may still vary from what the teacher expects.

Epilogue

Unfortunately, few decision-making activities currently available to social studies teachers possess all the components needed to be consistent with this approach. All too often, teachers use very incomplete and nonacademic decision-making activities and expect them to work as cooperative learning strategies. As this chapter and its sample episodes reveal, not all decision-making activities are created equal. In fact, few activities posited as highly effective will generate the positive student outcomes likely from episodes designed like those described here.

This cooperative learning approach is unique in that nearly all of its components are manifested in the episodes that are created and in the manner in which students, as individuals and as members of a group, are required to think and work as they progress through the tasks integrated into the short-story episodes. When accompanied by teacher formation of heterogeneous groups, sufficient time, supportive teacher monitoring, and appropriate follow-up activities, these episodes generate results that are compatible with widely used cooperative learning strategies.

The structure and components for the episodes in this approach, as a cooperative learning alternative, evolved over three years. More years were spent refining these components so that when constructed according to the guidelines, nearly all students cannot complete the episodes without sharing, cooperating to help one another comprehend and learn, working together as a group, and learning the academic content targeted. In effect, the episodes are designed to guide cooperative learning tasks as students progress to attain a collaborative consensus solution to a contrived problem.[5]

Finally, this chapter was not written to describe how to design episodes such as the ones provided here. Step-by-step guidelines for generating the short-story episodes require much more space than available in this chapter. Instead, a strategy that enables students to meet cooperative learning expectations within carefully constructed small-group short-story episodes was presented as a viable option for teachers seeking an alternative approach to cooperative learning instruction in the social studies classroom.

---

[5] Nearly all the episodes may be completed without having students complete written responses to all the Predecision Forms or having students reach a group decision by consensus. When these are allowed, the teacher moves away from the strong tie-in with cooperative learning and converts these episodes into activities in which students primarily cooperate to complete the assignment. While many positive results *may* occur in such situations, the most powerful and enduring results occur as these episodes are used as described, along with teachers ensuring that the other elements of cooperative learning described in the chapter are also included.

Sample Episodes

The episodes on the following pages were originally developed with the assistance of Nancy Webster-Miller for use in her seventh-grade history classes in Columbus, Mississippi. Nearly all students were reading two or more grades below grade level. Her success with this and other similar activities convinced her of the effectiveness of this approach to instruction. Other episodes like those featured here, along with lesson plans, are available from the author. Incidentally, these episodes have been highly successful in sixth-grade to graduate-level classrooms, and in in-service teacher workshops, gifted education programs, and advanced placement courses. Teachers may design and create their own episodes to fit the subject matter content, outcome objectives, and concepts they have selected for students to attain. The details on how to construct such episodes are beyond the scope of this chapter.

Big Bad John

The year is 1215. You are a baron living in England during the rule of King John. King John has acted like a tyrant—a king who often does not obey the laws. The people of England view him as selfish, greedy, and only interested in using his position to benefit his friends and himself.

There is plentiful evidence that he has acted in ways consistent with the people's view of him. He has punished people without allowing them a trial. He has collected taxes from the poor—often selling their property to get the tax money. He has levied heavy taxes on barons he dislikes and few taxes on his friends. He has taxed people as he wanted. He has even refused to ask his council of barons, the Great Council, for permission to raise taxes. In every way, King John has acted above the law to get what he can't get using the laws properly. To make matters worse, he has selected people very much like himself to carry out his orders.

A large portion of the population of England is very unhappy with King John. As a baron, you too are upset because King John has not obeyed the law. Other barons agree with you. Most of the barons have become sick and tired of the way the king has acted. The feeling among the population, including many barons, is that now is the time to limit this king and all future kings in their abuse and misuse of royal power.

You decide to meet with a number of barons to write up a set of rules for the king to follow. Your group decides to make the king sign the rules by forcing him to agree to obey and enforce the list of rules. The nine rules you have agreed upon as a group are:

1. The king may not collect any taxes without the permission of the Great Council of Barons.

2. The king cannot think up any new or special taxes and begin collecting them without the permission of the council.

3. The king cannot take anyone's property without paying a fair price to the owner for the property.

4. The king cannot take bribes (payments from people so that they can get what they want from the king or get special favors from the king).

5. The king cannot put people in prison or jail unless they have had a trial by jury (peers) and been sentenced by the court.

6. The king has to obey the laws just like everyone else in England.

7. The king cannot force people to go to war in another country when they don't want to go to war.

8. The king must stop interfering in Church affairs by telling priests and bishops what to do and say.

9. The king must stop granting special favors and privileges to barons who like him while treating barons unfairly who don't like him.

After some hard work and debate, the group of barons agrees to these rules.*

As a group, you are able to surround King John on a field near Runnymede. John refused and still refuses to sign the agreement. He says he will not be forced to obey the law. He says a king can break the law when and if he wants. King John threatens to have all the barons arrested and their leaders imprisoned.

After several days, John says he will agree to sign the charter, but that he will not follow all the rules. He asks the barons to take some of the rules out. Meanwhile, the king has received word that his army is approaching. If the army arrives, then you and the other barons will either have to fight or surrender.

Suppose King John offers you a compromise. He says he will agree to follow three of the rules immediately. He will think about three other rules that he might accept later. But three of the nine rules he will never follow under any conditions. As barons, you can agree to his wishes or continue to demand that all nine rules be accepted. To wait any longer, you and your fellow barons would only run the risk of fighting the king's army and losing all nine rules included in this charter.

The barons agree to the king's compromise plan. Also, you agree that if his army does not show up, you will continue to demand he agree to all nine rules.

---

* This set of rules will eventually be called the Great Charter or its Latin equivalent, *Magna Carta*.

To follow the king's plan, your group agrees to select:

1. The three rules you believe the king must follow. These three rules you believe are the most important for you and for all of England. These three rules the king must follow and enforce fairly.

2. The three rules you believe are not that important and which you will give up in order to make sure the first three rules are followed. These rules are important but are not that important. These will be the rules the king said he would never agree to or would ever enforce.

3. The three remaining rules that the king has agreed to consider at a later time. He may or may not ever agree to these rules.

Stop here. Before going any further take time to review the above. Then answer these questions for yourself and as part of your group.

- *Within the feudal system of England, what were the roles, duties, and obligations of a baron?*

- *As described in this story so far, what is the present situation for the barons? As a baron, what do you want to accomplish?*

- *As a group of barons, what have you agreed to do?*

Share your answers to these questions before going on to complete the Predecision Sheets on your own. Make sure all the barons in the group have clear, adequate answers to these questions before moving on.

Teacher's Note. Have students complete any two of the three Predecision Sheets shown on the next pages. (Provide each student with one copy of each of the sheets you select.) Hand each student a copy of Decision Sheet 1 and each group one copy of Decision Sheet 2. Be sure that you delete this note from the copy of the episode you give each student to complete.

Predecision Sheet 1: Big Bad John

To be completed by each student as an individual baron.

In the space provided below, write in at least one possible good and one possible bad result or consequence of each of the nine rules.

Proposed Rule	Possible Good Results	Possible Bad Results
1.		
2.		
3.		
4.		
5.		
6.		
7.		
8.		
9.		

Once each person in the group has written a possible good and bad result in each space, share your responses with each member of your group. Add to your list any results suggested by the other barons. Explain each of the results you listed to the group. Take steps to make sure that each baron in your group comprehends all the results suggested.

Predecision Sheet 2: Big Bad John

To be completed by each student as an individual baron.

In the space provided below, write in at least one possible advantage and disadvantage of each of the nine rules *for the common people of England*.

Proposed Rule	Possible Advantages	Possible Disadvantages
1.		
2.		
3.		
4.		
5.		
6.		
7.		
8.		
9.		

Once each person in the group has written a possible advantage and disadvantage in each space, share your responses with each member of your group. Add to your list any advantages and disadvantages suggested by the other barons. Explain each of the statements you listed to the group. Take steps to make sure that each baron in your group comprehends all the advantages and disadvantages suggested.

Predecision Sheet 3: Big Bad John

To be completed by each student as an individual baron.

In the space provided below, write in at least one possible advantage and disadvantage of each of the nine rules *for the barons*.

Proposed Rule	Possible Advantages	Possible Disadvantages
1.		
2.		
3.		
4.		
5.		
6.		
7.		
8.		
9.		

Once each person in the group has written a possible advantage and disadvantage in each space, share your responses with each member of your group. Add to your list any advantages and disadvantages suggested by the other barons. Explain each of the statements you listed to the group. Take steps to make sure that each baron in your group comprehends all the advantages and disadvantages suggested.

Decision Sheet 1: Big Bad John

Before the group decides on its three most-wanted and three least-wanted rules, the barons agree that each baron should first rate these rules as an individual. After this is done, they will begin discussing the rules and make their final choice as a group.

- ▪ *Use the form below to organize these nine rules into three groups: the three you <u>most want</u> to be made into laws and enforced (mark with the letters MW); the three you are willing to <u>give up</u> to get the three you most want (mark with the letters GU); and the three that represent the <u>remaining rules</u> (mark with the letters RR). You may want to approach this task by assigning a 1 in the space next to the rule you want most to keep; a 2 next to the second-most-important rule, and so on until your least-important rule has a 9 next to it. Once done, review these choices before writing the letters MW, RR, and GU.*

- ▪ *Record your decisions on the line to the left of the rules listed below.*

Remember that in making your decisions and in selecting the final three rules that the king will agree to follow, the common people of England may either be helped or hurt by what you decide. However, since you are a baron, you may decide to consider helping the position of the barons before you consider the position of the common people.

The nine rules you have agreed upon as a group are:

_____ 1. The king may not collect any taxes without the permission of the Great Council of Barons.

_____ 2. The king cannot think up any new or special taxes and begin collecting them without the permission of the council.

_____ 3. The king cannot take anyone's property without paying a fair price to the owner for the property.

_____ 4. The king cannot take bribes (payments from people so that they can get what they want from the king or get special favors from the king).

_____ 5. The king cannot put people in prison or jail unless they have had a trial by jury (peers) and been sentenced by the court.

_____ 6. The king has to obey the laws just like everyone else in England.

_____ 7. The king cannot force people to go to war in another country when they don't want to go to war.

_____ 8. The king must stop interfering in Church affairs by telling priests and bishops what to do and say.

_____ 9. The king must stop granting special favors and privileges to barons who like him while treating barons unfairly who don't like him.

The best reason I can give for having my top three choices made into law for the king to follow is:

_____

_____

_____

_____

The best reason I can give for giving up the three rules I am willing to give up is:

_____

_____

_____

_____

Decision Sheet 2: Big Bad John

In the space provided below, your group is to record its final decisions for its three most-wanted and three least-wanted rules. You are to decide by achieving a consensus. You do not vote and decide by majority rule. Rather, all members must agree on the decision for each of the nine rules. All members must also agree on each of the reasons for the group's decision for each rule. In addition, each member must be able to support the group's final decisions.

- Use the form below to organize these nine rules into three groups: the three you <u>most want</u> to be made into laws and enforced (mark with the letters MW); the three you are willing to <u>give up</u> to get the three you most want (mark with the letters GU); and the three that represent the <u>remaining rules</u> (mark with the letters RR).

- Record your decisions on the line to the left of the rules listed below.

The nine rules you have agreed upon as a group are:

_____ 1. The king may not collect any taxes without the permission of the Great Council of Barons.

_____ 2. The king cannot think up any new or special taxes and begin collecting them without the permission of the council.

_____ 3. The king cannot take anyone's property without paying a fair price to the owner for the property.

_____ 4. The king cannot take bribes (payments from people so that they can get what they want from the king).

_____ 5. The king cannot put people in prison or jail unless they have had a trial by jury (peers) and been sentenced by the court.

_____ 6. The king has to obey the laws just like everyone else.

_____ 7. The king cannot force people to go to war in another country when they don't want to go to war.

_____ 8. The king must stop interfering in Church affairs by telling priests and bishops what to do and say.

_____ 9. The king must stop granting special favors and privileges to barons who like him while treating barons unfairly who don't like him.

The best reasons we can give for having our top three choices made into law for the king to follow are:

_____

_____

_____

The best reasons we can give for giving up the three rules we are willing to give up are:

_____

_____

_____

As barons and citizens of England, we expect the following benefits of our actions:

_____

_____

_____

If the king fails to follow these rules, then as barons and citizens of England, we may have to take the following action in the future:

_____

_____

_____

As barons, we may have lost the following things as a result of our actions against the king:

_____

_____

_____

Big Bad John*

Sample follow-up questions to focus and guide inquiry and learning.

1. According to legend, what is the name of the famous outlaw-hero who lived during the time of King John?

2. What is a baron?

3. What is meant by the term *compromise?*

4. Within a feudal system, what is the relationship between a king and a baron?

5. What should be the relationship between a king and the people?

6. In this story, who had more power—the king or the barons?

7. According to this story, in what ways did King John not obey the law?

8. In what ways is a king like a president? A dictator?

9. In what way is it good to have a powerful king rule a country?

10. To what extent should people ever allow a weak king to rule their country?

11. To what extent should people be able to force a king to agree to follow certain rules?

12. If you were King John, would you be upset or pleased by the demands of the barons?

13. Suppose King John agreed to follow all nine rules. Suppose further, that he later followed none of these rules. If this happened, what would be your feelings toward this king?

14. If you were a peasant in England, would you be happy or angry with what the barons were trying to do to your king?

15. In what ways would the Magna Carta be like the Bill of Rights, the amendments to the United States Constitution?

* This episode used by permission of the author.

Letter for Florence

The time period is the Renaissance. The place is Florence, Italy. In the city, life is dangerous. Public officials have openly defied the law. Numerous city workers are known to be corrupt. Robbers, arsonists, beggars, murderers, and blackmailers threaten the safety of the people. The citizens of Florence do not feel safe on the streets. Many do not feel safe even in their homes or businesses. The ruler of Florence, the mayor or "Doge," has just died. His death was unexpected, with rumors that he may have been assassinated.

The leader of the temporary city government, Guido Bernini, must appoint a new ruler or mayor. The position of mayor is important and powerful. The mayor has control over the government, taxes, businesses, education system, and even the army. He is the most powerful person in the city. However, if he does a poor job, he may be killed by an angry mob.

Guido announces that those people who want the job of mayor must write a letter stating why they think they should be mayor. After all the letters have been read, Guido will select the new mayor.

Guido has read the works of Niccolo Machiavelli. He has stated publicly that he believes what Machiavelli has written about what makes a "good" prince. He even has stated that what Florence needs is a "prince" much like that described in Machiavelli's book, *The Prince*. Among the ideas that Guido believes are that:

a. A city should never stand still; it must either expand (grow) or decay (rot).

b. In the real world, power counts far more than lofty ideals. Being nice and worrying about what is right or wrong don't count for much.

c. Only what a ruler does that brings success is important. The idea that a ruler should have a conscience and should consider what is right or moral is ridiculous. A ruler is not bound by any man-made or moral law.

d. Rulers should keep their city together (safe and strong) by whatever means they think necessary and should not be bothered about being honest, fair, just, or honorable.

e. In general, most people are liars and will do anything and everything in order to get what they want.

f. Rulers should use any method no matter how cruel, mean, or ruthless in order to get what they want.

g. During times of peace, a ruler should be making military preparations in case of another war.

h. A ruler should be both feared and loved, but being feared is much more important than being loved.

i. In general, men and women are ungrateful, dishonest, cowardly, and covetous.

j. If you help people and be good to them, they will do what you want them to do.

k. Religion is not important.

Before going further, stop and take time to paraphrase these important ideas of Machiavelli. Make sure everyone in your group comprehends these statements before anyone in the group goes on to complete the story.

_____

_____

_____

_____

_____

_____

_____

_____

_____

_____

_____

Once your group has finished, complete Predecision Sheet 1.

Predecision Sheet 1: Letter for Florence

Imagine you were Guido Bernini. Imagine further a friend has asked you to deliver a lecture at the local university on the ideas of Machiavelli as included in *The Prince*. To help prepare for this lecture, write answers to the following questions:

1. From the ideas of Machiavelli listed in the story and in paraphrased form, what five ideas do you consider to be the most important ones to remember?

    a. _____

    b. _____

    c. _____

    d. _____

    e. _ _____

2. If all of Machiavelli's ideas were accepted by the Doge of Florence,

    a. what would life in the city be like?

    _____

    b. what words would best describe the Doge?

    _____

3. Give at least two reasons why a person would like and actually follow the ideas of Machiavelli.

    _____

    _____

4. Give at least two reasons why a person would reject and avoid following the ideas of Machiavelli.

    _____

    _____

Once everyone in your group has written answers to the above, share your answers with them. Add additional information on your form to fit these four questions. You should also be able to paraphrase the reasons given by other students that are different from your own.

Letter for Florence, *continued*

Lorenzo Verde is a citizen of Florence. He is a wealthy, intelligent, strong, 40-year-old merchant. He has two grown sons. One is a priest and the other is his chief accountant in his merchant business. Because he and his family are "Humanists," they spend some of their money on items of beauty and personal learning.

Fortunately, Lorenzo Verde is wealthy enough to have a group of armed guards that protect his property and the lives of his family. Even with all his money, Lorenzo does not feel very safe.

Three years ago, Lorenzo's wife, Sophia, gave birth to a beautiful daughter—something that Lorenzo had always dreamed of but had not realized. His prayers and dreams were answered with the birth of the baby girl. Sophia became very weak and almost died while giving birth to the baby. For some reason, Sophia never recovered completely. Then, last month, Sophia's condition grew worse.

As she lay dying and with the entire family and many of their friends present, Sophia asked Lorenzo to promise that he would do everything he could do to become the Doge of Florence. She wanted the city to once again be a safe and beautiful place for people to live. She especially wanted her daughter to grow up in such a place. Lorenzo promised to Sophia and everyone else that he would try to become the next Doge of Florence. Shortly afterwards, Sophia died.

Because he is a Humanist, some of the things Lorenzo believes are:

a. A city should be beautiful with architecture in the style of classical Greece.

b. Art is a pleasure in itself. (In medieval times, art was seen as something to be used only to glorify God. No other legitimate purposes were given to art.)

c. Individual accomplishment and learning are important for one's own growth. (In medieval times, only a select few were formally educated or were given the opportunity for personal accomplishments.)

d. Each person should know what is going on in the world and should care about the world and other people.

e. Each person is worthy and important as a human being, and his or her life is valuable.

f. The individual is much more important than the government.

g. New inventions, attitudes in politics, and ways of waging war should be developed and used.

h. Each person should work within the system for beneficial changes. He or she should not just accept whatever is going on.

i. The good life on Earth consists of embracing beauty, comfort, possessions, material objects, etc., rather than rejecting these things in favor of more spiritual things.

j. Human life is important and should be preserved.

k. Changes in the [Catholic] Church must be the result of working within the Church rather than leaving it or trying to destroy it.

Before going any further, stop here and take time to paraphrase these important ideas of the Humanists of the Renaissance. Make sure everyone in your group comprehends these statements before anyone in the group goes on to complete the story.

_____

_____

_____

_____

_____

_____

_____

_____

_____

_____

_____

Once your group has finished, complete Predecision Sheet 2.

Predecision Sheet 2: Letter for Florence

Imagine you were Lorenzo Verde. Imagine further that a friend has asked you to deliver a speech at the steps at your place of business on the ideas of the "Humanists." To help prepare you for this speech, write answers to the following questions:

1. From the ideas of the Humanists listed in the story and in paraphrased form, what five ideas do you consider to be the most important ones to remember?

   a. _____

   b. _____

   c. _____

   d. _____

   e. _____

2. If all of these Humanists' ideas were accepted by the Doge of Florence,
   a. what would life in the city be like?

   _____

   b. what words would best describe the Doge?

   _____

3. Give at least two reasons why a person would like and follow the ideas of the Humanists.

   _____

   _____

4. Give at least two reasons why a person would reject and not follow the Humanists' ideas.

   _____

   _____

Once everyone in your group has written answers to the above, share your answers with them. Add additional information on your form to fit these four questions. You should also be able to paraphrase the reasons given by other students that are different from your own.

Letter for Florence, *continued*

Lorenzo Verde has read Machiavelli's *The Prince* very carefully. He doesn't agree with the author's point of view. To Lorenzo Verde, the ideas of Machiavelli don't agree with the ideas of the Humanists.

Lorenzo Verde knows that the position of Doge of Florence is open. He has read Guido's announcement. If he wants to become the Doge, Lorenzo Verde must write a letter. Lorenzo Verde wants to keep his promise to Sophia. He knows that the letter he writes will either get him selected as the Doge or cost him the position. If he doesn't get the position, he will not be able to make Florence the safe and beautiful city he wants it to become.

However, if he just writes a letter, will he have done *everything he could do* to become the Doge? Would he be keeping his promise to his dead wife Sophia?

You are Lorenzo Verde. You know what you believe. You know that the position of the Doge of Florence is a very powerful political office. You know what a strong person in that office can do to help the city and its people. You know what may happen if someone else gets selected as the Doge. You know what Guido believes. You know that you promised to do what you could to become the next Doge. *You must write a letter*.

As Lorenzo Verde, write your letter to Guido Bernini on Decision Sheet 1. Before you write that letter, answer the questions provided on Predecision Sheet 3.

Once you have completed your individual letter, work with all members of your group to reach a consensus decision. Everyone in the group must agree on the content and wording of this group letter.

Teacher's Note. Have students get together in their small groups after they have completed their individual letters for the purpose of writing one letter to Bernini that represents the consensus of the group. Decision Sheet 2 provides an outline for this assignment. Run off copies of Decision Sheet 2 for each group. Delete this footnote before running off copies of this episode and passing them out to students.

Predecision Sheet 3: Letter for Florence

Before you write the letter as Lorenzo Verde to Guido Bernini, you should take some time to consider what should go into the letter. To help you with your decisions, write answers to the questions below:

1. What reason(s) do you have for writing this letter?

   _____

   _____

2. What do you expect to accomplish by writing this letter?

   _____

   _____

3. What are your expectations for the city of Florence?

   _____

   _____

4. What particular ideas of Machiavelli and/or the Humanists are appropriate for you, as Lorenzo, to include in this letter?

   _____

   _____

5. What particular ideas of Machiavelli and/or the Humanists should you, as Lorenzo, *not include* in this letter?

   _____

   _____

   _____

6. What would your family and friends say were they to read the letter you are planning to write?

   _____

   _____

   _____

   _____

Decision Sheet 1: Letter for Florence

In the space below, write the letter you would write as Lorenzo Verde to Guido Bernini.

Decision Sheet 2: Letter for Florence

In the space below, write a letter to Guido Bernini that represents the decision all members of your group believe must be made in this instance. This decision must be a consensus decision and not one made by democratic voting. Information such as that contained in Predecision Sheet 3 is to be included in this letter. *The bottom of this form must be signed by all members of the group showing that all accept the final decision and letter as written by the group.*

———————
———————
———————

———————
———————
———————

———————————— :

————————————————————
————————————————————
————————————————————
————————————————————
————————————————————
————————————————————
————————————————————

Signatures of group members:

———————————   ———————————
———————————   ———————————
———————————   ———————————

*Letter for Florence**

Sample follow-up questions to focus and guide inquiry and learning.

1. From what is stated, to what extent did Machiavelli say that a ruler was "above the law"?

2. According to the story, what were at least four negative things about living in Renaissance Florence?

3. What is the name of one modern-day person who believes or believed in the same things as Lorenzo Verde?

4. Which ideas of the Humanists are similar to Machiavelli's?

5. If someone like Machiavelli's Prince were to get the position of Doge, what would probably happen to the city of Florence? To men like Lorenzo Verde?

6. If someone who knew of your promise to Sophia read your letter to Guido, would he or she be upset or pleased with you?

7. Would it be better for our nation if our next (or current) president ruled like Machiavelli's Prince or like the Humanists?

8. In what ways are you like the Humanists? Like "the Prince"?

9. For the Prince, power counts more than lofty ideas. In your own words, what does this mean?

10. What is a good definition of the term *power*?

11. Why would a ruler rather be feared than loved?

12. What did the Humanists mean by the "good life"?

13. What is the connection between power and government?

14. According to other sources,
    a. what are five additional important ideas of the Humanists?
    b. what are at least five additional important ideas that characterize a "Prince"?
    c. what are at least five additional characteristics of the city of Florence during the Renaissance period?

15. In your own words, what was the Renaissance?

* This episode used by permission of the author.

References

Casteel, J. D., and R. J. Stahl. 1975. *Value clarification in the classroom: A primer.* Santa Monica, CA: Goodyear.

————. 1989, revised 1992. Doorways to decision-making: A handbook for designing decision-making activities. (Tentative title. Manuscript submitted for publication.)

Hunt, B. S. 1981. Effects of values activities on content retention and attitudes of students in junior high social studies classes. Tempe, AZ: Arizona State University. Unpublished Ph.D. dissertation.

Stahl, N. N., and R. J. Stahl. 1992. Science and society, up close and personal: Decision-making activities for the integrated study of science and society. (Tentative title. Manuscript submitted for publication.)

Stahl, R. J. 1979. A blueprint for designing structured group decision-making episodes: An introductory module. Tempe, AZ: Arizona State University.

————. November, 1979. The effects of values dilemma activities on the content retention and attitudes of social studies students: An empirical investigation based upon the Casteel-Stahl approach to values education. Paper presented at the annual meeting of the National Council for the Social Studies, Portland, OR.

————. 1981. Achieving values and content objectives simultaneously within subject-matter-oriented social studies classrooms. *Social Education* (7, November/December) 580-85.

————. June, 1987. The Casteel-Stahl model as an alternative cooperative learning strategy. Workshop conducted at Curtin University of Technology, Perth, Western Australia.

————. October, 1990. Using small-group decision-making activities to achieve a cooperative learning classroom: A model and examples. Workshop presented at the annual Fall Conference of the Arizona Council for the Social Studies, Mesa, AZ.

Stahl, R. J., P. Hronek, N. Webster-Miller, and A. Shoemake-Netto. 1992. Doorways to the past: Group decision episodes. (Manuscript submitted for publication.)

10.

What Do We Want To Study? How Should We Go About It? Group Investigation in the Cooperative Social Studies Classroom

YAEL SHARAN AND SHLOMO SHARAN

"How can government action reduce pollution?"

"Are the natural resources in our area endangered?"

"Why are teenagers rebellious?"

"How does growing up in the city differ from growing up in the country?"

In each field subsumed under the title of social studies—geography, history, sociology, anthropology, government, and so forth—teams of practitioners and researchers set out to answer questions such as these. The substance of their work deals with how people interact with one another, with their social environment, and with the institutions in society. The method by which they carry out their work requires cooperation among people, frequently across disciplinary boundaries. It is paradoxical to have students in social studies classrooms sit isolated from one another and study about social issues in a totally *asocial* way!

Moreover, the classroom itself is a miniature social organization. Cooperative learning methods take this fact into account and incorporate the social dimensions of the classroom into their organizational strategies. Cooperative learning enables teachers and students to collaborate in creating the ways and means of organizing how they go about achieving academic goals. Group Investigation in particular encourages

257

students' initiative and responsibility for their work, as individuals, as members of study groups, and as members of an entire class.

Overview of the Group Investigation Strategy

What Is Group Investigation?

A Group Investigation project begins when the teacher presents a challenging, multifaceted problem to the class and invites students to suggest a topic they want to study in order to explore the problem and the issues it suggests. Working together, students sort their questions into subtopics and form small groups on the basis of common interest in a subtopic. Group members cooperate in planning their inquiry and in carrying out their plans. Their plans generally involve a division of work among group members so that the investigation combines independent study as well as work in pairs and in small groups (from three to five students). When they complete their search, groups integrate and summarize their findings and decide how to present the essence of their work to their classmates. Throughout the process, teachers facilitate the development of social and academic skills that make it possible to investigate a topic in groups (Joyce and Weil, 1986; Miel, 1952; Sharan and Hertz-Lazarowitz, 1980; Sharan and Sharan, 1990, 1992; Thelen, 1981).

Why Group Investigation?

Instead of presenting a topic for students to study as the teacher organizes it, Group Investigation gives students the opportunity to seek information, discuss and analyze it, and relate it to knowledge and ideas they already have. Thereby they transform this information into new knowledge for themselves. Instead of being passive consumers of others' ideas and information, students take an active part in choosing topics for study, in identifying and selecting sources of information, and in deciding on ways to organize, interpret, and summarize their findings. Group Investigation maximizes students' opportunities to:

- ask questions about what interests them.
- search for answers in a wide variety of sources.

- plan together the content and process of their inquiry.

- interpret the answers in light of their personal experiences and prior knowledge.

- interact with their peers in a constant exchange of information and ideas.

Group Investigation incorporates the basic features of cooperative learning. At all stages of the investigation, group members meet to discuss their findings. Together they clarify, expand, and modify their understanding of the material. They help one another, share ideas and information, and work together to achieve their common goal.

There is one more element of cooperation that is required in order to implement Group Investigation: cooperative planning. Students should have had some practice in cooperative planning before undertaking a Group Investigation project. Actually they engage in a great deal of spontaneous planning outside of school when they plan games or social events. With systematic guidance, they will be able to apply this skill to learning situations.

Before introducing a Group Investigation project, the teacher should make sure the students have had some experience in short-term learning tasks based on cooperative interaction. Many of the ways to provide this experience are described in other chapters in this book.

The next section describes cooperative planning and demonstrates how to develop it as part of the social studies curriculum. A later part of the chapter describes Group Investigation in detail and presents an example of an investigation project completed in a social studies classroom.

Cooperative Planning

At the heart of the students' involvement at every stage of Group Investigation are the plans group members formulate together. Together they specify the steps they will take in order to study what it is they want to know about a topic. During the planning discussions, the rule is that everyone must have a turn and that all suggestions are to be heard without rejection. One group member serves as recorder and notes all suggestions. Another group member serves as discussion leader and guides the group in the decision-making process.

While discussing their plans together, students listen to one another; exchange ideas, information, and points of view; elaborate and expand on one another's ideas; and get feedback on their understanding of the material.

Students also make independent and joint choices about how to proceed with their work, how to divide the work among themselves, and how to integrate everyone's contributions into a group product. These choices determine the goals and scope of their inquiry, thus giving them a great deal of control over their behavior. This control is a major component of the motivation that sustains them throughout the project. Cooperative planning of class and group goals draws additional motivating power from the interaction among group members.

Developing Cooperative Planning Strategies and Skills

The combined intellectual, motivational, and social features of cooperative planning develop and improve with practice and teacher guidance. At every grade level and in every subject, teachers can make cooperative planning a part of the ongoing repertoire of learning activities. Teachers can provide opportunities for the class to engage in planning discussions as a whole, in pairs, or in small groups. Cooperative planning can be practiced in any of the following ways.

Planning a Nonacademic Activity

There are a number of activities or tasks that students might plan together, such as the program for a class party, the questions to ask a visitor, the agenda for a student council meeting, the care of a class pet, or an exhibit at the end of a unit. Planning these events provides students the necessary practice in anticipating the sequence of actions that will help them reach their goal. They must also anticipate problems that may spoil their plans and suggest ways of dealing with them.

Planning How To Locate Information in a Variety of Sources

Where should we look if we want to plan a trip to another state? Where can we find information about the customs of another nation? How can we learn about the changes in population in our city? With the teacher's guidance students learn that in addition to their textbooks there is an endless pool of resources available to them—people, sites, stamps, magazines, books of all kinds, stores, factories, offices, maps, television programs, and so forth. Many of these sources are part of the students' lives outside of school. Incorporating them in their schoolwork helps lower the barriers between the two worlds and is compatible with the goals of the social studies curriculum.

Planning a Study Task

Students participate in determining what they will study and how they plan to go about it. They anticipate and specify the actions that will enable them to reach their goal. Individually, in pairs, and in groups of three to five members, students have to ask:

1. What will we study?

2. What resources do we have?

3. How will we divide the work among us?

4. How will we summarize our findings?

Answers to these planning questions are determined either by (a) all groups when tackling the same study task or (b) each group undertaking to study a different task. An example of each of these planning options is described below.

All Groups Plan the Same Assignment. Mr. Hopkins' seventh-grade geography class was learning about data gathering. He conducted an introductory discussion with the class and then showed the telecast *Gathering Data*, from TV Ontario's series on geography skills. The program clarifies basic terms and demonstrates a variety of ways that data can be gathered and recorded.

In order to have his students experience data gathering as well as cooperative planning, Mr. Hopkins posed two questions: How were methods of transportation in the 1930s different from those we use today? Most important, what have these changes meant for our lives?

He asked the students to form groups at random and gave them an assignment that incorporated planning questions 2, 3, and 4 from the list above. The initial instructions were:

> Plan where to gather data about methods of transportation in the 1930s and today.

Think of three kinds of data: data you can get by observation, data gathered by others, and data gathered and summarized by others.

Groups spent a whole period generating ideas about where they might find information. Everyone's ideas were heard and recorded by one group member. Each group made a chart of possible sources they agreed upon. Toward the end of the period the teacher asked the groups to divide the work among their members so that individuals or pairs would seek data from different sources. Mr. Hopkins allotted the class a week for gathering data and asked that each group member write a short summary of what he or she learned.

Students gathered data from books, newspapers, old movies, stamps, and so forth. A representative from each group formed a team and interviewed several veteran car salespeople. One group went to the public library to look up information in magazines from the 1930s, and to find, at Mr. Hopkins' suggestion, what material the library had from the Smithsonian Institution in Washington. Members also went to a local museum to see an exhibition of old railroad cars and automobiles.

When they completed their search, Mr. Hopkins asked group members to share their findings with one another and write a paragraph summarizing the changes that have taken place in methods of transportation since the 1930s and another paragraph to indicate some implications of these changes for our lives today.

For the final step in this assignment, Mr. Hopkins asked each group to plan how to present their findings to the class. Several groups prepared posters of photographs and tables depicting the changes. One group set up a display of model cars, trains, and planes. Another group prepared two separate posters. One showed "How They Traveled in the 1930s" and one showed "How We Travel Today."

The final activity in this project was to get a glimpse of what the future might bring. Mr. Hopkins arranged for the class to meet with a team of researchers in the local university to hear about their efforts to develop an electric car.

Each Group Plans a Different Assignment. As part of their study of geography skills, Mr. Hopkins taught his class map-reading skills. He combined this unit with the opportunity to practice another aspect of cooperative planning, i.e., students generate their own questions for study. After learning how distance is measured and recorded on different types of maps, Mr. Hopkins asked his class to consider the problem: How can maps be useful to us? In investigating and then formulating an answer to this question, students completed the following tasks.

Determining Subtopics. Each student wrote down all the ways he or she thought maps might be useful. Pairs of students compared what they wrote and, finally, two pairs compared notes. One student from each foursome reported their ideas as Mr. Hopkins wrote them on the board. He then asked the class to sort the list of ideas into categories.

This procedure resulted in five categories: 1. selecting a route; 2. finding natural resources; 3. locating historical and archaeological sites; 4. learning about the weather; and 5. selecting vacation sites. These categories became the subtopics of the general problem.

Forming Groups and Asking Questions. Unlike the former task, this time groups were formed on the basis of interest in a subtopic. Students signed up to study the subtopic of their choice and spent one period planning what to study. They chose one member to record their questions. Then they noted how they might find resource materials for their inquiry. Mr. Hopkins helped out with some suggestions based on what he had prepared before the inquiry began. Group members divided the work among themselves.

Searching for Answers. Groups spent two class periods searching through all the materials for answers to their respective questions. Available to them were encyclopedias, various textbooks, a catalog of maps, games based on maps, and many different types of maps. At the end of each period, group members met to discuss their findings. They shared their information by describing what they had learned and explaining whatever was unclear. Each group member could see what he or she contributed to the group's search, and what others contributed to his or her understanding of the topic.

Summarizing Their Findings. In the third class period, groups summarized the information they had gathered. Each group had a good idea of how useful different types of maps can be. They prepared a short statement describing the ways maps can be useful in the particular category they studied.

Presenting Their Findings. All groups planned how to present their findings to the class. They chose what they considered to be the best way to convey what they had learned. The presentations included a map of several different routes that lead from their town to Disney World; a large puzzle of a map highlighting the state's natural resources; a pictorial map of all the archaeological sites in the state; a poster showing different kinds of weather maps and their uses; and a vacation packet for each class member containing a map of different vacation sites in the area. Mr. Hopkins capped the presentations with a short whole-class discussion to integrate what the class had learned.

Individual Evaluation. Mr. Hopkins gave the class a test based on the new facts and terms students had acquired during the course of their investigation. He also wanted to test the students' abilities to integrate their new knowledge and apply it in a new situation. Therefore, the test included a map of a city that the students had not seen before. They were asked to write whatever they could learn from looking at the map and to mark a route for a tour of the main sites of the city.

Components of Cooperative Planning

Although there is no predetermined specific sequence by which teachers should develop cooperative planning skills, it is important to make sure that students have ample opportunities to practice them all. A checklist of the components of cooperative planning is helpful. When the teacher plans an assignment, he or she can check off those components of the task for which students will be responsible. The checklist should include the following items:

___ 1. group composition

___ 2. procedures

___ 3. assignment of roles in the group

___ 4. questions that will be studied

___ 5. subtopics

___ 6. resource materials

___ 7. type of presentation

___ 8. content of the presentation

Teachers must judge which components of cooperative planning to incorporate in their teaching and how often to do so, based on the amount of time available, on the level of their students' planning skills, and on the nature of the subject matter. Obviously, simple tasks do not require elaborate planning. When teachers feel that their students have had substantial practice in cooperative planning, they may expand the acquired skills by applying them to the systematic implementation of a Group Investigation project.

Group Investigation in Action: A Classroom Example

What the Group Investigation strategy might look like in an actual classroom is illustrated in the scenario that follows. The reader should note how the example illustrates the guidelines and descriptions provided above as well as those at the end of this chapter.

Choosing the Problem To Investigate

A critical element affecting the success of the Group Investigation strategy is the problem that is presented for students to research and address. The problem may stem from the students' particular interest or may be related to a timely issue. Most often it is part of the curriculum. The teachers in our example chose a problem from their content area that was suitable for cooperative inquiry because it was a multifaceted one: it called for more than a single answer. Moreover, the answers could be found in a variety of resource materials. Another factor to consider when choosing a problem is its *relevance to the students' lives in and out of school*. The issue put to the class should be one that in some way concerns the larger society.

Preparing for a Group Investigation Task

Mr. Swain and Ms. Lulkin, tenth-grade social studies teachers in a Milwaukee junior high school, teamed up to plan a unit on the environmental problems of Lake Michigan. They began their preparation by asking the school librarian what was available on the subject, and spoke with the head of the science department to see what resources she could recommend. They found a few pertinent articles in back copies of *National Geographic* magazine. They wrote away to all the agencies mentioned in the articles they read, asking for written information, pictures, films, and so forth. The more they found out, the greater their enthusiasm for the subject. At one point the teachers even went to interview some people who lived on the lake front, to learn firsthand what problems they faced.

From time to time during their planning sessions, the two teachers voiced the wish that their students would also find the subject so compelling. "After all," they said, "it's the environment they live in!" One day Mr. Swain suggested that they have their students go through the same experience: "Let's hear what the kids want to know. They can ask questions and look for answers. They can use the material we've collected . . . and maybe they'll find more." Ms. Lulkin felt that it would be interesting to see what the students made of it all. The two teachers eventually decided to conduct a group investigation of the general problem: What are the environmental problems of Lake Michigan?

Introducing the Project

In order to arouse the students' interest, the teachers brought many of the materials to class two weeks *before* the beginning of the project. All the materials were placed on a table under a sign that read:

> Look through the magazines, pictures, and brochures. Which pictures are familiar to you? Have you been to any of the places you see or read about? Try to get an idea of what you'd like to know in order to understand more about what threatens Lake Michigan.

Teacher's Role During the Group Investigation Lesson

The teacher has two major roles in the course of a Group Investigation project: to guide and facilitate the process of investigation and to help maintain norms of cooperative behavior. How did Mr. Swain and Ms. Lulkin carry out these roles?

Guiding the Students and Facilitating the Process of Investigation. Ms. Lulkin's and Mr. Swain's preparation was by no means a waste of time. They were now able to convey their genuine enthusiasm for the subject. Because they were aware of many aspects of the general problem, it was easy for them to help their students make the connection between their attempts to formulate questions and the key concepts of the general topic. The teachers' initial search for material also enabled them to suggest a broad range of resources for their classes. As the investigation progressed, the teachers continued to help their students make plans and carry them out.

Helping Maintain Cooperative Norms of Behavior. The teachers also helped groups interact effectively. They circulated from group to group to see where help was needed. They intervened when they felt that groups couldn't come to an agreement or when they noticed that not all group members were participating. In these cases they chose one of several ways to help the students:

- They asked questions that encouraged students to suggest their own solutions. One such question was: What is a good way to make sure everyone gets a turn?

- They supported and reinforced the students' efforts to solve their own problems.

- They suggested that a group take a short break and conduct an exercise that would strengthen their ability to listen to one another, paraphrase one another's comments, reach consensus, and so forth (Cohen, 1986; Graves and Graves, 1990; Kagan, 1989).

Bringing Closure to the First Phase of the Group Investigation

At the end of the two-week period, the teachers arranged for the classes to visit two of the families the two teachers had interviewed. The visit was the culminating activity of the first phase of Group Investigation strategy. The latter phase involved students taking charge of the investigation after the problem has been posed by the teachers.

The Stages of Group Investigation Once a Problem Has Been Posed

The six stages of the Group Investigation strategy that follow served as general guidelines for the continued implementation of the project.

Stage 1. The Whole Class Determines Subtopics and Organizes into Research Groups. After the teacher presents the general problem, students scan sources, propose questions, and sort the questions and related issues into categories. The categories become subtopics. Students form and join the particular group that is studying the subtopic of their choice.

Stage 2. Groups Plan Their Investigations. Group members plan their investigation cooperatively, including deciding what they will investigate, how they will go about it, and how they will divide the work among themselves.

Stage 3. Groups Carry Out Their Investigations. Group members gather, organize, and analyze information from several sources. They pool their findings and form conclusions. Group members discuss their work in progress in order to exchange ideas and information, and expand, clarify, and integrate their findings.

Stage 4. Groups Plan Their Presentations. Group members determine the main idea of their investigation. They plan how to present their findings. Group representatives meet as a steering committee to coordinate plans for final presentation to the class.

Stage 5. Groups Make Their Whole-Class Presentations. Group members present their findings to the class in a variety of forms: skits, quizzes, role play, posters, and so forth. The audience evaluates the clarity and appeal of each presentation.

Stage 6. Teacher and Students Evaluate Their Projects. Students share feedback about their investigations and about their affective experiences. Teachers and students collaborate to evaluate individual, group, and classwide learning. Evaluation includes assessment of higher-level thinking processes.

Let's follow Ms. Lulkin's class as they plan and carry out the investigation of the problem put to them.

Stage 1. The Whole Class Determines Subtopics and Organizes into Research Groups. Scanning the materials and visiting the families aroused the students' interest. A few even found some relevant material at home and brought it to class. Ms. Lulkin introduced the cooperative planning part of the investigation. She asked each student to write what he or she wanted to find out in order to know more about the problems of Lake Michigan. Minutes later the students paired up, compared lists, and compiled one comprehensive list. After ten minutes, the pairs formed quartets and again compared their lists and combined their questions.

A representative of each group read the final list, taking care not to repeat questions already mentioned. Ms. Lulkin led the class in the final step of this stage, the sorting of the questions into subtopics. She wrote these on the chalkboard and asked each student which subtopic he or she was most interested in investigating. Everyone signed up for the subtopic he or she found most appealing, and groups were formed accordingly. Ms. Lulkin photocopied the questions for each student.

Stage 2. Groups Plan Their Investigations. When the students came to class the next day they found that the desks were organized in small clusters. On one desk in each cluster was a card with one question, such as: What are the dangers of the rising water level of Lake Michigan? How are people affected by the pollution of Lake Michigan? Why is the lake considered a "toxic hot spot"?

Each student knew where to go to join his or her study group. Groups spent one period discussing their ideas about the scope of their inquiry. They referred to the list of questions generated by the whole class in Stage 1. They chose those questions they felt best reflected their respective interests and at the same time were most relevant to their subtopic. As the discussion proceeded, a few questions were deleted and a few were added, as each group determined exactly what it would investigate.

Dividing the work. The cooperative planning at this stage allowed each group member to choose to investigate what seemed most interesting about the subtopic and in the way that suited him or her most. Some preferred to look up information in reference books; others chose to interview people. Some felt that they would learn best by studying diagrams and maps.

Choosing group roles. Each group also chose members to fill the following roles:

Group leader:	To lead all discussions and help the group stay on task.
Secretary:	To keep a record of everyone's specific area of investigation and remind group members of the timetable for reporting back to the group.
Resource person:	To obtain the resources the group requires.

Groups also chose one member to represent them on the steering committee that will meet toward the end of Stage 4, in order to coordinate the groups' whole-class presentations.

In her role as facilitator, Ms. Lulkin went from group to group and offered help to those who needed it. One group was unhappy with its original plan, so the teacher discussed alternatives and helped members redirect their goal. When she saw that one group was struggling with a plan that was too ambitious, she helped it formulate a more realistic plan. She also helped draw out one particularly shy student who was having difficulty expressing what he wanted to investigate.

All groups' final plans were posted so that the class could see how each individual's question related to the group's subtopic and how each group's subtopic related to the class's general problem.

Stage 3. Groups Carry Out Their Investigations. This stage lasted three weeks, as groups carried out their plans. They located information, organized it, and conducted several discussions to interpret and integrate their findings.

At the beginning of every session, Ms. Lulkin reviewed what each group had planned for that day. Their activities varied from day to day. Students went to the library; wrote interim summaries; prepared questions for an interview; read magazine articles, newspapers, and books; drew diagrams; and discussed a point with a friend or with the teacher. At the end of every class period, groups convened to share their findings and see what sense they could make of them.

Ms. Lulkin circulated among the groups. She helped groups find suitable material and reinforced study skills and cooperative interaction when and as necessary. She helped one group find an expert to help answer the question: Why is Lake Michigan considered a "toxic hot spot"?

At first, the five students in the group that addressed this question divided the subtopic into three parts: wind borne toxics, marine parasites, and toxics in the food chain. Further along in their reading they broadened the scope of their inquiry by uncovering three more causes of contamination: rainfall runoff, leaching through subsoil, and, unexpectedly, dredging. As they learned more about these causes, the group members discussed the relative impact of each cause on the toxification of the lake. When Ms. Lulkin walked over to see how they were doing, she heard them debating which phenomenon was the most threatening and what should be done about it.

She suggested that they invite someone from the state Department of Public Health to tell them what action had been taken. The students agreed and prepared specific questions to ask the expert. During their discussion with the official they learned about the Great Lakes toxic-waste agreement and how difficult it was to enforce it. Undaunted by the enormity of the problem, members of this group wrote a summary of their findings wherein they detailed the sources of contamination of Lake Michigan and recommended ways of controlling toxic pollution.

Stage 4. Groups Plan Their Presentations. Group discussions at this stage clarified what students considered the most significant findings of their investigation. Their next task was to plan how to present these findings in a way that would be both instructive and appealing to the whole class. Ms. Lulkin helped those who had trouble pinpointing the main idea of their combined findings. She also convened the steering committee and heard what materials each group needed in order to make its presentation. She asked committee members to make sure that the presentations included everyone in each group. Together the teacher and the committee coordinated the schedule of presentations.

Stage 5. Groups Make Their Whole-Class Presentations. The class assembled as a whole so that each group could contribute its expertise to the class's understanding of the general topic. Each student knew what his or her group had learned; now they could see what other groups could add to their knowledge.

The presentations illuminated the different aspects of the environmental problems of Lake Michigan. One group played taped interviews with people whose homes were destroyed by storm erosion. Another group showed a chart of all the fish and wildlife endangered by the lake's pollution. They distributed leaflets obtained from the State Department of Health detailing those species of fish that were safe to eat and those that were dangerous. The students who had investigated the causes of the toxic hot spots drew diagrams explaining each cause. They pasted the diagrams around the map of the lake. One by one, members of this group expanded on the specific cause of toxification he or she had studied. Another group focused on the way the increasing pollution endangered the recreational facilities of the lake. They showed slides obtained from the Department of Parks and took turns describing how pollution affects bird watching, fishing, camping, boating, and so forth. After each presentation, the audience commented on its clarity and appeal. The progression of Group Investigation projects is illustrated in Figure 10-1.

At the end of Stage 5, Ms. Lulkin and Mr. Swain teamed up again, and decided to have their classes collaborate in the production of an interactive project entitled *The Water Quality Magazine*. Both teachers felt that in this way each class would contribute its newly acquired specialization to the understanding of their common concern, the problems of Lake Michigan. The editorial board consisted of representatives from all groups.

Groups from both classes contributed their summaries, along with pictures, diagrams, and charts. Even though both classes had undertaken to investigate the same general problem, each class had emphasized different aspects. Within classes, each group produced a unique summary that reflected the group members' interests and showed how they had interpreted their findings. The magazine provided a varied and comprehensive overview of the environmental problems of Lake Michigan.

Figure 10-1 *The Group Investigation Project*

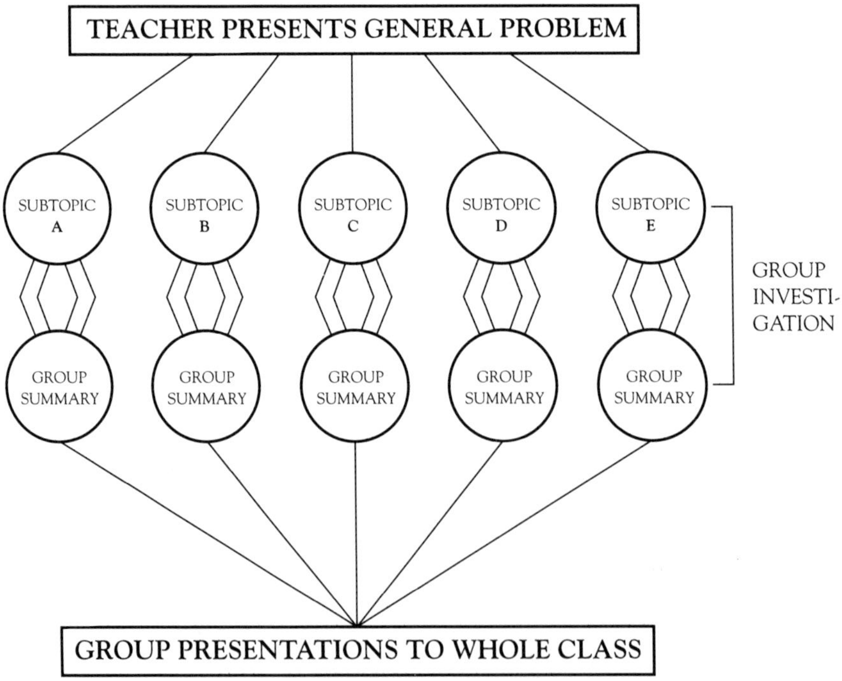

Stage 6. Teacher and Students Evaluate Their Projects. The students in Ms. Lulkin's class didn't have to wait till the end of the project to find out how they were doing. Throughout the project the teacher conducted ongoing evaluations as she circulated from group to group, talking with students about their academic and social progress and problems.

Individual evaluation took the form of a test based on *The Water Quality Magazine.* A copy was given to every student, and the class had a week to study its contents. The test included factual questions as well as a short essay question: What are your recommendations for improving the environment of Lake Michigan? The essays demonstrated the extent to which students had integrated the material and applied it to the solution of the problem.

Group Investigations Vary in Practice but Follow Identical Guidelines

This project illustrated above is but one example of how Group Investigation can be carried out. Huhtala and Coughlin (1991) describe a Group Investigation project in English and government classes. Examples of projects in geography and other subjects are detailed in Sharan and Sharan (1992). In these examples, the teachers and students follow the sequence of stages presented here, but with a great deal of variety and flexibility.

No two Group Investigation projects are alike. To the extent that teachers incorporate students' interests and plans in the design of the investigation, the project will not be just another series of predetermined steps imposed on the students. By combining personal, social, and academic meaning, Group Investigation offers students and teachers an authentic learning experience.

Implementing Group Investigation: A Checklist To Guide Decisions

The teacher is responsible for providing the leadership that will enable students to carry out Group Investigation competently and effectively. To this end, we suggest the following checklist in order to guide the implementation of Group Investigation.

___ 1. I need to find out what kinds of resources are available: textbooks, magazines, books, experts, film, libraries, museums, commercial firms, stores, industries, parks, and so forth.

___ 2. I need to list questions that come to mind as I scan the sources, visit a site, or talk with an expert.

___ 3. I need to choose a stimulating problem to present to the class—a problem that will be related explicitly to people's lives and will require the use of the varied resource materials I found.

___ 4. I need to bring as many materials to the class as possible and plan an appealing introductory activity that will stimulate the class's interest in the problem.

___ 5. I need to explain to the students exactly how the investigation will proceed and tell them how they will be evaluated.

___ 6. During Stage 1, I need to encourage students to generate questions for the investigation that interest them.

___ 7. During Stage 2, I need to help groups make realistic plans and make sure that all members' ideas are heard.

___ 8. During Stage 3, I need to help students with study skills. I need to check if there's a skill that the whole class finds difficult, and if so, take time out to have students practice that skill.

___ 9. During Stage 4, I need to help groups identify the main idea of their findings. I also need to convene the steering committee and coordinate the groups' presentations.

___10. During Stage 5, I need to lead the class in determining criteria for the evaluation of the presentations. After each presentation I need to lead the class's feedback discussion.

___11. For Stage 6, I need to choose ways of evaluating new facts and terms students acquired in the course of the investigation. I also need to determine what conclusions they reached from their inquiry and how they integrated their findings.

___12. I need to ask the students what meanings the investigation and its results had for them.

___13. I need to ask myself and the class what we did well during the investigation and what can be improved next time.

___14. Finally, I need to reflect on what Group Investigation means to me as a teacher. I also need to find other teachers in my school who will team up with me so that we can plan a new Group Investigation project.

REFERENCES

Cohen, E. 1986. *Designing groupwork: Strategies for the heterogeneous classroom.* New York: Teachers College Press.

Graves, N., and T. Graves. 1990. *What is cooperative learning? Tips for teachers and trainers,* 2nd ed. Santa Cruz, CA: Cooperative College of California.

Huhtala, J., and E. Coughlin. 1991. Group investigation, democracy and the Middle East: Team teaching English and government. *English Journal* (80): 5.

Joyce, B., and M. Weil. 1986. *Models of teaching,* 3rd ed. Englewood Cliffs, NJ: Prentice Hall.

Kagan, S. 1989. *Cooperative learning: Resources for teachers.* San Juan Capistrano, CA: Resources for Teachers.

Miel, A. 1952. *Cooperative procedures in learning.* New York: Teachers College Press.

Sharan, S., and R. Hertz-Lazarowitz. 1980. A group investigation method of cooperative learning in the classroom. In S. Sharan, et al., eds. *Cooperation in education,* 14-46. Provo, UT: Brigham Young University Press.

Sharan, Y., and S. Sharan, 1990. Group Investigation expands cooperative learning. *Educational Leadership* (47): 17-21.

———. 1992. *Group investigation: Expanding cooperative learning.* Colchester, VT: Teachers College Press.

Thelen, H. 1981. *The classroom society.* London: Croom Helm.

11.

Co-op Co-op: A Student Interest-Based Cooperative Study/Learning Strategy

ROBERT J. STAHL, JOHN R. MEYER, AND NANCY N. STAHL

Context and Philosphical Base of the Co-op Co-op Strategy

The comprehensive term *cooperative learning* is a generic one for more than twenty approaches or strategies to effective small-group teaching and academic achievement. Each strategy is based on a particular orientation or belief system about how students and student tasks need to be structured in order to increase learning. One orientation, the transformation model (Miller and Seller, 1985), stresses personal and social change through the person's active interaction and interrelations with his or her environment. The aim of this model is self-actualization, with an emphasis on the integration of subject matter, creative writing, and holistic learning.

The orientation of Miller's transformation model is highly compatible with the Group Investigation strategy (Sharan and Sharan, 1976).[1] During Group Investigation and its complement, Co-op Co-op (Kagan, 1985, 1992), students cooperate in small groups or teams in order to cooperate with the entire class in its joint study of one topic.

---

[1] See also Chapter 10 by Yael and Shlomo Sharan in this book.

The Co-op Co-op strategy emerged within the context of a postsecondary environment in which an entire class of students promoted learning and the motivation to study in one area by accepting the challenge to organize first into small teams and eventually to contribute to the entire class using the principle of effective division of labor. Subsequent applications and refinement have confirmed that this strategy could be used at all age and grade levels with appropriate adaptations according to the abilities of the students. When the guidelines are followed, this strategy in practice implements a democratic, cooperative philosophy that is highly valued in the social studies community (Meyer, 1992).

The name Co-op Co-op emerges from the fact that students cooperate within and as small groups to produce something of benefit to share with the entire class. In doing this, "they are cooperating in order to cooperate" (Kagan, 1992, page 19:1). Students volunteer to study a particular aspect of a topic they are personally interested in investigating with other students who are interested in the same aspect. Since the entire class has a single academic area to be studied, the small groups function as subcommittees of the whole class. After their study of a subtopic of mutual interest, each group of volunteers, now knowledgeable in its respective subarea, informs all others in the same class through one or more timed presentations. Students then are called upon to learn what their classmates representing other subtopics have studied and consider important to share. Different options are available to hold students accountable for what each learned in the small groups as well as for what they acquired from the presentations of the many small groups.

Philosophical Base of Co-op Co-op

Connecting group academic study with student interest is an integral part of the philosophy upon which the Co-op Co-op strategy was built. As Kagan[2] puts it in his *Co-op Co-op: A Flexible Cooperative Learning Technique*, page 366:

> . . . *the aim of education is to provide conditions in which the natural curiosity, intelligence, and expressiveness of students will emerge*

---

[2] Spencer Kagan is the creator of the Co-op Co-op strategy. Besides his publications, his videotapes that explain this strategy in action are available from Resources for Teachers, Inc., 27128 Paseo Espada, Suite 602, San Juan Capistrano, CA 92675.

and develop. The emphasis in this philosophy is on bringing out and nourishing what are assumed to be natural intelligent, creative, and expressive tendencies among students.

A major assumption of Co-op Co-op is that

> *. . . following one's curiosity, having new experiences—especially with one's peers—are inherently satisfying, and that no extrinsic reward is needed to get students to engage in these activities, which are the most important forms of learning* (Clarke, et al., 1990, page 439).

The idea that propels this strategy is that quality education provides the conditions under which the assumed natural curiosity, intelligence, and expressiveness of students emerge and develop (Kagan, 1992). Part of these conditions may include appropriately structured and focused communications about topics of mutual interest through sharing with peers.

To be effective, teachers must learn the philosophy, basic principles, essential elements, and instructional steps compatible with Co-op Co-op's philosophy. Using well-structured Co-op Co-op tasks, students' academic, affective, and social achievements have increased noticeably.

Co-op Co-op in Light of Required Elements of Cooperative Learning

Like all cooperative learning strategies, the positive consequences of the Co-op Co-op strategy are enhanced as more of the following elements are met.

- Students work in small academically and socially heterogeneous groups that are periodically reconstituted.

- Students work in an environment of positive interdependence within their group or team.

- Students learn and use necessary collaborative skills (e.g., listening, productive discourse, constructive criticism) that are emphasized, taught, monitored, and rewarded.

- Students are accountable both as individuals and as groups.

- Students learn through structured opportunities that allow for purposeful discourse.

- Students are provided with class (large-group) or small-group incentives as internal and/or external rewards are aligned with the quality of their individual learning.

This last element, rewards, might be provided in such ways as: oral or printed public praise and recognition for the groups that produce the highest quality products; showcasing particularly good group efforts; bonus points that earn other rewards; elimination of a homework assignment; or buttons or stickers for the winning group(s) members.

To help with determining the quality of the products and presentations within Co-op Co-op, an administrator or colleague occasionally may be asked to act as a judge. Such outsiders tend to provide an additional motivation for students to do well and help ensure that academic standards are not sacrificed for the sake of showy presentations that lack substance, clarity, accuracy, or cohesiveness.

While Co-op Co-op activities within a particular classroom *may be structured* to fulfill all the above elements, the strategy is often used in situations where, for one or more reasons, many of the critical cooperative learning elements are not fully accomplished. In many Co-op Co-op classrooms that do not meet all the elements, the academic results have tended to be more positive than when the teachers' routine teaching strategies and resources have been used. These findings do not warrant the conclusion that the critical elements of cooperative learning can be ignored. They do suggest that teachers who cannot meet every critical element can still use this alternative cooperative strategy to generate high levels of academic learning.

Four Often-Asked Questions Regarding the Use of the Co-op Co-op Strategy

What Areas of Student Learning Outcomes Are Appropriate for This Strategy?

If the social studies teacher desires one or more of the following student outcomes, then appropriately structured Co-op Co-op structures are likely to work.

- Cognitive skills achievement: Students gain higher abilities for classifying, forming connections, thinking in divergent ways, collecting relevant data, selecting resource materials, analyzing and interpreting content, synthesizing components or aspects of a topic into a coherent whole, and communicating interpretations to team members and to the class or large group.

- Self-directed learning abilities.

- Peer tutoring skills: This is especially likely when the teacher has provided systemic information relative to critical characteristics of effective tutoring behaviors.

- Social skills development: Students enhance their abilities to work within the division of labor situations, improve their interpersonal and intergroup relationship abilities, improve their empathic listening skills, learn to respond more empathetically to others' points of view, share resources, practice distributive justice, develop abilities to recognize and control harmful bias, deal with public affirmation and constructive criticism from others, and develop more positive cooperative attitudes.

- Self-actualization gains: Students achieve increased levels of motivation, self-esteem enhancement, and feelings of empowerment as well as higher self-concepts.

In What Subject Areas May Co-op Co-op Be Used?

Like nearly all cooperative learning strategies, Co-op Co-op is applicable to all content areas. All areas of the social studies, behavioral sciences, and humanities are appropriate for this cooperative learning strategy. This strategy is particularly appropriate in situations in which the content and abilities to be learned are conducive to small-group work and where the instructional variables, e.g., time, space, and outcomes, can be structured to facilitate group work.

At What Levels of Schooling May This Strategy Be Used?

Co-op Co-op may be used from lower elementary grades through graduate-level university classes and in in-service staff development environments. Such factors as the complexity of the topic chosen, students' reading and writing abilities, time available, the availability of relevant resources, and students' ability to make presentations will affect how well students complete this strategy in any particular course at a given grade level.

When this strategy is used a number of times in the same year and over several years, nearly all students at all grade levels significantly improve the quality of their study efforts, intragroup behaviors, and group presentations with each Co-op Co-op unit.

How Much Class Time Is Required To Complete This Strategy?

Major factors that affect the extent of the time required for successful completion of a Co-op Co-op group strategy are: (a) breadth or difficulty of the topic selected; (b) project organization/preparation; (c) availability and difficulty of instructional resources; (d) requirements for the small-group delivery or presentations to the entire class; and (e) evaluation. Mini Co-Op Co-op projects may be as brief as one class period. A unit could extend from as brief a time as one week to a semester or to a school year, depending on how the courses within the school are organized. Some teachers have these groups meet once or twice a week for a six- or nine-week term, with the week before the final exam used for the class presentations that wrap up the group work. As the teacher becomes more familiar with this strategy and students become more accomplished in its use, this element of time becomes far more flexible.

The Essential Steps of the Co-op Co-op Strategy

Co-op Co-op was invented as a simple and very flexible strategy. Teachers are expected to grasp the basic philosophy and then adapt the strategy to their own circumstances. However, the inclusion of the elements below increases the probability of success in the classroom (Kagan, 1992).

Announcement of the Teacher-Selected Focus for the Academic Unit[3]

The teacher selects and then announces the topic serving as the focus of study and of learning outcomes for the unit. For instance, the teacher

---

[3] This element is added by the authors to emphasize the planning decisions teachers must make and the teacher's role in getting the Co-op Co-op unit started.

may decide to study an era such as the Middle Ages or the Age of Exploration, a nation, or a particular region of the world. In some instances, the teacher may have the flexibility of allowing even the initial topic to be jointly selected with the whole class.

Student interest in the topic can be stimulated by requiring one or more relevant readings, experiences, or lectures immediately before or on the first day the topic is introduced. The teacher's introduction may include a lecture, handouts, a video, or any other resources that are likely to stimulate student interest. A second purpose of this presentation is to provide a core of information that students can use in the student-centered discussion that is to follow. These resources and initial tasks are especially useful when students lack either prior knowledge or have dysfunctional conceptions of the area to be studied.

Student-Centered Whole-Class Discussion

Students engage in creative thinking as they brainstorm about their particular interests in the topic as well as possible subtopics that could be examined. The discussion must be student centered and focus driven. They should be asked to share what they know about the topic or its subtopics as well as discuss the information encountered through the teacher's presentation and materials. Students must become actively interested in the topic or a significant subtopic. The discussion is not directed at leading students to particular subtopics for study but to stimulate their interest, curiosity, and motivation in the topic selected.[4] The teacher may find that more time is needed than originally planned for this discussion since students need to leave this discussion highly interested in pursuing an area of interest within the broad topic selected for study.

The teacher may help students to reconsider all the brainstormed subtopics and select the ones that might really need to be studied. The important thing is that this list is student generated. Often there are more subtopics, even after this boiling-down process, than there will be groups in the class. This is fine. Not every subtopic needs to be studied at this time. The teacher should be prepared to consider alternative ways many of the remaining subtopics might be studied in the future.

---

4 This step is similar to the cognitive skill of "Focus" as incorporated in the 1988 Ontario History and Contemporary Studies Guidelines.

Whenever possible, the teacher with the help of students should highlight the ideas generated during this discussion on the chalkboard, overhead, or newsprint as a record of the brainstorming session. If recorded on newsprint, these ideas can be posted for display throughout the unit and reviewed at the end.

Initial Topic Selection Toward Forming the Learning Teams

One of the strengths of the Co-op Co-op strategy is that students with similar interests in the same subtopic are likely to learn a great deal about their selected area, share what they find as individuals, and do a good job in presenting their findings to the whole class. Students need to know that giving them the opportunity to select their own teammates places responsibility on them for making appropriate choices so that they can complete the academic study and presentation tasks still ahead. Students must also know that the teacher reserves to right to adjust group size and membership to ensure balance, avoid problems, and help every student to be successful.

In most instances the teacher will want to maximize the heterogeneity among student Co-op Co-op groups. Consequently, students will be assigned to teams. Such heterogeneity is the most desirable approach given the increasing variability and pluralism in our schools. Among the benefits of such mixed groups are positive peer-tutoring attitudes, improved ethnic and social interrelations, increased role-taking abilities, and improved self-esteem.

When building upon and taking advantage of pre-existing (or just-generated) interest are paramount, then students should select their own teams as much as is possible. In this case, then, once the list of options is ready, students may be asked to raise their hands if they are interested in a particular subtopic. This gives students an initial sense of who in the class is interested in particular subtopics. Students then may be asked to move to designated areas of the room to meet with their potential teammates for their study teams. However, the teacher needs to monitor this selection process to ensure that teams have about equal numbers, are based on mutual interests rather than friendships, and are not made up exclusively of one type of student.

Once groups are formed, they are encouraged to begin a discussion of the subtopic of interest so that they get an idea of just how interested everyone is in that subtopic and whether everyone agrees about what is involved in the subtopic. Each team is directed to select and elaborate upon one subtopic. This initial movement to teams allows students to get a sense of the groups and often of other subtopics, since some will move around in this stage until they find a subtopic and group more to their liking.[5]

Team Building

To be very successful in this cooperative strategy, students need to trust their group members and to use appropriate social skills for working within and as a group. Initial team-building experiences are usually needed so that students develop a genuine sense of being a "we." Team-building experiences will be most necessary in situations where students have had little or no previous structured group work. Team building is particularly important at the secondary level because personal sharing and helping relationships tend to deteriorate or be lost after leaving the elementary school. Strategies are available to introduce students quickly to one another for the purpose of building the camaraderie needed to function as an effective cooperative learning study and presentation team (Kagan, 1985, 1992). The teacher also encourages a spirit of class unity by urging every student to do his or her best to ensure attainment of the class goal of everyone mastering the content and skills associated with the targeted topic and subtopics.

Group Subtopic Selection and Refinement

Teams are encouraged to further discuss and elaborate upon the subtopics. Although each team is to select one subtopic, we suggest that each team select and rank its top three choices.[6] This process of selecting preferred subtopics from the brainstormed list contributes to the creation of a division of labor among class members. In order to avoid

---

5 Johnson and Johnson (1975) suggest that the number and type of teams depend on the needs of the particular classroom.
6 The ranking of a team's top three choices allows some room for negotiation in case two or more teams select the same subtopic as their number-one choice.

duplication of another team's selection, the teacher circulates among the teams and facilitates the selection process. This step ends when each group has one clear subtopic for study and believes this is a very important and highly interesting topic for its members to study.

Minitopic Selection and Delegation of Work

Each team member now selects a minitopic or aspect of the team's subtopic that he or she will be responsible for studying. This decision often requires the whole team to analyze collectively the subtopic, sometimes resorting to the same brainstorming technique used earlier by the whole class. Each member of the group is responsible for gathering sufficient information and resources on his or her minitopic and then sharing it with the entire team. Whenever possible, the selection of the minitopic is based upon the interest of the particular student, although this is not always feasible. Minitopics are not assigned, although they are subject to teacher approval (Kagan, 1992). Each minitopic is to provide a unique contribution to the team effort. Everyone is expected and encouraged to contribute to the group's study on the basis of his or her abilities. Eventually, each student will prepare and present a personal report on his or her minitopic. Students are informed that within their groups they are expected to evaluate the contributions of their teammates, assign tasks to individual team members, and monitor each member's contribution.

Individual Minitopic Study and Preparation

The team members, individually and sometimes collectively, spend on-task time studying their minitopics by a variety of means: reading available resources, gathering data using various strategies, completing library research, completing computer searches, conducting interviews, reflecting upon what they have found, or planning individual projects. Students may be given two or three days or longer in order to collect, analyze, and organize data relevant to their minitopics. Furthermore, each must prepare a five- to seven-minute presentation of his or her findings for the entire team.

Minitopic Presentations

Sharing and forming a coherent whole for a team topic are crucial to the success of a Co-op Co-op unit. Students interacting with peers on a topic of common concern provides the potential for significant, long-lasting learning to occur. Basic principles of listening, interviewing, and supportive questioning are applied by students as they consider and reflect upon what their teammates provide. Nonpresenting members assume specific roles—*Critic, Discussant, Notetaker*—in order to improve the quality of the information presented by their teammates. Time limitations are carefully observed.

The pieces provided by the individual members are organized into a coherent whole for a successful team presentation to the entire class. Thus, following the individual presentations and team discussion, there is a period for further research, rethinking, and synthesis. Priorities are determined and less-critical information is dropped from the presentation agenda.

Preparation of Team Presentations

Team members collectively formulate a list of the most important information, concepts, and ideas they have discovered about their subtopic. We suggest they make this decision in response to questions such as: If all members of the class could learn only the ten most important pieces of information or ideas about the subtopic we studied, what information or ideas should they learn? or If all members of the class forgot everything we presented to them except the ten important pieces of information or ideas about our subtopic, what information or ideas should they remember? The presentation should also describe how the particular subtopic fits in with the larger topic of study for the unit.

Teams must plan a timely, informative, and interesting presentation. Student presentations should make sure that what has been selected to be learned is stated in clear language and that all members of the class are informed that these items are the most important things to learn and remember about their group's subtopic. In addition, the presentation should suggest how each group's subtopic fits into the overall topic and should provide reasons why the particular subtopic is important to study.

Students are encouraged to use a wide range of instructional aids and avoid turn-taking panel presentations and lectures.[7] The teacher makes sure that all teams work to keep their presentations within the announced time limit for each presentation. This time is usually five, six, or seven minutes.

Even though teachers have taken a number of courses in how to plan for instruction and how to teach, many think nothing of asking students to plan quality personal and group presentations and then to teach their peers with virtually no help in doing either. We have heard from teachers in a number of subject areas who spent the major part of one or two class periods teaching the whole class some important points in planning, preparing visuals and handouts, working with transparencies, and organizing their presentations. Some even mentioned that they shared five or six ideas about teaching included in Madeline Hunter's *Essential Elements of Instruction*. All mentioned that taking this time to help students learn how to teach resulted in higher confidence levels on the part of their students, more focused and higher quality presentations, more varied usage of audiovisual aids, and greater whole-class attention to the presentations than when students were given no such advice. It also reaped benefits that more than made up for the time taken. Teacher and team members' sharing, consultating, and giving feedback after one or more practice sessions are encouraged.[8]

Whole-Class Presentations by All Teams

Each presenting team is responsible for how time, space, and resources are managed during the presentation. Since the management of time is crucial, it is wise to have a highly visible clock with a second hand along with a class timekeeper. The teacher and class may conduct a postpre-

---

[7] If the teacher has not used a variety of instructional aids and has stuck primarily to using minilectures, the textbook, and the chalkboard, students are going to need help in developing and delivering presentations that include a wide range of instructional aids. For instance, students may be taught how to make transparencies, how to use the overhead projector, and how to make a relevant short videotape.

[8] More than one practice session may be needed, especially during the first two units in which students are to make presentations. In addition, students need to learn to monitor and assess their own presentations, or each group is likely to wait for the teacher's approval for everything it decides about its presentation.

sentation activity so that growth (for that group) by means of feedback can occur immediately after the presentation.

Evaluation and Reflections

One of the unusual features of Co-op Co-op is that the teacher has an extremely wide range of options regarding the evaluation of student efforts in their groups and presentations. Evaluation can involve elaborate multiple methods of evaluation to no evaluation at all to formal quizzes or games-tournaments as in TGT. The safest bet is to provide some form of testing of individual student achievement, as well as assessing the quality of each group's presentation. Remember that no formal assessment is required for this strategy.

Multiple options of evaluation are available so that both team and individual contributions can be assessed in order that accomplishments are recognized and areas where progress is needed are made clear. To be most effective, the teacher and students should determine the evaluation procedures and standards well in advance of the group study and presentations. Merit or grades should be assigned to both group and individual work in a reasonably fair distribution. A typical combination is group self-evaluation = 40 percent and teacher evaluation = 60 percent of the final grade for the group study and presentation. This grade is in addition to grades on individual tests for what was learned from all group presentations (Meyer, 1992).[9]

Given the previous socialization of students into exclusive teacher-evaluation procedures, the implementation of student-involved evaluations of group presentations may take considerable practice, time, and perseverance before it really takes hold. A checklist and set of open-ended statements about cooperative small-group work (such as those in Figure 11-1 on page 290)[10] serve to focus on the essential components of quality group study and a quality whole-class presentation.

Teachers who want to ease into having students evaluate other group presentations may prepare students by having them practice

---

9 If students are not graded in terms of what they learned from other group presentations, they are not likely to pay much attention to these presentations and ignore what is provided by their peers.

10 Extensive modification made of the checklist in Clarke, et al. (1990).

Figure 11-1   *Sample Evaluation Form to Assess the Quality of the Group Presentations*

GROUP PRESENTATION ASSESSMENT FORM

Group Name _____   Date of Presentation_____

Group Topic _____

	Not at all		Thoroughly		
Points:	0	1	3	5	7

The group

a) had a clear focus of what was important about its subtopic or area.

b) appeared prepared and organized.
— — — — —

c) was knowledgeable about its section.
— — — — —

d) made it clear what was important for me to learn about its subtopic or area.
— — — — —

e) worked together as a group.
— — — — —

f) really did want me to learn what it thought was most important.
— — — — —

g) provoked active participation of the class that focused on what we were to learn.
— — — — —

h) demonstrated patience and helpfulness in guiding our comprehension of its subtopic.
— — — — —

i) used appropriate and attention-keeping teaching strategies.
— — — — —

j) used appropriate and attention-keeping instructional aids.
— — — — —

k) Each group member knew the subtopic equally well.
— — — — —

One part of your presentation that was particularly *helpful*:

_____

Two important reasons why this part of your presentation was particularly *useful*:

_____

_____

Suggestions that would have improved your presentation:

_____

_____

_____

evaluating preliminary presentations within their own groups. Students cooperate to learn how to apply the teacher's evaluation standards by using these to assess rehearsals by members of their own groups. An informal paired activity might require that two group members paraphrase and elaborate the evaluative standards and questions prior to beginning their individual assessments of a presentation rehearsal of one of their teammates. The two then jointly review their assessments, making sure that the focus is on evidence consistent with the teacher's printed evaluative standards. Some teachers report forming pairs made up of one member from two groups to complete this same activity so that students have a sense that the evaluation that will be made of their own group's presentation will focus on how closely they adhere to the printed evaluative standards rather than being based on personality or other criteria.

Self-evaluation by individuals and by groups is another type of evaluation that is being promoted in some educational systems. Structured and standard-based self-reflection is important for both the group as a group and for individual student corrections, growth, and sense of accomplishment. Standards to guide this reflective process should be made public and then applied by students in discussing and writing about the group's study, cooperative learning, and group maintenance behaviors as they operated as a group. Individually, students might focus on helping, explaining, demonstrating, listening, discussing, and sharing skills. More academic-focused reflection might include giving reasons for their ideas/positions, explaining clearly what points they make, thinking and reporting using more visual words, and reporting in concise terms. Sample questions that evoke descriptive comments to focus this reflection are provided in Figure 11-2 on page 292.

During and after a team presentation, the social studies teacher may use an additional form to provide additional information to guide the team's future work as a team. An example of what this form might contain is provided in Figure 11-3 on page 293.

Co-op Co-op has worked well without team evaluation, but only in those cases in which intrinsic motivation and/or informal peer pressure was such that concerns about quality participation by nearly all students were absent.

Figure 11-2   *Sample Questions for Use in Helping Students Reflect upon and Assess the Extent and Quality of Their Performances Within Their Respective Teams*

SAMPLE QUESTIONS FOR SELF-ASSESSMENT

FOR GROUPS

- What did the group learn about procedures for operating as a group to investigate a topic?

- What is at least one idea or point of view you learned from a teammate?

- What were the problem-solving steps used to improve the quality of your team's report?

- To what extent did members of your group see themselves as being members of a team?

FOR INDIVIDUALS

- In order to ensure that your teammates learned what you discovered about your minitopic, what are at least two specific things you tried that were successful?

- What is one piece of information or one idea your teammates learned from you?

- What is one ability you learned from your teammates tutoring you? How did you learn this ability?

- What is one idea you learned from observing and asking questions about your teammates' research?

Figure 11-3   *Sample Form To Guide Student Reflection of Behaviors and Attitudes for Productive Team Work*

PRODUCTIVE TEAM ATTITUDES AND BEHAVIORS

Team Name _____   Date of Presentation_____

Team Topic _____

	Not at all		A great deal		
Points:	0	1	3	5	7

a) We checked with peers to be sure that they understood the work expected of each person.   — — — — —

b) We practiced our ability to work with others by listening and contributing ideas to the group.   — — — — —

c) We were all responsible for sharing the work to be done.   — — — — —

d) We worked hard to ensure that every member accepted responsibility for what we all learned about the topic.   — — — — —

e) We demonstrated patience when explaining concepts to all group members.   — — — — —

f) We worked to create a clear presentation.   — — — — —

g) We worked hard to ensure that every member accepted responsibility for good or poor quality of the presentation .   — — — — —

What specific things *did* members of your team do that were particularly effective in helping the team complete its many tasks?

_____

_____

What specific behaviors were *counterproductive* to your team's success?

_____

_____

What specific things *should* members of your team do to be more effective in future team study activities?

_____

_____

Alternatives Within the Basic Co-op Co-op Strategy

The previous section provided a somewhat detailed account of the essential steps and elements of the Co-op Co-op strategy. Options available to vary elements of this strategy without losing those features that make Co-op Co-op an effective group-learning alternative include:

- using a minilength format in which teams are given only from one to fifteen minutes to prepare a five-minute presentation on a subtopic and on materials studied as part of an ongoing unit.[11]

- using a term-long format in which teams are given a semester or year to prepare a detailed presentation.

- using this strategy to complement the routine teaching format for a unit.

- using this strategy as the only strategy for an entire unit.

- using this strategy with an emphasis on group investigation, stressing the gaining of insight and disclosure on the selected subtopic.

- using this strategy for the acquisition of basic information about the topic.

- varying the product(s) to be generated as a result of the team study and presentation needs: a thesis, an experiment, a mural, or a slide show may be required. (Suggestions for team products are as varied as one's imagination: audiotapes, videotapes, gameboards, soap operas, skits, T-shirts, public service or commercial ads, graffiti boards, telegrams, and so forth.)

Co-op Co-op presentations may also be followed by a games-tournament such as that used in the TGT strategy discussed in Chapter 8.

Tips for Teachers New to the Co-op Co-op Strategy

This strategy is among the simplest cooperative learning strategies for teachers to use. However, its apparent simplicity can be deceiving. We

---

[11] This option is recommended only (a) after students have been in the same groups over an extended period of time working on other subtopics; (b) in situations in which the presentation is not expected to be of the same quality as when longer periods are provided; and (c) when resources to complement the groups' presentations are available in the time allowed for preparation.

urge teachers to study the steps and guidelines very carefully and imagine themselves leading one of their classes through this strategy before ever trying it out in an actual classroom setting. We suggest they visualize what students are expected to do during each step, and then what they (the teachers) will be doing during each step. The following tips will help the social studies teacher find success in using this strategy.

- Start with a topic and subtopics that have high-interest appeal and are likely to motivate students to engage in the study needed prior to the presentations.

- Start with simple tasks of short duration, not a major project, until both teacher and students are comfortable with the steps and are ready for longer group study. Gradually increase the complexity of the tasks with regard for the appropriate timelines.

- Use teambuilding activities early in order to develop a positive classroom climate. Then proceed with peer monitoring and evaluation. Students must get to know one another, communicate accurately and unambiguously with one another, accept and support one another, and resolve conflicts constructively.

- Be reflective and analytical about your own teaching. Work with a trusted colleague, if possible, in order to share experiences planning, using, and assessing your use of this strategy.

- Announce the evaluative standards that are to be used. Hand out copies of the standards.

- As necessary, spend some time helping students to learn how to plan for instruction (their presentations), to develop appropriate props and audiovisual materials, and to teach.

- Whatever the topic and group-task demands, build in time for student reflection on what they studied, how they studied it, and how they cooperated.

The Co-op Co-op Strategy: A Practical Classroom Example

To illustrate this strategy as it may look in a particular classroom, we will take you through the essential steps of Co-op Co-op within Ms. Yirga's history of Florida course. This practical example will not include all the options that are available, but it will highlight what is likely to be found in the typical Co-op Co-op classroom.

The first part of the course, stressing Florida's Native American history prior to the European exploration, has just concluded. Ms. Yirga knows that students in the past have not been excited by the textbook version of Florida's history from European exploration to 1800. This year she decides that she will use the Co-op Co-op strategy to help students learn about this 250-year period. She selects this period as the topic to be studied by the whole class. Using Co-op Co-op, she assumes that she can get her students interested in studying parts of this history on their own.

Announcement of the Teacher-Selected Focus for the Academic Unit

On the first day of the unit, to stimulate student interest in this topic of Florida's past, Ms. Yirga brings in reproductions of two artifacts, one from a Native American society and one from the Spanish settlement in St. Augustine in 1567. She shows three large photographs of Fort San Marcos and excerpts from correspondence written by three different original settlers of the fort. These attract the attention of most of her students. In addition she pulls down a large map of the state and asks students to imagine being at this site. She follows a short introductory lecture with five carefully worded questions to engage her students in a discussion to further stimulate their interest. A second purpose of her multimedia presentation is to provide a core of information that students can use in the student-centered discussion she knows is to follow. These resources and initial tasks are especially useful, since her students lack the knowledge to discuss this period of the state's history on their own. After most of the class period has passed with these initial activities, Ms. Yirga senses that her students are excited, intrigued, and interested enough in this period of history that she can move smoothly into the next phase of her Co-op Co-op strategy.

Student-Centered Whole-Class Discussion

Ms. Yirga engages all her students in a brainstorming task to get as many students as possible to talk about their particular interests in the topic. She also asks them to mention possible subtopics that they or someone else in the class could study and share with the class. As required, the brainstorming discussion is very student centered and focused on the topic and relevant subtopics. By answering her questions, students share what they know about the topic or its subtopics as well as discuss the information contained in her presentation and materials.

Ms. Yirga keeps in mind how important it is that this list of possible subtopics be student generated. She keeps busy asking questions and writing comments and subtopic names on three sheets of newsprint. Student suggestions are not evaluated or voted upon, although several students are asked to provide greater details on their suggestions. She asks four students to define key terms they used in their comments and one to clarify the meaning of a statement he made about the settlers' inhumane treatment of the Native Americans.

As she had hoped, students become more and more actively interested in the topic or a significant subtopic. Ms. Yirga works hard to help students move from casual interest toward being personally motivated to study the subtopics. Sensing that students need more time and that little time is left in the period, she instructs students that, for homework, they are to think about all the things they would like to know about this period in Florida's past. She wants to move to the next step only after her students are committed to pursuing an area of interest within this broad topic.

At the start of the next day, students reconsider all the brainstormed subtopics, adding any more to the list they generated the day before. Everyone is asked to think about all the subtopics listed. Ms. Yirga then asks them to consider the one or two they would really like to study on their own. The class is also told that students who are interested in the same subtopic will form a study group to investigate their subtopic and to make a group presentation to the entire class. No student will have to study the entire subtopic by himself or herself.

Ms. Yirga then asks students to raise their hands when they consider a particular subtopic to be really interesting to them. She goes down the list for each subtopic. This process weeds out those topics that will not be studied by the class, at least at this time. Even after this weeding-out task, there are far more subtopics than there will be groups in the class. There is no requirement that every subtopic be studied at one time. (Ms. Yirga knows she has time to plan alternative ways besides this Co-op Co-op strategy to help students learn important details concerning some of the remaining subtopics.)

Initial Topic Selection Toward Forming the Co-op Co-op Teams

Since this is the first time she has used this strategy, Ms. Yirga takes time to tell the class that she is using a new approach to teaching this unit. She also announces that she expects that students with similar interests in the same subtopic should learn a great deal about their selected area, share what they find as individuals with their teammates, and do a good job in presenting their findings to the whole class. She reminds them that in giving them the opportunity to select their own topics and teammates, they are responsible for making appropriate choices so that they can complete the academic study and presentation tasks still ahead. However, as the teacher, she reserves the right to shift group members around so that everyone can be successful.

With the shortened list of options ready, students are instructed to raise their hands if they are interested in each particular subtopic. This gives each student another chance to determine the particular subtopic(s) in which he or she is personally most interested. Students then are asked to move to designated areas of the room to meet with their potential teammates for their study teams. Each group begins a discussion of the subtopic of interest so that everyone in each group gets an idea of just how interested everyone else is in that subtopic and whether everyone agrees as to what is involved in the subtopic. Each team is directed to select and clarify its one subtopic.

Some students decide to move to another interesting subtopic and its corresponding group. Since she wants to build upon and take advantage of her students' interest, Ms. Yirga wants her students to select their own teams as much as is possible.

Finalizing the Permanent Student Learning Teams

After five minutes, Ms. Yirga reassigns two students to their next favorite but different subtopics after she realizes that they got together on the basis of their friendship rather than high interest in the subtopic. Two males and two females are reassigned from groups that were all male or all female. Ms. Yirga announces that the membership in the teams, which number seven teams among her thirty-three-student class, are now set. She notices that some teams have four while others have as many as six.

Subtopic Selection and Refinement

The teams are now instructed to further discuss and elaborate upon their subtopic as a team. Each team is to select one subtopic, but Ms. Yirga knows that sometimes this clarification leads teams to broaden their subtopics to include those studied by one or more other groups. Although the process of selecting one preferred subtopic from the original brainstormed list was supposed to avoid overlapping, Ms. Yirga finds that two groups defined their subtopics in the same way. She talks to the two groups, one of which selected "Early European Settlements" and the other "Forts," and finds they really were interested in studying the city of St. Augustine. She works with them and helps them to study related topics. One will study "St. Augustine as the First Permanent Settlement." A second group will study "The Defense of Spanish Florida," and include Fort San Marcos as part of the defense system of the Spanish empire in this area of the world. Both groups like their topics. Ms. Yirga is pleased that the compromise worked and that both groups are satisfied. Now that each group has one clear subtopic for study, Ms. Yirga is ready to move to the next step of the strategy—a step she expects will enable her students to form and to see themselves as members of a team.

Teambuilding

Ms. Yirga knows that to be very successful in this cooperative strategy, students need to trust their group members and to use appropriate social skills for working within and as a group. Since this is the first time that students will work for an extended time as a study and learning team, highly relevant and activity-oriented team-building experiences are needed. She uses a strategy to build the camaraderie needed to function as an effective cooperative learning study and presentation team.

In addition, she encourages a spirit of class unity by urging every student to do her or his best to ensure attainment of the class goal of everyone mastering the content and skills associated with the targeted topic and subtopics. She imagines herself as a coach who gets together with a team for the first time and tries to excite the players into seeing themselves as a team and each player as a teammate who is expected to contribute to the success of the entire team as well as substantially improve his or her own knowledge and skills.

Minitopic Selection and Delegation of Work

Each team collectively analyzes the subtopic and generates a list of relevant minitopics, sometimes resorting to the same brainstorming technique used earlier by the whole class. Each member of the group is responsible for gathering sufficient information and resources on his or her minitopic and then sharing it with the entire team. As much as is possible, the minitopic each student selects is based upon the interest of the particular student. In the group, he or she will be solely responsible for studying that minitopic. All but five students find minitopics they are highly excited about studying. After Ms. Yirga spends several minutes with each of the five, each finds a minitopic he or she accepts as worth studying.

Students are reminded that sharing of resources and references among teammates and with other groups is required and that each minitopic is to provide a unique contribution to the team effort. Each student is instructed to prepare and present a personal report to the team on what was found from his or her minitopic investigation. Students are also informed that within their groups they are to evaluate the contributions of their fellow teammates, assign tasks to individual team members, and monitor each team member's contribution. To make sure her point gets across to the class, Ms. Yirga writes "Everyone is expected to contribute to the team's study and success on the basis of his or her abilities" on the chalkboard. She has the class read it aloud.

Individual and Team Study and Learning

The team members, individually and sometimes collectively, spend on-task time studying their minitopics on Florida's past by a variety of means. During this time students read textbooks, look over maps of Florida during this time period, complete library research that locates numerous chapters and articles on Florida from 1565 through 1800, and watch two videotapes and two filmstrips. Some students locate drawings, photographs, and even excerpts from diaries and ships' logs that are helpful. Ms. Yirga smiles as her students do far more reading than most would have done using the textbook and the one filmstrip she has used in the past. After five days, the students move from investigating, analyzing, prioritizing, and organizing to systematically informing their teammates as to what they have found relative to their minitopics.

Minitopic Presentations

Students are now required to make short presentations to their teammates on what they found during their inquiry and organization work. Ms. Yirga's students know that the data the individual team members contribute must be synthesized into a coherent whole for a successful team presentation to the entire class.

Important principles of listening, interviewing, and supportive questioning are used by team members in reaction to each member's minitopic presentation. As per Ms. Yirga's instructions, team members assume specific roles such as critic, discussant, notetaker. Supplementary resources such as maps, charts, and pictures are critiqued as well. To ensure that everyone has time to finish, a seven-minute time limitation for each presentation is carefully observed.

Preparation of Team Presentations

Each team collectively formulates a list of the most important information, concepts, and ideas they discovered about its subtopic. To help her students during this first-time effort using Co-op Co-op, Ms. Yirga asks that each team answer the following questions: If all members of the class could learn only the ten most important pieces of information or ideas about the subtopic we studied, what information or ideas should they learn? What are at least two reasons why information on our subtopic is important in understanding Florida's past? What are two effects or reminders of our subtopic that can be observed in modern-day Florida?

Teams are reminded that their presentations are to focus on making sure that the information they have selected is stated in clear language and that these are the most important data to learn and remember about their subtopics. In addition, each presentation is to report how each group's subtopic fits into the overall topic and provide reasons why the particular subtopic is important to study. Ms. Yirga reemphasizes that each team is to use a wide range of instructional aids while avoiding turn-taking reading presentations. All teams know they are to keep their presentations within the seven-minute time limit.

To help her students be successful during this first team presentation effort, she spends the major part of the next class period teaching the whole class some important points in planning, preparing visuals and handouts, working with transparencies, and organizing their presentations. She helps three students actually make transparencies for the overhead and add color for effect. Students are given an extra day for rethinking their presentations in light of her input and their practice.

Whole-Class Presentation by Each Team

Ms. Yirga randomly assigns the order of the group presentations. In the next unit she knows the presentations will be made using another system for determining order. Each team is announced by name, given one minute to prepare, and then given seven minutes to complete its presentation. A highly visible clock with a second hand is provided, and a timekeeper is selected.

To help the students who served as the audience for the presentation, the whole class is given two minutes following each presentation to review their notes and to interact with peers sitting next to them to clarify their understanding. Ms. Yirga has found this activity to be very effective in helping the entire class attend to the important information just presented. Each team then fields questions from the class for two minutes after the presentation and study time are completed. Finally, Ms. Yirga and the class provide two minutes of feedback and reaction following each team's presentation.

Evaluation

Ms. Yirga is well aware of the fact that one of the unusual features of Co-op Co-op is that there is an extremely wide range of options regarding the evaluation of student efforts in their groups and presentations. She had already decided to give students an individual test over the academic content, concepts, and skills they were to acquire and a grade on their performance within their respective groups. She selected multiple options of evaluation so that both team and individual achievements are assessed, accomplishments are recognized, and areas where progress is needed are made clear.

To ensure that students consider their efforts as part of an inquiry and presentation team, Ms. Yirga provides for a structured and standard-based self-reflection task for both the team as a team and for individual student corrections, growth, and sense of accomplishment. She wants to make public the standards to guide this reflective process and ensure that students apply these by discussing and writing about the team's study, cooperative learning, and group maintenance behaviors as they operated as a team. Using questions such as those presented in Figure 11-2 on page 292, her students spend time and conscious effort focusing on how they helped, explained, demonstrated, listened, discussed, questioned, and shared within their teams. Their equally important academic-focused reflection included giving reasons for their ideas/positions, explaining clearly what points they make, thinking and reporting using more visual words, and reporting in concise terms.

Ms. Yirga decides that she will use an additional form (Figure 11-3 on page 293) before the next Co-op Co-op unit to provide even more information to guide the teams' future work as teams. She then grades the students' individual tests and recognizes the highest-achieving students and teams. With these accomplished, her Co-op Co-op unit is completed. Ms. Yirga spends two more days on this period in Florida's past to furnish information not provided by the student teams.

Epilogue

As the above makes clear, the Co-op Co-op strategy requires students to cooperate first in small interest-based teams and then cooperate as a collection of teams to ensure that the entire class learns significant information, concepts, and abilities related to a teacher-selected major academic topic. The teacher's tasks involve keeping students interested in their subtopics and minitopics, conducting research investigations of relevant resources, and working together to generate the best possible presentation so that all members of the class learn important details about the topic.

Surprisingly, we have found many teachers who advocate curriculum and instructional practices centered around student interest shying away from this strategy even though it is designed to take advantage of this very interest. One explanation is that other cooperative learning strategies are available for such purposes. Another is that teachers used to traditional approaches find it uncomfortable and difficult to adopt a nontraditional strategy such as Co-op Co-op to achieve the interest-based classroom they envision. Co-op Co-op can work for teachers willing to take the time to master the steps and to allow students to explore topics according to their interests. Not only will many students learn the content they are studying, they tend to become more interested in many aspects of the topic and other related topics yet to be studied.

In Co-op Co-op, students complete tasks and learn in order to satisfy their own curiosity about a topic, themselves, and the world—and to share with others what their search has revealed (Kagan, 1992). The structure makes it clear that the teacher values students' personal interests, abilities, and capacities for being responsible for their own learning, as individuals, as members of a small group, and as members of a cooperating whole-class investigation.

References

Clarke, J., R. Wideman, and S. Eadie. 1990. *Together we learn: Co-operative small group learning.* Scarborough, Ontario: Prentice Hall Canada.

Johnson, D. W., and R. T. Johnson, 1975. *Joining together.* Englewood Cliffs, NJ: Prentice Hall.

Kagan, S. 1985. Co-op Co-op: A flexible cooperative learning technique. In R. E. Slavin, S. Sharan, S. Kagan, R. Hartz-Lazarowitz, C. Webb, and R. Schmuck, eds. *Learning to cooperate, cooperating to learn.* New York: Plenum.

———. 1992. *Cooperative learning.* San Juan Capistrano, CA: Resources for Teachers.

Meyer, J. R. 1992. Co-op co-op: A student-based cooperative learning approach. Windsor, Ontario: University of Windsor (a working paper).

Miller, J. P., and W. Seller. 1985. *Curriculum perspectives and practice.* New York: Longman.

Sharan, S., and Y. Sharan. 1976. *Small-group teaching.* Englewood Cliffs, NJ: Educational Technology Publications.

Slavin, R. E. 1984. Students motivating students to excel: Cooperative incentives, cooperative tasks, and student achievement. *The Elementary School Journal,* 85 (1): 53–63.

12.

The Pro-Con Cooperative Group Strategy: Structuring Academic Controversy Within the Social Studies Classroom

DAVID W. JOHNSON AND ROGER T. JOHNSON

Have you learned lessons only of those who admired you, and were tender with you, and stood aside for you? Have you not learned great lessons from those who braced themselves against you, and disputed the passage with you?

—WALT WHITMAN, 1860

In a social studies class, students are considering the issue of civil disobedience. They learn that in the civil rights movement, individuals deliberately broke the law to gain equal rights for minorities. In numerous instances, such as in the civil rights and antiwar movements, individuals wrestle with the issue of breaking the law to redress a social injustice.

In order to study the role of civil disobedience in a democracy, students are placed in a cooperative learning group of four members. The group is then divided into two pairs. One pair is given the assignment of making the best case possible for the constructiveness of civil disobedience in a democracy. The other pair is given the assignment of making the best case possible for the destructiveness of civil disobedience in a democracy. In the resulting conflict, students draw from such sources as the Declaration of Independence by Thomas Jefferson, "Civil Disobedience" by Henry David Thoreau, "Speech at Cooper Union, New York" by Abraham Lincoln, and "Letter from Birmingham Jail" by Martin Luther King, Jr., to challenge one another's reasoning and analyses concerning when civil disobedience is, and is not, constructive.

This unit would typically take five class periods to conduct. During the first class period, each pair develops its position and plans how to present the best case possible to the other pair. Near the end of the period, pairs are encouraged to compare notes with pairs from other groups who represent the same position. During the second class period, each pair makes its presentation. Each member of the pair has to participate in the presentation. Members of the opposing pair are encouraged to take notes and listen carefully. During the third class period, the group members discuss the issue following a set of rules to help them criticize ideas without criticizing people, differentiate the two positions, and assess the degree of evidence and logic supporting each position. During the fourth hour, the pairs reverse perspectives and present one another's positions, drop all advocacy, and begin developing a group report that synthesizes the best evidence and reasoning from both sides. During the fifth period, the report is finalized. The teacher evaluates each report on the quality of the writing, the logical presentation of evidence, and the oral presentation of the report to the class. During this same period, the group's conclusions are presented to the class with all four members of the group required to participate orally in the presentation. Then students each take an individual test and, if every member of the group achieves up to criterion, they all receive bonus points. Finally the group processes how well it worked together and how it could do even better next time.

Such intellectual disputed dialogues generate higher achievement (characterized by critical thinking, higher-level reasoning, and metacognitive thought), more positive interpersonal relationships, and greater psychological health when they *occur within cooperative learning groups* and *are carefully structured* to ensure that students manage them constructively. Social studies teachers need ways to enable differences of opinions and interpretations to foster positive interactions, productive inquiry, and academic achievement within their classrooms.

As Thomas Jefferson noted, "Difference of opinion leads to inquiry, and inquiry to truth." Despite Jefferson's faith in conflict, however, many social studies teachers have been reluctant to spark disagreements in the classroom. Teachers often suppress students' academic disagreements and consequently miss out on valuable opportunities to capture their own audiences and enhance learning.

Over the past twenty years, we have developed and tested a theory of controversy (Johnson, 1970, 1979; Johnson and Johnson, 1979, 1987,

1989; Johnson, Johnson, and Smith, 1986). We have also developed a series of curriculum units on energy and environmental issues, structured for academic controversies, which have been field tested in classrooms throughout the United States and Canada. This chapter describes the nature of controversy, a strategy to use controversy, the effects of this strategy on desired instructional outcomes, the process by which the strategy works, and how teachers can structure controversy within their classrooms.

The Nature of Controversy

Imagine a social studies teacher asking students to think about what problems hunting and gathering societies had to solve. Immediately, Jim jumps up and states that the major problem was how to hunt better so that they could have more food. Jane disagrees. She says the major problem was how to store food so that it would last longer. Juan stands up and tells both Jim and Jane that they are wrong; the major problem was how to domesticate the wild grains that grew in the area so that the people would be less dependent on hunting. Jim, Jane, and Juan begin to argue forcefully, bringing out the facts supporting the reasons why each thinks he or she is right.

Controversy exists when one student's ideas, information, conclusions, theories, and opinions are incompatible with those of another, and the two seek to reach an agreement. *Structured academic controversies* may be contrasted with concurrence seeking, debate, and individualistic learning. For instance, students can inhibit discussion to avoid any disagreement and compromise quickly to reach a consensus while they discuss the issue (*concurrence seeking*). Or students can appoint a judge and then debate the different positions with the expectation that the judge will determine who presented the better position (*debate*). Finally, students can work independently with their own set of materials at their own pace (*individualistic learning*).

Concurrence seeking is close to the groupthink concept of Janis (1982), in which members of a decision-making group set aside their doubts and misgivings about whatever policy is favored by the emerging consensus so as to be able to concur with the other members. The underlying motivation of groupthink is the strong desire to preserve the harmonious atmosphere of the group on which each member has become dependent for coping with the stresses of external crises and for maintaining self-esteem.

Structured controversies are resolved by engaging in deliberate discourse aimed at synthesizing novel solutions (e.g., creative problem solving, in Follet, 1940). When controversies are apppropriately structured, participants are required to research and prepare a position; rehearse orally the relevant information; advocate a position; teach their knowledge to peers; analyze, critically evaluate, and rebut information; reason both deductively and inductively; take the perspectives of others; and synthesize and integrate information into factual and judgmental conclusions that are summarized into a joint position to which all sides can agree.

Controversies are typically resolved by engaging in a structured discussion of the advantages and disadvantages of proposed actions to attain novel solutions. During controversy there is advocacy and challenge of each other's positions in order to reach the highest possible quality synthesis of both perspectives. Argumentative clashes develop, clarify, expand, and elaborate one's thinking about the issues being considered.

A key to the effectiveness of conflict procedures for promoting learning is the mixture of cooperative and competitive elements within the procedure (see Figure 12-1 on the following page). The greater the cooperative elements and the fewer the competitive elements, the more constructive the conflict (Deutsch, 1973).

Cooperative elements alone, however, do not ensure maximum productivity. There has to be both *cooperation and conflict*. Structured controversy activities are characterized by both positive goal and resource interdependence as well as by conflict. Debates feature positive resource interdependence, negative goal interdependence, and conflict. Within concurrence-seeking activites, there is only positive goal interdependence, whereas in individualistic learning situations there is neither interdependence nor intellectual conflict. The characteristics of these four methods are outlined in Figure 12-2 on page 311.

How Students Benefit

Over the last twenty years, the research on structured controversy, with one exception, has all been conducted within an experimental and

Figure 12-1 *Process of Controversy*

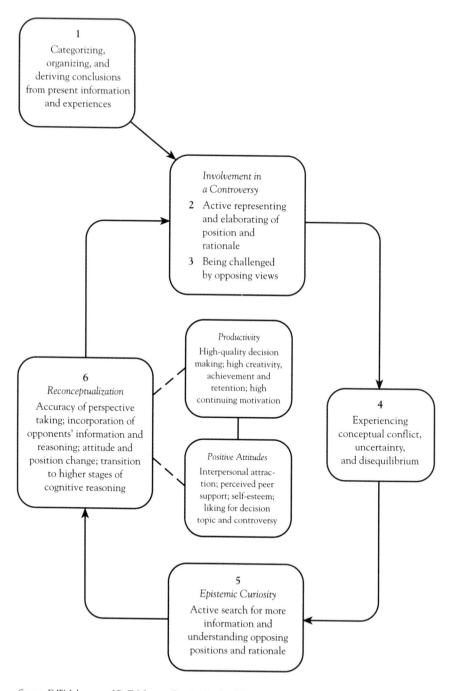

Source: D.W. Johnson and R. T. Johnson. *Creative Conflict*. Edina, MN: Interaction Book Company, 1987

Figure 12-2 *Characteristics of Four Controversy-Oriented Instructional Approaches*

Characteristic	Structured Controversy	Debate	Concurrence Seeking	Individualistic Learning
Positive Goal Interdependence	Yes	No	Yes	No
Positive Resource Interdependence	Yes	Yes	No	No
Negative Goal Interdependence	No	Yes	No	No
Conflict	Yes	Yes	No	No

field-experiment format. All studies randomly assigned subjects to controversy or noncontroversy classroom situations. The twenty-three studies, conducted using intermediate-elementary through college level, took from one to thirty hours of instructional time. The results of these studies provide a sound rationale for using this strategy in social studies classrooms.

These results may be grouped into three broad outcomes: achievement, positive interpersonal relationships, and psychological health and social competence. A number of other significant effects also found for the use of this strategy are described in this section.

Academic Achievement and Retention

In a meta-analysis of the available research, Johnson and Johnson (1989) found that controversy produced higher achievement and retention than did debate (effect-size = 0.77), individualistic learning (effect-size = 0.65), and concurrence seeking (effect-size = 0.42). The dozens of studies conducted indicate that students who participate in an academic controversy recall more correct information, are better able to transfer learning to new situations, use more complex and higher-level reasoning strategies in recalling and transferring information learned, and are better able to generalize the principles they learned to a wider variety of situations.

Quality of Problem Solving

If students are to become citizens capable of making reasoned judgments about the complex problems facing society, they must learn to use the higher-level reasoning and critical-thinking processes involved in effective problem solving, especially in those problems for which different viewpoints can plausibly be developed. To do so, students must enter emphatically into the arguments of both sides of an issue, ensure that the strongest possible case is made for each side, and arrive at a synthesis based on rational, probabilistic thought. Participating in structured controversy teaches students of all ages how to find high-quality solutions to complex problems.

Compared with concurrence-seeking, debate, and individualistic efforts, controversy tends to result in higher-quality decisions and solutions to complex problems for which different viewpoints can plausibly be developed. An interesting question concerning controversy and problem solving is what happens when erroneous information is presented by participants. Simply, can the advocacy of two conflicting but wrong solutions to a problem create a correct one? A number of studies with both adults and children have found significant gains in performance when erroneous information is presented by one or both sides in a controversy. Ames and Murray (1982) compared the impact of controversy, modeling, and nonsocial presentation of information on the performance of nonconserving, cognitively immature children on conservation tasks. The cognitively immature children were presented with erroneous information that conflicted with their initial position. Ames and Murray also found modest but significant gains in conservation performance. For instance, three children with scores of 0 out of 18 on the first test scored between 16 and 18 out of 18 on the posttest while eleven other children with initial scores of 0 scored between 5 and 15. They concluded that conflict *qua* conflict is not only cognitively motivating, but that the resolution of the conflict is likely to be in the direction of correct performance. In this limited way, two wrongs came to make a right.

Enhanced Creativity

> By blending the breath of the sun and the shade, true harmony comes into the world.
>
> —Tao Te Ching

Controversy tends to result in more frequent creative insights into the issues being discussed and in synthesis combining both perspectives (Johnson and Johnson, 1989). Structured controversy increases the number of ideas, the quality of ideas, the creation of original ideas, the use of a wider range of ideas, originality, the use of more varied strategies, and the number of creative, imaginative, and novel solutions. Studies have further demonstrated that particular controversy strategies encouraged group members to dig into a problem, raise issues, and settle them in ways that showed the benefits of a wide range of ideas being used. Structured controversy also resulted in a high degree of emotional involvement in and commitment to solving the problems the group was working on.

Exchange of Expertise

Controversy tends to result in greater exchange of expertise (Johnson and Johnson, 1989). Students often know different information and theories, make different assumptions, and have different opinions. Within any cooperative learning group, students with a wide variety of expertise and perspectives are told to work together to maximize each member's learning. Many times, students study different parts of an assignment and are expected to share their expertise with the other members of their group. Conflict among their ideas, information, opinions, preferences, theories, conclusions, and perspectives is inevitable, although not always public. Yet such conflicts are typically avoided or are handled destructively. Having the skills to manage controversies constructively to exchange information and perspectives among individuals with differing expertise is essential for maximal learning and growth.

Task Involvement

Task involvement refers to the quality and quantity of the physical and psychological energy that individuals invest in their efforts to achieve. Task involvement is reflected in the attitudes participants have toward the task and toward the controversy experience. Individuals who engage in controversies tend to like the tasks and the procedures better and generally have more positive attitudes toward the experience than do individuals who engage in concurrence-seeking discussions, individualistic efforts, or debate.

In addition, making and sharing knowledge through disagreement usually arouses emotions and increases involvement. Structured controversy tends to result in high task involvement, reflected in greater emotional commitment to solving the problem, greater enjoyment of the process, and more feelings of stimulation and enjoyment (Johnson and Johnson, 1989).

Intrapersonal Attraction Among Participants

It is often assumed that (1) the presence of controversy within a group will lead to difficulties in establishing good interpersonal relations while promoting negative attitudes toward other group members; and (2) arguing automatically leads to rejection, divisiveness, and hostility among peers (Collins, 1970). Within structured controversy and debate there are elements of disagreement, argumentation, and rebuttal that create difficulties in establishing good relationships. On the other hand, conflicts have been hypothesized potentially to create positive relationships among participants (Deutsch, 1962; Johnson, 1970). The evidence from classroom studies indicates that appropriate controversy promotes greater liking and social support among participants than does debate, concurrence seeking, no controversy, or individualistic efforts (Johnson and Johnson, 1989).

Psychological Health and Social Competence

A number of components of psychological health, such as academic self-esteem, perspective-taking accuracy, managing disagreements and conflicts constructively, and coping with the stresses involved in interacting with a variety of other people, are significantly strengthened by participating in academic controversies (Johnson & Johnson, 1989).

The Process of Structured Controversy

Since the general or prevailing opinion on any subject is rarely or never the whole truth, it is only by the collision of adverse opinion that the remainder of the truth has any chance of being supplied.

—JOHN STUART MILL

The hypothesis that intellectual challenge promotes higher-level reasoning, critical thinking, and metacognitive thought is derived from a number of premises.

1. When individuals are presented with a problem or decision, they draw an initial conclusion based on categorizing and organizing incomplete information, their limited experiences, and their specific perspective.

2. When individuals present their conclusion and its rationale to others, they engage in cognitive rehearsal, deepen their understanding of their position, and discover higher-level reasoning strategies.

3. Individuals are confronted by other people with different conclusions based on other people's information, experiences, and perspectives.

4. Individuals become uncertain as to the correctness of their views. A state of conceptual conflict or disequilibrium is aroused.

5. Uncertainty, conceptual conflict, and disequilibrium motivate an active search for more information, new experiences, and a more adequate cognitive perspective and reasoning process in hopes of resolving the uncertainty. Berlyne (1965) calls this active search *epistemic curiosity*. Divergent attention and thought are stimulated.

6. When a new, reconceptualized, and reorganized conclusion is derived, novel solutions and decisions are detected that are, on balance, qualitatively better than what otherwise would have been proposed.

Steps in the Process of Structured Controversy

Each of the above premises can serve as a step in the process of structured controversy as it may occur in the social studies classroom. These six steps are:

1. organizing information and deriving conclusions

2. presenting and advocating positions

3. being challenged by opposing views

4. conceptual conflict and uncertainty

5. epistemic curiosity and perspective taking

6. reconceptualization, synthesis, and integration

Each of these is elaborated below, along with examples as appropriate.

STEP 1: *Organizing Information and Deriving Conclusions*

In order to make high-quality decisions, individuals have to think of the proper alternatives, evaluate them, and choose the most promising one. When individuals are presented with a problem or decision, they form an initial conclusion based on categorizing and organizing incomplete information, their limited experiences, and their specific perspective. Using the framework of their perspective, individuals organize their current knowledge and experiences into a conceptual framework to derive a conclusion (through the use of inductive and deductive logic). The conceptual frameworks formed, however, often lead to inaccurate conclusions because of the limitations of one's existing perspective and one's expectations and mental set at the time. In essence, there is a tendency to allow one's prevailing perspective to dominate one's response to a situation, or to fix on the first seemingly satisfactory solution generated.

In thinking of proper alternative solutions and evaluating them, divergent, rather than convergent, thinking is required. Divergent thinking includes more ideas (fluency) and more classes of ideas (flexibility). To ensure that divergent thinking takes place and all major alternatives to a problem are given a fair hearing, each alternative needs to be presented in a complete and persuasive way within a receptive group.

Structured controversy begins by assigning the major alternatives to advocacy subgroups and having each subgroup develop its alternative in depth and plan how to present the best case possible for its alternative to the rest of the group.

Preparing a position to be advocated within a problem-solving group has clear effects on how well the position is understood and the level of reasoning used in thinking about the position. Higher-level conceptual understanding and reasoning are promoted when individuals have to teach one another a common way to think about problem situations. The preparation of a position involves the following.

1. *Formulating a thesis statement or claim.* A *thesis statement or claim* is a statement that the person wants accepted but which he or she

expects to be challenged. These statements often include qualifiers and reservations. *Qualifiers* are ways of communicating the confidence of the speaker in his or her claim; they involve words such as "probably," "sometimes," "never," and "always." *Reservations* are the circumstances under which the speaker would decide not to defend a statement; they involve words such as "unless" and "until." The thesis statement may be presented as a policy issue, a moral-value issue, a definitional issue, or as a fact-explanation issue, or some combination of all four.

2. *Listing and detailing the facts, information, and theories gathered that validate the thesis statement.*

3. *Linking the facts together in a logical structure that leads to conclusions.* The isolated facts are arranged, composed, and structured into conceptual systems that make the case for the thesis statement. The person strives for solid evidence, sound reasoning, and conclusions based on the principles of scientific inquiry and deductive and inductive logic.

There are conditions under which individuals will gather and organize facts, information, and theories into a rationale to support a thesis statement, and there are conditions under which they will not. Three of the conditions that may affect the adequacy of a person's rationale follow.

1. *The social and cognitive skills involved in formulating a rationale to support the thesis statement.* The person needs the skills of searching out relevant evidence and organizing it into a coherent and logical rationale. Doing so as part of a team requires a wide variety of interpersonal and small-group skills (Johnson, 1990; Johnson and F. Johnson, 1991).

2. *The effort expended in formulating a rationale.* The more effort expended, the more the position is valued. Individuals generally have an enhanced regard for their own productions relative to others', and the effort spent in preparing a position may be a source of enhanced regard for one's position.

3. *The ego- or task-orientation underlying the person's efforts.* Ego-oriented efforts tend to focus on proving one is "right" and "better," whereas task-oriented efforts tend to focus on contributing to a process of making the best decision possible.

Thus, adequate preparation of the position to be advocated is dependent on (a) being skilled in searching out relevant evidence and reasons; (b) working with others to organize the supportive data into a coherent and logical rationale; (c) one's willingness to expend considerable effort; and (d) being task oriented.

STEP 2: *Presenting and Advocating Positions*

Most students get few opportunities to present and advocate a position. Within the structured controversy strategy, students present and advocate positions to others who, in turn, are advocating opposing positions. *Advocacy* may be defined as presenting a position and providing reasons why others should adopt it. Decisions and conclusions are then reached through a process of argument and counterargument aimed at persuading others to adopt, modify, or drop positions. Advocating a position and defending it require engaging in considerable cognitive rehearsal and elaboration, increased understanding of the position, and the use of higher-level reasoning processes. Under certain conditions, disagreements within a group have been found to provide a greater amount of information and variety of facts as well as changes in the salience of known information than when less disagreement existed.

STEP 3: *Being Challenged by Opposing Views*

> *"Has anything escaped me?" I asked with some self-importance. "I trust there is nothing of consequence that I have overlooked?"*
>
> *"I'm afraid, my dear Watson, that most of your conclusions were erroneous. When I said that you stimulated me I meant, to be frank, that in noting your fallacies I was occasionally guided towards the truth."*
>
> —From *The Hound of the Baskervilles* by
> SIR ARTHUR CONAN DOYLE

In controversy, individuals' conclusions are challenged by the advocates of opposing positions. Members critically analyze one another's positions in attempts to discern weaknesses and strengths. They attempt to refute opposing positions while rebutting attacks on their position. At the same time, they are aware that they need to learn the information being presented and understand the perspective of the other group members.

The direct evidence indicates that individuals engaged in appropriate controversy are motivated to know the others' positions and to develop understanding and appreciation of them (e.g., Johnson and Johnson, 1989). Furthermore, hearing opposing views stimulates new cognitive analysis and frees individuals to create alternative and original conclusions. When contrary information is not clearly relevant to completing a task, it may be ignored, discounted, or perceived in biased ways in favor of supporting evidence. When individuals realize, however, that they are accountable for knowing the contrary information sometime in the near future, they will tend to learn it. Even being confronted with an erroneous point of view can result in more divergent thinking and the generation of novel and more cognitively advanced solutions.

STEP 4: *Conceptual Conflict and Uncertainty*

Hearing other alternatives being advocated, having one's position criticized and refuted, and being challenged by information incompatible with one's conclusions lead to conceptual conflict and uncertainty. The greater the disagreement among group members, the more frequently controversy occurs. The greater the number of people disagreeing with a person's position, the more competitive the context of the controversy. The more affronted the person feels, the greater the conceptual conflict and uncertainty the person experiences (Johnson and Johnson, 1989).

STEP 5: *Epistemic Curiosity and Perspective Taking*

When faced with intellectual opposition within a cooperative context, students ask one another for more information. Conceptual conflict motivates an active search for more information (called *epistemic curiosity*) in hopes of resolving the uncertainty. Indices of epistemic curiosity include individuals actively searching for more information, seeking to understand opposing positions and rationales, and attempting to view the situation from opposing perspectives.

STEP 6: *Reconceptualization, Synthesis, and Integration*

Andre Gide said, "One completely overcomes only what one assimilates." Nothing could be more true of controversy. When overt controversy is structured within a problem-solving, decision-making, or learning group by identifying alternatives and assigning members to advocate the best case for each alternative, the purpose is not to choose the best alternative. The purpose is to create a synthesis of the best reasoning and conclusions from all the various alternatives.

Synthesizing occurs when individuals integrate a number of different ideas and facts into a single position. It is the intellectual bringing together of ideas and facts and engaging in inductive reasoning by restating a large amount of information into a conclusion or summary. Synthesizing is a creative process involving seeing new patterns within a body of evidence, viewing the issue from a variety of perspectives, and generating a number of optional ways of integrating the evidence. This requires probabilistic (knowledge is available only in degrees of certainty) rather than dualistic (there is only right and wrong, and authority should not be questioned) or relativistic thinking (authorities are seen as sometimes right but that right and wrong depend on your perspective). The dual purposes of synthesis are to arrive at the best possible decision or solution and to find a position on which all group members can agree and commit themselves.

There is evidence that controversy handled in the ways described here leads to accuracy of perspective taking, incorporation of others' information and reasoning into individuals' own position, attitude and position change, and transition to higher stages of cognitive reasoning, all of which contribute to the quality of individuals' reconceptualization, synthesis, and integration.

Within the social studies classroom, students need sufficient time and guidance to complete the structured controversy and learning tasks designated for each step, completing step one before moving to the next step.

Conditions Determining the Constructiveness of Structured Controversy Guidelines for the Classroom

> *He that wrestles with us strengthens our nerves, and sharpens our skill. Our antagonist is our helper.*
>
> —EDMUND BURKE in *Reflection of the Revolution in France*

Although controversies can operate in a beneficial way, they will not do so under all conditions. As with all types of conflicts, the potential for either constructive or destructive outcomes is present. Whether there are positive or negative consequences depends on the conditions under which controversy occurs and the way in which it is managed. These conditions and procedures follow.

The first is the *goal structure* within which the controversy occurs. Communication of information is far more complete, accurate, encouraged, and utilized in a cooperative context than in a competitive context. Controversy within a cooperative context promotes more open-minded listening to the opposing position. Within a competitive context, controversy promotes a close-minded orientation in which individuals are unwilling to make concessions to the opponents' viewpoints and refuse to incorporate any of the opponents' viewpoints into their own positions.

The second condition is the *heterogeneity of participants*. Heterogeneity among individuals leads to potential controversy and to more diverse interaction patterns and resources for achievement and problem solving.

The third condition is the *amount of relevant information distributed among participants*. The more information individuals have about an issue, the more successful their problem solving is likely to be. Individuals, however, need the required interpersonal and group skills to ensure that everyone involved contributes his or her relevant information and that the information is synthesized effectively.

The fourth condition is the *ability of participants to disagree with one another without creating defensiveness*. For controversies to be managed constructively, individuals need a number of conflict-management skills, such as disagreeing with others' ideas while confirming one another's competence, and seeing the issue from a number of perspectives.

The fifth condition is *students' ability to engage in rational argument*. Rational argumentation includes generating ideas, collecting and organizing relevant information, using inductive and deductive logic, and making tentative conclusions based on current understanding.

Structuring Academic Controversies: Classroom Example

What might a well-structured academic controversy look like were you to visit a classroom where this strategy was being used? An example of an appropriately structured controversy follows.

The social studies teacher assigns students to groups of four and asks each group to prepare a report entitled "The Role of Regulations in the Management of Hazardous Waste." There is to be one report from each group representing the members' best analysis of the issue. The groups are divided into two-person advocacy teams, with one team given the position that More Regulations Are Needed and the other team given the position that Fewer Regulations Are Needed. Each advocacy team is given articles and technical materials supporting its assigned position.

They are then given time to read and discuss the material with their partner and to plan how best to advocate their assigned position so that (a) they learn the information and perspective within the articles and technical reports; (b) the opposing team is convinced of the soundness of the team's position; and (c) the members of the opposing team learn the material contained within the articles and technical reports. To accomplish this, students proceed through five steps.

First, students research the issue, organize their information, and prepare their positions. Learning begins with students gathering information. They then categorize and organize their present information and experiences so that a conclusion is derived.

Second, the two advocacy teams actively present and advocate their positions. Each pair presents its position and reasoning to the opposition, thereby engaging in considerable cognitive rehearsal and elaboration of its position and the rationale. When the other team presents, students' reasoning and conclusions are challenged by the opposing view, and they experience conceptual conflict and uncertainty.

Third, students engage in a general discussion in which they advocate their position, rebut attacks on their position, refute the opposing position, and seek to learn both positions. The group discusses the issue, critically evaluates the opposing position and its rationale, defends positions, and compares the strengths and weaknesses of the two positions. When students are challenged by conclusions and information that are incompatible with and do not fit with their reasoning and conclusions, conceptual conflict, uncertainty, and disequilibrium result. Because of their uncertainty, students experience epistemic curiosity. Therefore, students actively search for more information and experiences to support their position and seek to understand the opposing position and its supporting rationale. During this time, students' uncertainty and information search are actively encouraged and promoted by the teacher.

Fourth, students reverse perspectives and present the opposing position. Each advocacy pair presents the best case possible for the opposing position.

Fifth, the group of four reaches a consensus and prepares a group report. The emphasis during this instructional period is on students reconceptualizing their position and synthesizing the best information and reasoning from both sides. The group's report should reflect its best reasoned judgment. Each group member then individually takes an examination on the factual information contained in the reading materials.

Structuring the Academic Controversy Task: Planning and Implementation Decisions

> *The best way ever devised for seeking the truth in any given situation is advocacy: presenting the pros and cons from different, informed points of view and digging down deep into the facts.*
> —HAROLD S. GENEEN, Former CEO, ITT

The basic format for structuring academic controversy tasks is the focus of this section. The task must be structured cooperatively and so that there are at least two well-documented positions (pro and con). The choice of topic depends on the interests of the instructor and the purposes of the course.[1] Once the topic has been selected, the teacher would engage in and complete the tasks associated with the three stages of this instructional strategy.

Preparation of Instructional Materials

Instructional materials must be prepared in advance so that group members know what position they have been assigned and where they can find supporting information. The following materials are needed for each position:

1. a clear description of the group's task

2. a description of the phases of the controversy procedure and the interpersonal and small-group skills to be used during each phase

---

[1] A more detailed description of conducting academic controversies may be found in Johnson, Johnson, and Smith (1986) and Johnson and Johnson (1987).

3. a definition of the position to be advocated with a summary of the key arguments supporting the position

4. resource materials (including a bibliography) to provide evidence for the elaboration of the arguments supporting the position to be advocated

Structuring the Controversy-Related Classroom Tasks

The principal requirements for a successful structured controversy are a cooperative context, skillful group members, and heterogeneity of group membership. The social studies teacher structures the learning tasks for these to occur as follows:

1. *Assigns students to heterogeneous groups of four* and divides each group into two pairs. A high- and a low-ability reader may be assigned to each pair. The responsibility of the pair is to comprehend the information supporting its assigned position and prepare a presentation and a series of persuasive arguments to use in the discussion with the opposing pair.

2. *Assigns pro and con positions* to the pairs and gives students supporting materials to read and study. A bibliography of further sources of information may also be given. A section of resource materials may be set up in the library.

3. *Structures for positive interdependence* by highlighting the cooperative goals. All group members will reach a consensus on the issue, master all the information relevant to both sides of the issue (measured by a test), and participate in writing a quality group report and making a presentation to the class. The teacher also ensures *resource interdependence* (materials are jigsawed within the group) and *rewards interdependence* (bonus points are given to members if all of them learn the basic information contained in the two positions and score well on the test).

4. *Structures for individual accountability* by ensuring that each student participates in preparing the assigned position, presenting the position, discussing the issue, reversing perspectives, preparing the report, presenting the report, and taking an individual test on the material.

Conducting the Structured Controversy Tasks

1. *Assign each pair the following tasks:*

    a. Learn its position and the supporting arguments and information.

    b. Research all information relevant to its position.

    c. Give the opposing pair any information found supporting the opposing position.

    d. Prepare a persuasive presentation to be given to the other pair.

    e. Prepare a series of persuasive arguments to be used in the discussion with the opposing pair.

    The group members research and prepare their positions, presentation, and arguments. To facilitate student completion of these tasks, the following instructions should be given.

    "Plan with your partner how to advocate your position effectively. Read the materials supporting your position. Find more information in the library reference books to support your position. Plan a persuasive presentation. Make sure you and your partner master the information supporting your assigned position and present it in a persuasive and complete way so that the other group members will comprehend and learn the information."

2. *Have each pair present its position to the other.* Presentations should involve more than one medium and should persuasively advocate the "best case" for the position. Announce to students that there is no arguing during this time. Students should listen carefully to the opposing position. Students are told:

    "As a pair, present your position forcefully and persuasively. Listen carefully and learn the opposing position. Take notes, and clarify anything you do not understand."

3. *Have students openly discuss the issue by freely exchanging their information and ideas.* As this phase of the strategy begins, students are reminded to:

    "Argue forcefully and persuasively for your position, presenting as many facts as you can to support your point of view. Listen critically to the opposing pair's position, asking for the facts that support their viewpoint and then present counterarguments. Remember, this is a complex issue, and you need to know both sides to write a good report."

For higher-level reasoning and critical thinking to occur, it is necessary to probe and push one another's conclusions. Students are to ask for data to support one another's statements, clarify rationales, and show why their position is a rational one. Students evaluate critically the opposing position and its rationale, defend their own position, and compare the strengths and weaknesses of the two positions. Students refute the claims being made by the opposing pair and rebut the attacks on their own position. Students are to follow the specific rules for constructive controversy. Students should also take careful notes on and thoroughly learn the opposing position. Sometimes a time-out period needs to be provided so that pairs can caucus and prepare new arguments.

Social studies teachers should encourage more spirited arguing, take sides when a pair is in trouble, play devil's advocate, ask one group to observe another group engaging in a spirited argument, and generally stir up the discussions.

4. *Have the pairs reverse perspectives and positions* by presenting the opposing position as sincerely and forcefully as they can. It helps to have the pairs change chairs. They can use their own notes but may not see the materials developed by the opposing pair. Students' instructions are:

"Working as a pair, present the opposing pair's position as if you were they. Be as sincere and forceful as you can. Add any new facts you know. Elaborate their position by relating it to other information you have previously learned."

5. *Have the group members drop their advocacy and reach a decision by consensus.* Then they:

a. Write a group report that includes their joint position and the supporting evidence and rationale. Often the resulting position is a third perspective or synthesis that is more rational and comprehensive than the two assigned. All group members sign the report indicating that they agree with it, can explain its content, and consider it ready to be evaluated.

b. Take a test on both positions. If all members score above the preset standard of excellence, each receives five bonus points.

c. Process how well the group functioned and how their performance may be improved during the next controversy. Teachers may wish to structure the group processing to highlight the specific conflict-management skills students need to master. The social studies teacher would also instruct students to summarize and synthesize the best arguments for *both* points of view. Students should reach consensus on a position that is supported by the facts and change their minds only when the facts and the rationale clearly indicate they should do so. Students should write their reports with the supporting evidence and rationale for the synthesis that the group has agreed on. When students are certain the report is as good as they can make it, they should sign it. Reports should be organized and presented to the entire class.

Teach Students Conflict Skills

No matter how carefully teachers structure controversies, if students do not have the interpersonal and small-group skills to manage conflicts constructively, the controversy does not produce its potential effects. The *social skills* emphasized are those involved in systematically advocating an intellectual position and evaluating and criticizing the position advocated by others, as well as those skills involved in synthesis and consensual decision making. Students should be taught to:

1. Emphasize the mutuality of the situation and avoid win-lose dynamics. To do this, focus on coming to the best decision possible, not on winning.

2. Confirm others' competence while disagreeing with their positions and challenging their reasoning. Be critical of ideas, not people; i.e., challenge and refute the ideas of the members of the opposing pair, but do not reject these members personally.

3. Separate your personal worth from criticism of your ideas.

4. Listen to everyone's ideas, even if you do not agree with them.

5. Bring out the all the ideas and facts supporting both sides; then put them together in a way that makes sense. Sort out the differences between positions before attempting to integrate ideas.

6. Take the opposing perspective in order to understand the opposing position. Try to understand both sides of the issue.

7. Change your mind when the evidence clearly indicates that you should.

8. Paraphrase what someone has said if it is not clear.

9. Emphasize rationality in seeking the best possible answer, given the available data.

10. Follow the golden rule of conflict: *Act toward your opponents as you would have them act toward you.* If you want people to listen to you, then listen to them. If you want others to include your ideas in their thinking, then include their ideas in your thinking. If you want others to take your perspective, then take their perspective.

Summary

Social studies may be taught by giving answers or by asking questions. It is within social studies classes that students can consider the great questions that have dominated our past and determine our present and future. Leaving such questions out can create the impression that social studies is simply a series of events and people. If students are to consider the great questions, these must be presented in a way that clarifies possible alternative answers and opposing points of view.

When teachers lecture about events and people and structure competition among students, they in fact create the conditions under which students will avoid listening to different points of view and defensively reject ideas and people that might prove them wrong. In order to avoid close-minded attempts to "win" in answering the great questions, social studies teachers must structure the learning situation in ways that promote interest, curiosity, inquiry, and open-minded problem solving. To do so, social studies teachers need to interrelate two powerful instructional procedures: cooperative learning and academic controversy.

Controversy exists when one student's ideas, information, conclusions, theories, and opinions are incompatible with those of another, and the two seek to reach an agreement. Controversies are an inherent aspect of inquiry, decision making, problem solving, reasoned judgment, and critical thinking, and are inevitable. When students become intellectually and emotionally involved in cooperative efforts, controversies will occur no matter what teachers do. Controversies are critical events that may bring increased learning, creative insight, high-quality problem solving, and decision making. They also may bring closer and more positive relationships, greater social competence, and enhanced psychological health. Or they may bring closed minds and poorly conceived decisions, lasting resentment and smoldering hostility, psychological scars, rigidly ineffectual behavior, and a refusal to change or learn.

Whether positive or negative outcomes result depends on how effectively teachers structure the controversy process. Within well-structured controversies, students make an initial judgment, present conclusions to other group members, are challenged with opposing views, become uncertain about the correctness of their views, search for new information and understanding, incorporate others' perspectives and reasoning into their thinking, and reach a new set of conclusions.

Although this process sometimes occurs naturally within cooperative learning groups, it may be considerably enhanced when teachers structure academic controversies. This structure involves dividing a cooperative group into two pairs and assigning them opposing positions. The pairs then develop their position, present it to the other pair, listen to the opposing position, engage in a discussion in which they attempt to refute the other side and rebut attacks on their position, reverse perspectives and present the other position, and then drop all advocacy and seek a synthesis that takes both perspectives and positions into account.

Controversies tend to be constructive when the situational context is cooperative, there is some heterogeneity among group members, information and expertise are distributed within the group, members have the necessary conflict skills, and there is rational argumentation.

It is vital for citizens to seek reasoned judgment on the complex problems facing our society. Especially important is educating individuals to solve problems for which different points of view can plausibly be developed. To do so, individuals must enter empathetically into the arguments of both sides of the issue, ensure that the strongest possible case is made for each side, and arrive at a synthesis based on rational thought.

Structured academic controversies are now being used in numerous elementary, secondary, and college classrooms to enable individuals to learn how to address the great questions of our (and previous) times and ensure that high-quality solutions are found to complex problems.

References

Ames, G., and F. Murray. 1982. When two wrongs make a right: Promoting cognitive change by social conflict. *Developmental Psychology* (18): 894-97.

Berlyne, D. 1965. Curiosity and education. In J. Krumholtz, ed., *Learning and the educational process*. Chicago: Rand McNally.

Collins, B. 1970. *Social psychology*. Reading, MA: Addison-Wesley.

Deutsch, M. 1962. Cooperation and trust: Some theoretical notes. In M. Jones, ed., *Nebraska symposium on motivation*, 275-319. Lincoln, NE: University of Nebraska Press.

———. 1973. *The resolution of conflict*. New Haven, CT: Yale University Press.

Follet, M. 1940. Constructive conflict. In H. Metcalf and L. Urwick, eds., *Dynamic administration: The collected papers of Mary Parker Follet*, 30-49. New York: Harper.

Janis, I. 1982. *Groupthink: Psychological studies of policy decisions and fiascoes*. Boston, MA: Houghton Mifflin.

Johnson, D. W. 1970. *Social psychology of education*. Edina, MN: Interaction Book Company.

———. 1979. *Educational psychology*. Englewood Cliffs, NJ: Prentice Hall.

———. 1980. Group processes: Influences of student-student interaction on school outcomes. In J. McMillan, ed., *The social psychology of school learning*. New York: Academic Press.

———. 1990. *Reaching out: Interpersonal effectiveness and self-actualization*, 4th ed. Englewood Cliffs, NJ: Prentice Hall.

Johnson D. W., and F. Johnson. 1991. *Joining together: Group theory and group skills*, 4th ed. Englewood Cliffs, NJ: Prentice Hall.

Johnson, D. W., and R. T. Johnson. 1979. Conflict in the classroom: Controversy and learning. *Review of Educational Research* (49): 51-61.

———. 1987. *Creative conflict*. Edina, MN: Interaction Book Company.

———. 1989. *Cooperation and competition: Theory and research*. Edina, MN: Interaction Book Company.

―――. 1992. *Creative controversy.* Edina, MN: Interaction Book Company.

Johnson, D. W., R. T. Johnson, and K. Smith. 1986. Academic conflict among students: Controversy and learning. In R. Feldman, *Social psychology of education.* New York: Cambridge University Press.

13.

The Cooperative Group Research Paper Project: Using Cooperative Learning Principles for Classroom Research

A. MICHAEL JACKSON

The research paper in its various forms and mutations has long been an integral part of middle- and high-school social studies curriculums. Since research papers are a tradition in American education, nearly every mainstream student has at some point in his or her education been asked (assigned, commanded, forced?) to write a research paper. However, in an informal survey of social studies students, I found that only about 50 percent of those coming into eleventh-grade American history had ever completed any form of formal research paper and less than 5 percent classified the experience as positive. This overview should not imply a negative view of the formal research paper or of the necessary skills involved in conducting quality research and writing a quality research paper, even though many research experiences are less than pleasant.

Research papers are not traditionally fun, and if by chance they do turn out to be rewarding experiences, students assume that the topic chosen was responsible for the positive outcome, not the techniques for searching and documenting that are entailed in completing a research paper. The "aftertaste" that many carry for research (due in part to the failure to understand the potential benefits of acquiring research skills) motivates them to take any means to avoid the research and the dreaded paper that follows.

Cooperative learning offers a powerful solution for this dilemma. A cynic might call cooperative learning activities "sharing the misery"; I call it "sharing the burden" through peer-assisted cooperation. My experience has been that acquiring research-related skills and fostering positive attitude change toward research expand exponentially when work on acquiring the research skills is shared.

The particular cooperative research project described here incorporates many principles of cooperative learning, some principal elements of Learning for Mastery, and the standard guidelines of the formal topical research paper. I developed this cooperative learning strategy in response to my students' lack of prior research skills and their negative attitude toward research and the research paper. This cooperative research project can be used within as well as across the social studies, humanities, and language arts classrooms. Finally, this research-group strategy emerged from my concerns that my students could not (or would not) complete a standard research paper despite grade histories showing they had adequate background knowledge to do the assignment. This strategy's primary purposes were to help students (a) acquire and refine appropriate research and writing abilities; (b) improve long-term retention of research-related skills; and (c) develop positive attitudes toward research and its benefits for individual learning success.[1]

This cooperative learning approach helps students master many abilities needed to complete acceptable library prewriting research as well as to write an acceptable research paper. Specific decisions that teachers will need to consider are described below in order to enable them to construct an image of what this cooperative research project might look like in their classroom situations. Combined with the teacher's current background information about study, library research, and research writing knowledge, this chapter should enable teachers to establish and structure cooperative groups that will significantly increase the quality of student research. My experiences with this cooperative research strategy have been far more positive than any other strategy I have to used for this purpose.

Background and Context

Much of the technical and philosophical structure for the cooperative learning part of this project was drawn from *Circles of Learning:*

---

[1] Robert J. Stahl was instrumental in helping to clarify, modify, and fine-tune many of the steps and guidelines of this cooperative learning project.

Cooperation in the Classroom and the concept of *positive interdependence* (Johnson, Johnson and Holubec, 1986). The balance between the individual competitive drive to succeed and the responsibility of each group member to perform assigned tasks in order for the group to reach its goals seemed just the right mix of peer pressure and team spirit. The skeleton of this project sprang from reading an elaborated lesson plan for a middle-school social studies project written by Flora Wyatt (1988).

The details concerning the specificity of what information and abilities students were to learn relative to the research, study and library skills, and writing a formal paper were drawn from the literature on Mastery Learning and Outcome-Based Education (OBE) (Block, Efthim, and Burns, 1989; Spady, 1987) and the work in learning theory and instructional design of Stahl (1989; 1992, in press). The ideas in these sources that were especially helpful were those associated with (a) describing the outcome abilities that students were to acquire and (b) determining the information base students had to acquire and apply if they were to master the targeted research skills.

Planning—and Faculty Interdependence if Possible

The social studies teacher may carry out this cooperative research project as part of his or her course activities and requirements. This project may be integrated with units on library research skills offered by, or team taught with, media specialists and/or librarians. It may also be used in cooperation with one or more members of the language arts department. Objectives for the unit subsection on library research skills can be selected jointly with the media specialist or English teacher.

This strategy is enhanced when the classroom teacher has the strong cooperation of the media specialist. He or she can be responsible for instructing students on the technical library skills necessary for effective research. When this instruction occurs, the teacher is free to monitor data collection and documentation for the research paper as students move about the library. Since there are three major outcome abilities targeted for student learning—library skills, conducting the research, and writing the formal research paper—the likelihood of student success increases when the teacher coordinates his or her course and unit objectives with the librarian or media specialist.

To successfully complete this planning phase of research instruction, library skill-related objectives, performance expectations, time schedules, group rosters and seating charts, topic assignments, role assignments, formative and summative tests, as well as evaluation criteria are agreed upon with the librarian *prior to* the first day of the project. The more committed the media person is to this cooperative research project, the more assistance students will have in attaining the library-related skills and locating topic-related reference materials.

The participation of the librarian is an effective means of systematically approaching and teaching resource awareness, indexing in various sources, cross-referencing, subject categorizing and sorting, technologies available, library systems in general, and physical location of materials on site. Working in advance and collaborating with the librarian(s) helps him or her to know up front what students are expected to do and what topics they are to research.

The target reference sources that students are to use include, but are not limited to, the following:

1. card catalogue (and/or the computer referencing system)

2. *Readers' Guide to Periodical Literature*

3. vertical files

4. *News Bank*

5. *SIRS* (Social Issues Resources Series)

6. reference sources/shelves (encyclopedia, almanac, and so forth)

Diagnosing and Providing Prerequisite Information and Skills

Student avoidance of, or failure to complete, research may be attributable to a lack of adequate reference search skills and abilities that are necessary before they can successfully complete the actual research paper. They may lack adequate study and organization skills *prior to* writing the actual research paper. Prerequisite abilities such as note taking and outlining are equally necessary to complete adequate research. However, all too often teachers assume that these abilities are already part of their students' prior knowledge and abilities. As many social studies teachers can attest, the abilities most students do have in these prerequisite skills are generally faulty, if not missing, even among students who believe these skills have been mastered.

Accurate assessment of prerequisite knowledge and skills about how to use library tools, to do formal research, and to construct a research paper is difficult without a formal instrument. For the English classroom, this usually would not be a problem, but social studies teachers rarely take the time or have the materials to adequately preassess students' research abilities. The social studies teacher may visit with members of the English department or the librarian in order to obtain both the details on these skills and the evaluation instruments to check the extent to which each student has each prerequisite ability. As necessary, taking a day or more providing and reviewing basic research guidelines with the entire class and within cooperative learning groups can greatly improve students' research performances, especially when mastery of these guidelines is attained *prior to* starting the written research paper.[2]

Formation of Heterogeneous Groups

Cooperative learning views student heterogeneity as a resource to be taken advantage of rather than as a problem to be solved. In cooperative groups, students are expected to share a broad range of perspectives and understandings to help one another master academic content (Slavin, 1987). Research supporting the advantages of heterogeneity of small-group membership is overwhelming, especially when the cooperative groups are given the all-important factors of clear learning objectives and sufficient on-task time to work together toward a common goal. Therefore, as much as is possible, social studies teachers should ensure a mixture of *heterogeneous ability grouping* (based on reading scores, pre-assessments, grade histories, and so forth) and *heterogeneous gender/ethnic/racial grouping* in order to distribute skills and points of view.

I must admit that I had my reservations about setting up heterogeneous groups, since the theory sounded better than what I imagined would happen in real classroom settings. *In this case, the theory did work in practice.* I am very pleased with all the positive things that happened within and as a result of the heterogeneous groups that would not have happened had I grouped in more traditional and convenient ways.

---

[2] If time permits, a very good slide/tape presentation entitled *How to survive in school: Note-taking and outline skills* sequences the procedures for taking notes and transferring those from lecture/articles to formal outlines in a lively rehearsal-oriented presentation (The Center for Humanities, Inc., 2 Holland Ave., White Plains, N.Y. 10603).

For this group strategy, I have found a three-member group to be the most manageable and effective. An ABC jigsaw pattern, such as illustrated in Figure 13-1, allows an operational structure of a director and two assistants within each group. (Figure 13-2 on the following page describes the roles of the director and assistants.) Within these heterogeneous groups, responsibilities are distributed accordingly, with the director providing and maintaining focus as well as monitoring assignments and progress within the group.

Figure 13-1 *The Name of the Three Primary Task Roles of Members of Each Cooperative Learning Research Group*

The Cooperative Research Groups at Work

Once groups are established, the teacher distributes a topic list for group discussion and decision making (see Figure 13-3 on page 339). The topics listed are drawn from social and historical genres and should be developed in conjunction with the school media specialist in order to verify that information on each specific topic will be available in the reference sources located in the school library.[3]

The availability of in-school resources and confirmation of resource material are key factors in ensuring success, since prior confirmation

---

[3] This requirement is especially important in small schools or schools located in places where students are not likely to have access to many resources outside their school library.

Figure 13-2   *List of Responsibilities for Each Member of the Research Group**

COOPERATIVE GROUPS: ROLE ASSIGNMENTS

Group Director (10 percent bonus role—subject to teacher evaluation)

1. Is responsible for project organization and presentation
2. Is responsible for final draft of written research
3. Is responsible for assigning tasks within the group
4. Lists responsibilities assigned to individual members of the group
5. Evaluates each member's performance when project is complete by distributing 30 cooperation/participation points based on merit (10 percent of total project grade)
6. Collects article outlines from members and organizes a single master outline covering entire range of research
7. Oversees development of a group list of focus questions that the research paper will attempt to answer, approximately 10–15 total questions (questions will be mounted on posters for class presentation)
8. Directs decisions concerning which of the 18 sources collected by the group members will be used to present the most concise and comprehensive research paper
9. Makes rough-draft writing assignments

Assistant A

1. Is responsible for collecting bibliographic references from each member's article research and compiling a complete bibliography for the research project
2. Is responsible for presenting bibliographic references in the proper format suitable to the individual source
3. Is responsible for contributing half of the rough draft to the group project
4. Cites any material quoted in rough draft using the required bibliographic reference format
5. Contributes to the group project focus-question list
6. Completes all tasks assigned by the group director

Assistant B

1. Is responsible for creating a cover page listing title, group members, student numbers, dates, and class; and for placing the report in a binder
2. Is responsible for creating a table of contents that covers all materials within the group project
3. Is responsible for contributing half of the rough draft to the group project
4. Cites any material quoted in rough draft using bibliographic reference format
5. Contributes to the group list of focus questions
6. Completes all tasks assigned by the group director

---

*   This form is similar to the one used by the author. It may, of course, be modified for local needs and expectations. However, any responsibility list should be clearly delineated and precise, as in this example.

Figure 13-3   *Suggested Topics for Research Papers**

1. Achievement testing in schools
2. Acid rain
3. Advertising/Propaganda
4. AIDS
5. Air travel—accidents, safety
6. Alcoholism
7. Alternate energy resources
8. Automobile safety
9. Budget deficits
10. Capital punishment: Does it work?
11. Child abuse
12. Children of divorced parents
13. Defense industries: Fraud? Influence?
14. Droughts and food prices
15. Euthanasia
16. Farming—organic, future
17. Gambling—addiction, lotteries
18. Gun control
19. Housing for the poor
20. Illiteracy
21. Interfaith marriages
22. Iran hostage affair
23. Job stress
24. Medical research—animal
25. Medical research—human
26. Military bases—closings
27. Neo-Nazism
28. Nuclear energy
29. Nuclear weapons
30. Persian Gulf War (1990-1991)
31. Police brutality: Real or alleged?
32. Pollution and limiting pollution
33. Rain forest conservation
34. Sexual harassment
35. Smoking: Rights of smokers/non-smokers
36. Soviet Union breakup
37. Suicide
38. Teenage pregnancy
39. Toxic waste disposal
40. Unemployment
41. Violence—cultural
42. Violence—domestic
43. Water pollution
44. Wildlife conservation

---

* A list with a large number of options should be presented. Specific topics should be linked to the specific subject matter the teacher wants students to learn.

assures that groups will avoid the frustration that often confronts novice researchers when they "dead end."

With topic lists in hand, the groups are allowed to discuss (debate) the topics provided before reaching a consensus. Each group selects three prioritized choices, ranked one, two, and three, with these choices and rankings being unanimous. The second and third choices are made to avoid replication of topics and depletion of resources in the library. Group members negotiate both conflicts and learning tasks among themselves because all members will eventually be responsible for research in the area selected. At times I have observed students resort to a simple coin toss to settle claims about the topic to be researched.

Initial Group Dynamics and Empowerment

The group dynamics that evolve through the democratic and consensus-making processes are interesting. Heterogeneous grouping works amazingly well under these circumstances. Instead of a group dominated by the director (usually of high ability or academically aggressive), what typically develops is a moderator's role for the director with the two assistants advocating various topics. My personal experience is that there are surprisingly few instances of medium- or low-ability students acquiescing to high-ability students. In fact, most assistants speak with fervor once they realize they have the responsibility and power of choice—as well as the accountability that accompanies both.

The student empowerment that is characteristic of appropriately structured cooperative learning tasks is a dynamic factor that fundamentally alters the overall performance of the groups, as well as every member in each group. Empowerment in cooperative learning is *not* simply telling students to choose a topic of interest. Empowerment allows students to make decisions, to take risks, to assume responsibility, and to follow up decisions by actions for which they are individually and collectively accountable.

Empowerment through interdependence shapes the decision-making processes because a corporate goal places responsibility for topic choice, group role dispersement, style, editorial stance, data arrangement, problem solving, resource use, and any number of unexpected minutia choices within the group structure rather than in the traditional, externally imposed arena controlled by the teacher. Often groups, suddenly empowered, initially display a visible rush of power, often chaotic, as all members attempt to talk and act at once. This quickly dissipates as the *reality of responsibility* to peers and task settles in and brings reasoned and reasonable choices into focus.

Group empowerment also holds an unanticipated side effect for social studies teachers moving from traditional direct instruction to cooperative structures. Teachers act as facilitators and troubleshooters rather than "terminators," which is certainly a positive and welcome change. However, these new roles carry with them inherent anxiety resulting from letting go. Cooperative learning structures tend to initiate such anxiety for many teachers, especially when control and coverage have become highly prized commodities that ignore actual student outcomes. The teacher who empowers students must be willing to free students to make choices; to think, act, and feel responsible; and to pursue courses of independent action within the guidelines and structure provided to complete the group tasks. After all, if asked, most teachers would say that the creation of self-sufficient, successful young adults is an exit outcome all education strives to attain. Ironically, by using traditional methods that stress control and coverage, teachers prevent students from achieving one of the teachers' most valued goals: self-sufficient learners. As attainment of valued academic outcomes becomes more of a reality through cooperative learning, a positive and productive long-term student-teacher relationship emerges.

Becoming Skilled Users of Library Tools and References

The class visits the media center. When possible, the librarian and/or media specialist presents a detailed library orientation followed by an introduction to each of the targeted references. These presentations may include whole-group lectures, videos, handouts, demonstrations, overheads, student comprehension checking in groups of two, and hands-on rehearsal activities. For instance, the students may be given a map of the library with important areas marked out and a list of fifteen sources to locate. Students then move about the library and pick stick-on labels from various areas, placing these in proper locations on their maps. Simple yet effective tasks like these are needed at this stage.

The map is the first page of a library orientation packet that should be completed over the approximately five to ten days this portion of the project requires. Other material in the packet may include information about reference sources, rehearsal activities using these sources, and bibliographic documentation pages for use in writing the research paper later.[4] A new resource is presented approximately every two days. The first period is devoted to presentation and acquisition of critical information about the source; the second to researching the group topic in that source. Students work in their cooperative groups to master the information presented for that day and to help ensure that each member is able to apply the information stressed. They may even quiz one another over this content. They also work in these groups to locate topic-aligned reference sources and information for their final written research papers.

Formative quizzes over targeted must-learn information and skills are given on the first day after the introduction and orally checked. This quiz is kept by the student until the second day, when a second formative quiz is given using three of the original five questions and two new questions covering the same information and abilities. The attempt here is to focus the learning and teaching to specific must-learn information. All formative (or daily) quizzes are aligned with the summative (final) test given at the end of the library orientation phase of the project. *Interdependence* is maintained by giving an individual grade for the skills segment but offering a bonus for groups in which all members achieve the 80 percent mastery level on the formative and summative tests.

Return to the Classroom

With the completion of the data-gathering phase of the project and the summative test of library skills (administered while still in the library), each group member is required to have a minimum of six articles that have been copied and highlighted or notated, outlined, and documented for bibliographical citation. These materials are now carried to the classroom for selection, analysis, and synthesis.

It is in the classroom that the third phase of this cooperative venture occurs. Group directors assign writing and organization duties according to

---

[4] Nearly all school librarians have developed a guide similar to the one used at Mountain View High School in Mesa, Arizona. The social studies teacher should meet with the librarian to find out what is in the guide used in his or her school. As necessary, the social studies teacher can work with the librarian to modify this guide to make it more appropriate and thorough.

the role responsibilities delineated on the group guidelines. The cooperative will of the group is tested now as less-able or less-motivated students are challenged by peer encouragement, peer pressure, and individual pride to improve. Each group member is urged to follow the group guidelines and to meet the responsibilities set for himself or herself as an individual member and collectively as a team. Descriptions of responsibilities and tasks (such as those in Figure 13-4 below) should be distributed and reviewed in each group. All groups are responsible for ensuring that members comprehend and follow the guidelines.

Teacher's Classroom Responsibilities and Tasks

As work within groups is taking place, the teacher's role as a facilitator is made easier because of the jigsaw organization pattern. In order to disseminate necessary information to the groups and still maintain the

Figure 13-4   *List of General Responsibilities of All Cooperative Group Members*

General Responsibilities of All Cooperative Group Members

A. All members will keep a daily learning log listing specific activities and personal comments about material covered and personal reactions to that material.

B. All members will complete a Library Orientation and Research Guide.

C. All members will research and collect articles, books, pamphlets, and other material for contribution to the group research and writing project.

D. All members will read, take notes, and outline all individual material collected for contribution to the group project.

E. All members will take a library pretest and a posttest. The posttest grade will be averaged with the group project grade.

F. All group members will fulfill their assigned roles and responsibilities. Failure to do this will result in removal from the group and the assumption of all requirements and responsibilities of the group research project.

G. All group members will participate with their assigned groups in a class presentation of their research project.

---

interdependent structure, the jigsaw is used to conduct small-group instruction. For instance, when the teacher needs to review the group's general progress or to discuss writing formats, he or she can meet with just the directors without interrupting the flow of classwork. A meeting with assistants A might involve discussing the bibliographic citation format. A meeting with assistants B may review rough-draft requirements. The advantage of this procedure is that it presents information that all the group members need. At the same time, it maintains the interdependence by requiring that the students charged with each critical set of responsibilities in each group, after participating in the small-group instruction, return to the home group to share their newly acquired knowledge; hence, positive interdependence.

Monitoring and Evaluation

Evaluation that reinforces the interdependence of the group, yet maintains a fair and equitable reward system for all involved, should be the goal of any cooperative project. This is often easier said than done.

My experience has been that typically individual group members embrace the cooperative ideals with the zeal of a true believer until individual grades are perceived as being threatened. If not headed off before students go ballistic, cooperative groups may become mobs with mob mentality for "hang 'em first and we'll ask 'em questions later." Those contemplating cooperative units should understand from the start that no amount of social consciousness in just three to four weeks of cooperative learning is going to overcome a lifetime (however short) of conditioned responses about grades and individual rewards. My strongest suggestions are to monitor constantly, intervene quickly, and move away from the group before they know you've been there.

Social studies teachers considering a cooperative unit should begin with a clearly articulated plan for monitoring, guiding, and evaluating student accomplishments and in-group behaviors. Two methods for monitoring and focusing the groups are especially effective. One is the daily journal, an old standard in middle schools but a technique that is greatly underrated on the high-school level. In this cooperative unit, a few minutes are spent at the end of each hour having each student review and record the day's activities, either in the library or in the classroom (see the format for a daily learning log in Figure 13-5 on page 354). The journal enables students to rehearse the important daily information before it is lost in the mental jungle of the hallways and the next class period. Periodic checks of each student's log during the project will help verify the extent to which each objective is being met. In addition, the journal format provides space for students to say something positive about the day's activities. Positive attitudes produce positive results.

A second method of monitoring group progress is the cooperative group responsibility assessment, a long title for a short rating survey of individual group members' attitudes toward objectives of the unit, their progress, and member participation. Figure 13-6, on page 355, provides an example of one assessment form I have used. This assessment provides valuable insight into a group member's attitudes and relationships with his or her peer group. These surveys may be shared within the group as a means of allowing the group to self-monitor and assess its activities. However, the teacher is cautioned to be very careful in allowing such sharing, especially when this is only the first or second cooperatively structured experience these students have completed. There are two reasons for this caution. Students may fail to record actual opinions and beliefs to avoid possible negative consequences from their peers, so the survey is invalid, and sharing this information may cause more problems than it corrects.

What this type of assessment does provide is advance warning about potential trouble spots, as well as time to intervene in a low-key manner that is not disruptive to the overall group. These in themselves can be the difference between the success and failure of the cooperative research paper.

Grades

One of the keys to making cooperative learning strategies successful is the clear articulation of responsibilities and objectives for both the teacher and the students. For the teacher, early and clear descriptions of student outcome objectives, outcome-aligned assessment items, and criteria for achievement reduce confusion or indecision and translate into a projected sense of teacher competence and focus. Students who comprehend exactly what is expected to be learned, what is to be done in their groups, and the grade and reward structure will likely master the skills and work cooperatively within the group learning tasks (Slavin, 1987).

Since there are multiple outcomes for this project, there are a variety of grading responses used to evaluate individual and group progress. In my class, the entire library project is 30 percent of a student's term grade.

However, within this percentage all assignments carry individual assignment weights (see Figure 13-7 at the end of the chapter). Not all of the points are earned cooperatively. The pretest and posttest on the resource information and library research skills give an objective individual progress report. Grades on quizzes given on each of the six resource units are earned separately from the group. Bonus points can be earned for 100 percent group mastery both on the individual quizzes and the summative test.

The written portion of the research paper is graded for organization, variety of sources, outline format and thorough data gathering, writing (including coherence and unity), and citation-format correctness. The grade for this project is cooperatively given, with flexibility in the bonus points available for group leaders and in participation points given to group members by each team director. Part of the total is allocated to learning logs, library orientation packets, and homework. Teachers using this strategy should prioritize their student outcomes and assign grade and percentage weights reflecting their priorities.

The Evaluation Guide, which includes the grade-percentage break-downs aligned directly with the responsibility list, is carried with the student for the duration of the project (see Figure 13-7 on page 356). That each student has a copy from day one of the project ensures a clear comprehension of the criteria for assigning grades and reinforces the necessity of interdependence within the group work. Individuals and groups use this evaluation guide as a responsibility agreement, a reference source, and as a source of reassurance throughout the project.

Project Retrospect and Personal Reflections

Test results from one of my cooperative units revealed that these cooperative learning research groups were astoundingly successful. Of the 52 students in 16 groups working during one semester, only 8 individuals did not attain 80 percent mastery of the target content and skills for the unit.[5] More importantly, of the 16 groups, only 1 group failed to complete the project and attain the 80 percent target level of minimum proficiency. More students scored over the 90 percent level than had

---

[5] The lack of success of 8 individuals was directly attributable to their library knowledge and abilities test scores.

done so under all other strategies I have used in this area. A number of these students would likely not have even passed this assignment were I to have used traditional ways of teaching the research paper.

The only disaster I encountered was directly linked to the lack of attendance of one member of a group who collected all the group's work for final typing and then failed to return to class for three days, losing the file in the interim. Out of 52 students working together for an extended period of time on so many important skills, I consider this one problem to be minimal compared to what I normally encounter during similar projects. However, attendance can negatively affect success in cooperative learning groups just as it can affect success in traditional classroom strategies. On the positive side, I observed groups meeting outside of class time, group members doing extra work for another who broke his arm, very mature discussions with members behind on their deadlines, and a healthy competition among groups to be the best. Furthermore, it was obvious that students were genuinely concerned about their group members as people, learning colleagues, and learners regardless of their entering abilities, prior knowledge, and gender/eth-nic/racial background.

For a veteran teacher like myself, the success of this cooperative research strategy has forced a re-evaluation of my teaching practices and a commitment to expanding the use of cooperative learning wherever I can see application. The bottom line for myself and those contemplating using these techniques is the observable evidence that attitudes toward what once was an odious task become an enjoyable team goal that cre-ates a spirit of determination similar to the the little engine that kept saying, "I think I can." There is also a significant, positive carryover to other units in my course and, as seems to be the case in social studies classes, a marked increase in the number of students willing to partici-pate in and complete research projects in other subject areas.

These combined cooperative/mastery learning teams offer a clear alternative to the direct instruction or small-group activity methods most often used in the classroom. In this cooperative research project, cooperative groups are being used in tandem with elements of mastery learning as a means of focusing the teaching of targeted student abilities and providing a highly effective system for empowering students to be captains of their own learning. Cooperative learning approaches are not intended to replace direct instruction, only to complement a teacher's repertoire of effective instructional strategies.

Effective instruction is something like buying a good running shoe; not every foot is the same and careful matching of biomechanics with shoe structure is the key to comfort and successful running. So too is the use of cooperative learning in the classroom; comprehending its mechanics and requirements and then using it appropriately make the difference in success or failure.

Sequence of Steps for Implementing This Cooperative Group Research Strategy

Planning and Preinstruction Preparation

1. The first priority in using this cooperative unit is planning ahead. Schedule library time two to four weeks in advance of the anticipated starting date. A planning session with the media specialist should also be scheduled to discuss target outcomes, teaching roles, material needs, seating arrangements, available resources, copying access, grading policies, formative quiz procedures, instructional alignment with the summative test, rosters, topic lists, and projected time frame. I suggest a checklist that can be shared with your librarian.

2. Prior to implementing the research project, some assessment of students' *note-taking* and *outlining* abilities should be made. This can be done formally through pretesting or simply through an informal demonstration survey if time is short. Whether it is several days of intensive review, or a two-week unit, the time spent on helping all students attain these prerequisite basic organizational and information-gathering abilities will be well invested. One or more members of the school's language arts department may be enlisted to help in this area.

3. Since library research proficiency is one target outcome, a pretest emphasizing basic source knowledge and filing systems is given. The results from this test are used in part to aid in the formation of heterogeneous groups. If given a week or more before the unit actually begins, these results may be given to the librarian to help shape the presentations he or she prepares for the class.

Instruction: Introduction and Getting Started

4. After the pretesting and prerequisite skills units are completed, class time should be taken to explain thoroughly the cooperative unit. The justification and procedures for using cooperative learning should be explained so that each student clearly understands what is expected when doing group work and why you have chosen to use this method. This larger discussion is in addition to the more specific outcomes for the research project. The more the students understand what is expected, the more apt they are to strive to reach those expectations.

5. Groups of three are formed based on heterogeneous arrangements of prior knowledge, class ranking, gender, leadership, reading ability, or any combination of these and other individual data that might be available. Don't let students choose their own groups.

6. Hand out and go through the list of responsibilities of each of the members (see Figure 13-2 on page 338). The sequence of doing this is important because each member will be personally assessing his or her role and willingness to participate. Also, role responsibilities should be clearly outlined before each member decides who will lead and who will be an assistant.

7. Grading policies, incentives, and project requirements listed in the packet are now discussed in some detail. (In the future, models of completed projects will be very valuable, so some of the best should be saved for this occasion.)

8. Group members now agree on role responsibilities. Once these roles are decided, the director records the decisions with the teacher. This is necessary in order to evaluate member contributions and as a means of monitoring who may need special encouragement.

9. An overhead of a list of topics is displayed and groups are asked to choose a first-, second-, and third-ranked topic. As much as possible, duplication of topics is avoided. The teacher then approves and records the topic each group is to study.

10. With topics decided, the next step for the group is the formulation

of focus questions. These are preresearch questions for the group that give specific direction to their study and data collection. All of these questions may not be answered by the end of the project, but they are a place to start. Also, these questions and their resulting answers can be used as a basis for the class presentation after the project has been completed.

Instruction: The Library Phase

11. The class moves to the library from this point to the completion of the actual research portion of the project. Administrative duties are completed in the library each day, and time is not wasted in logistics. Students actually meet in the library rather than in the classroom.

12. Daily learning logs (see Figure 13-5 on page 354) are distributed to each student. At the end of each period, five minutes are allowed for recording and reflection on the day's events. This reinforcement of information helps to close the day and organize thoughts for what was accomplished and what is still to be done.

13. The library orientation is done either by the teacher or the media specialist, as agreed on prior to this project. For my purposes, the media specialist distributes a library orientation packet that each student is expected to complete. This packet includes maps, resource samples, resource application exercises, and bibliographical citation pages for each resource complete with page space for note taking. The packet also is the primary study source for quizzes and final tests on library-use abilities and resources.

14. For the next seven to ten days, the instructional routine is the same. A library resource, for example, the *Readers' Guide to Periodical Literature*, is introduced to the class as a whole. After introduction, individual and small-group exercises are completed from the packets that usually require some hands-on use of the resource. The teacher and the librarian jointly supervise student work. The exercises are then reviewed and graded for mastery. Remediation exercises and one-on-one attention are given to those not achieving mastery. As soon as mastery is achieved, the students are free to use that resource for their group topic.

15. On the day following the introduction and completion of a library

resource unit, a quiz is given and graded. When 80 percent mastery is achieved, the rest of the period is used for personal research. Nonmastery scorers are given the option of reviewing the quiz with either the teacher or the librarian and then taking a parallel quiz. Since research time is optimum, students are not required to make mastery. However, successful research depends on being able to use the library proficiently. Therefore, teachers should use their judgment on who needs to be retaught the resource material.

16. Some resources, because of their nature, require extended time. Therefore, catch-up time can be scheduled between resource units if it appears that a majority of students are not completing the required research.

17. After about a week into the project (choose time as you have it), I give the cooperative survey that gives me some idea of the perceptions and attitudes of individual group members toward other members (see Figure 13-6 on page 355). Where problems are apparent, interventions are possible that can prevent them from becoming critical.

18. At the end of the seven- to ten-day research time, the orientation packet is scanned for completion. This ensures that all material has been collected and groups have sufficient information to write the research paper. It also ensures that all students are prepared to take the final or summative test.

19. An objective, comprehensive summative test is given on the last day of the in-library portion of this project. Any students not achieving 80 percent mastery are offered the opportunity to meet with the media specialist (outside class time and as convenient for the media person) for remediation, review, and retesting, using a parallel test.

Instruction: Work in the Classroom To Complete the Written Research Paper

20. Classes now reconvene in the classroom for the completion of the project. All copied material, citation data, notes, and outlines are collected, organized, and distributed by the director of each group.

21. Group directors now re-review individual responsibilities, assign tasks, and set time schedules for deadlines (as per the teacher's overall time span).

22. Using the jigsaw pattern of cooperative grouping, I meet with representatives from each group for specific information instruction. For instance, I meet with all assistants B in order to go over the required citation format and to hand out excerpts from the style manual. Other groups meet to discuss outline formats, style formats, project organization, and directors meet to discuss group progress.

23. Class time for the next three to five days is given over to group work. I spend my time monitoring, doing small-group instruction, and intervening only as absolutely necessary.

24. Deadlines are set with some flexibility. Be aware of class progress. I sometimes plan for an extra day and, when nearing the deadline, *when* it appears necessary, I extend if all groups have worked diligently but still need time.

Instruction: What Follows the Completion of the Written Research Paper

25. If time permits and class presentations are to be made, these are scheduled immediately after the written paper is turned in. A lottery works well to determine the order in which the groups give their oral reports to the whole class. The groups will need to spend some time to prepare their presentations. I limit the scope and time (five to ten minutes) of these presentations to discussing sources, presenting focus questions with answers, personal conclusions, and a question and answer session with the class. Every group member must participate. The use of charts and graphs is optional.

26. My wrap-up duties include collecting the daily learning logs, collecting the library orientation packets (these can be required inside the project notebooks), and asking for directors' participation points distribution. Distribution of the directors' bonuses is also necessary now while their performance is fresh in my mind.

27. I reward individuals and groups in a public award ceremony. The emphasis is placed on the specific areas in which groups have met the standards of excellence.

28. When things have gone well, I give the class a collective pat on the back. If there were a few rough spots, I avoid criticizing the

class as a whole. Cooperative learning works, but for most (teachers and students alike), especially in the early stages, it is a new, risky, and uncertain experience. The more organized the project, and the more detailed the expectations, the smoother the operation will run, and the chances for learning success are increased significantly.

29. I then take some time to help students reflect upon their work as a group and in groups. They consider the advantages and benefits of working cooperatively and describe the behaviors and attitudes that helped the group succeed and those that were dysfunctional.

Figure 13-5   *One Format for a Daily Learning Log*

Name_____   Date:___/___/___

DAILY LEARNING LOG

Summary of Day's Activities (What we did)

_____

_____

_____

_____

_____

Focus (Information I need to remember)

_____

_____

_____

_____

_____

Personal Comments (Something positive to say)

_____

_____

_____

_____

_____

Figure 13-6 *One Cooperative Group Responsibility Assessment Instrument*

Date:_____/_____/_____

COOPERATIVE GROUP RESPONSIBILITY ASSESSMENT

Group #_____

Name: _____   Period: _____

Members: (A) _____

             (B) _____

             (C) _____

	LOW<<<<<<< >>>>>>>HIGH
I understand the objectives of this unit.	1——2——3——4——5
I work harder than my other group members.	1——2——3——4——5
All members of my group work well together.	1——2——3——4——5
Other members of my group listen to my input when offered.	1——2——3——4——5
I understand the responsibilities that have been assigned to me within the group.	1——2——3——4——5
All members are serious about making the group work.	1——2——3——4——5
My assessment of group member A's attempts to live up to the assigned responsibilities is:	1——2——3——4——5
My assessment of group member B's attempts to live up to the assigned responsibilities is:	1——2——3——4——5
My assessment of group member C's attempts to live up to the assigned responsibilities is:	1——2——3——4——5
My rating of the group's performance so far is:	1——2——3——4——5

Figure 13-7   *Suggested Guidelines and Standards for Individual and Group Evaluation*

EVALUATION GUIDE

A. All members of the group will receive a group grade.

B. Group grades will be evaluated by the following criteria:

1. overall appearance and presentation
2. proper outline structure
3. comprehensive outline coverage
4. extent and variety of research material
5. coherence and unity of the written research
6. writing mechanics
7. proper bibliographic and referencing format
8. group focus questions

C. Final project requirements are:

1. ink for cover page, table of contents, master outline, main body of written research (3–5 pages), and bibliography
2. binder
3. all collected material will be catalogued in the research project and listed in the table of contents as notes, outlines, copied materials, and so forth

D. Group research project grades will be averaged with posttest scores and library resource material to determine a final project grade.

E. Group member learning logs will be evaluated separately from the research project.

F. The library unit will comprise 30 percent of the final 9-week grade. Breakdown of this percentage is:

Cooperative Group Project . . . . 25 percent

- research paper/project (grade averaged with library skills)
- library skills grade (formative/summative)
- library skills 80 percent mastery level bonus points (if all members reach this level)
- director distributed participation points (30 points)
- director bonus (optional/extra up to 10 percent added to the individual's group grade)

Supplemental Library . . . . 5 percent

- library orientation activities and research guide
- learning logs

References

Block, J. H., H. E. Efthim, and R. B. Burns. 1989. *Building effective mastery learning schools.* White Plains, NY: Longman.

Johnson, D. W., R. T. Johnson, and E. J. Holubec. 1986. *Circles of learning: Cooperation in the classroom,* rev. ed. Englewood Cliffs, NJ: Prentice Hall.

Slavin, R. E. 1987. Grouping for instruction: Equity and effectiveness. *Equity and Excellence* (23): 31-6.

Spady, W. 1987. Outcome-based education: A summary of essential features and major implications (a workshop paper). San Carlos, CA: The Spady Consulting Group.

Stahl, R. J. April, 1989. Time alone does not mastery make: Extending Carroll's model of school learning in light of an information processing perspective. Paper presented at the annual meeting of the American Educational Research Association, San Francisco.

———. 1992 (in press). A context for "higher-order knowledge": An information-constructivist perspective with implications for curriculum and instruction. *Journal of Structural Learning and Applied Intelligence.*

———. (in preparation). Designing outcome-aligned curriculum units. Tempe, AZ: Secondary Education, Arizona State University.

Wyatt, F. 1988. Rethinking the research project through cooperative learning. *Middle School Journal* (September): 6-7.

Additional Resources

Cohen, Elizabeth G. *Designing Groupwork: Strategies for the Heterogeneous Classroom*. Colchester, VT: Teachers College Press, 1986.

This volume concentrates on practical and effective ways teachers can promote status equalization and greater active, on-task participation by all students within groups, regardless of gender, ethnicity, socioeconomic background, race, or entering academic abilities. Special attention is given to suggestions for working with bilingual students and in bilingual classrooms.

Davidson, Neil, ed. *Cooperative Learning in Mathematics: A Handbook for Teachers*. Menlo Park, CA: Addison-Wesley Innovation Division, 1990.

Written for the mathematics teacher, this volume contains a number of ideas and guidelines for cooperative learning that are generic across grade levels and content areas. If the reader mentally replaces the math problems and examples with social studies ones from his or her own classroom, this book has many fruitful and practical suggestions.

Johnson, David W., and Frank P. Johnson. *Joining Together: Group Theory and Group Skills*. 4th ed. Englewood Cliffs, NJ: Prentice Hall, 1991.

Group dynamics, especially knowledge about group dynamics and mastering the skills needed to operate effectively in and with groups, is the main thrust of this book. Besides the many examples, check sheets, and scenarios, the book presents a solid theoretical and practical framework for explaining group dynamics, interactions within groups, and ways in which groups can function more productively.

Johnson, David W., and Roger T. Johnson. *Learning Together and Alone: Cooperative, Competitive, and Individualistic Learning.* 3rd ed. Englewood Cliffs, NJ: Prentice Hall, 1991.

The book strongly reflects its title, describing the nature of, uses of, and places for, competition, individualism, and cooperation as well as competitive, individualistic, and cooperative learning in classroom situations. Filled with illustrative classroom examples and guidelines, the authors help teachers to work with all three of these approaches while making a strong case for emphasizing cooperative learning structures, tasks, and groups.

Johnson, David W., Roger T. Johnson, and Edythe J. Holubec. *Cooperation in the Classroom.* Edina, MN: Interaction Book Company, 1990.

The authors provide a very-easy-to-read introduction to cooperative learning for teachers, supervisors, administrators, and parents. Cooperation is described in light of two other goal structures — competitive and individualistic. Essentials for cooperative learning are also described, along with ideas to support the use of cooperative learning at all levels and in every content area.

Kagan, Spencer. *Cooperative Learning.* 27128 Paseo Espada, Suite 622, San Juan Capistrano, CA: Resources for Teachers, 1992.

A revision and expansion of the author's highly popular first volume, this book is a comprehensive handbook that provides extensive details on cooperative learning structures for classrooms on all levels. A number of examples and sample lessons are included, along with practical tips on classroom management, team building, and cooperative skills training. The information on a number of cooperative learning strategies complements and expands upon the descriptions provided in this book.

Sharan, Yael, and Shlomo Sharan. *Expanding Cooperative Learning Through Group Investigation.* Colchester, VT: Teachers College Press, 1992.

This is the definitive volume on group investigation, covering this strategy from A to Z. The authors describe practical classroom examples, scenarios, and details on the "how-to-do-its" and the theoretical framework upon which this strategy is based.

Slavin, Robert E. *Cooperative Learning: Theory, Research, and Practice*. Englewood Cliffs, NJ: Prentice Hall, 1990.

This volume provides an overview of many topics related to cooperative learning and many of the strategies and features that help to make cooperative learning work. Numerous examples are provided to highlight particular strategies that are introduced and described in varying degrees of detail. Provides a summary of research findings to date on this approach.

Slavin, Robert E. *Using Student Team Learning*. 3rd ed. Baltimore, MD: Center for Research on Elementary and Middle Schools, The John Hopkins University, 1986.

This volume is the most extensive "how-to-do-it" description of the Student Teams Achievement Divisions (STAD) and Teams-Games-Tournament (TGT) strategies available. Team Assisted Individualization (TAI) and Cooperative Integrated Reading and Composition (CIRC) are also introduced, along with general descriptions of other cooperative learning strategies.

Stahl, R. J., and R. L. VanSickle, eds, *Cooperative Learning in the Social Studies Classroom: An Invitation to Social Study*. 3501 Newark Street NW, Washington, DC 20016-3167: National Council for the Social Studies, 1992.

A set of nine chapters provides an extensive overview of cooperative learning relative to social studies education, written primarily from an introduction and invitation perspective. Three chapters written by teachers detail how they have used cooperative learning successfully in their respective elementary, middle, and high-school social studies classrooms.